Preface

In recent years the close relationships between management and the structure of their organizations have received increasing attention from theorists and practising managers alike. This book introduces readers to the various types of organizations that operate in the private and public sectors and analyses the management functions that are involved in their day-to-day operation. The contents are aimed both at students, who wish to gain an insight into the workings of organizations, and at practising managers who might wish to broaden their knowledge.

The book is particularly designed for students preparing for B/TEC Higher National Diploma and Certificate courses. It is aimed in particular at Study Areas B (People and Organizations) and C (Resources for Business Activity) in the core specification.

The book is also relevant for the CNAA Diploma in Management Studies syallabus and will be useful for students preparing for professional examinations of the following institutes:

The Institute of Chartered Secretaries and Administrators.

The Chartered Institute of Public Finance and Accountancy.

The Institute of Cost and Management Accountants.

The Association of Certified Accountants.

The authors have endeavoured to present the subject matter in a simple, factual manner in order to aid the reader's understanding. Each chapter is followed by a number of revision questions and exercises with which the reader can test his progress. These exercises also give scope for further development of some of the ideas introduced in the main body of the text. A recommended list of further reading is included at the end of each chapter so that readers can further increase their knowledge of the subject matter.

In most instances we have used the term 'he' when referring to managers. We are, of course, aware that there are many successful female managers; the term 'he' is used purely for convenience and we hope it will not offend our female readers.

We would like to thank, in particular, Mrs. Vivienne Reid for typing the manuscript so helpfully and efficiently and our friends and colleagues at Lancashire Polytechnic for their advice and support.

Contents

Part One
The Managerial and Organizational Environment

Part one sets the scene by describing the environment within which managers and organizations operate. In Chapter 1 we examine some of the pressures and challenges faced by managers and organizations. In Chapter 2 we discuss the growth in importance, in recent years, of the managerial function. Finally, in Chapter 3, we consider in more detail the organizational framework within which managers operate.

1

The Pressures and Challenges of Management

1.1 Introduction

Managers and organizations operate in an increasingly difficult environment. The pressures and challenges facing managers are becoming more complex. On the one hand managers must strive to increase their efficiency and — in commercial organizations — to maintain their profitability in a hostile economic climate. On the other hand they have to meet social, ethical and environmental requirements, and to try to achieve higher standards in the products and services they offer. These pressures often conflict, and all managers are constantly trying to maintain a balance between the two extremes.

In this chapter we examine some of these pressures, considering those that originate from the organization's external environment and those that are generated within the organization itself. Although we discuss each set of pressures in turn, readers should remember that the two often interact.

1.2 External pressures

1.2.1 Economic

The first quarter of a century after the end of World War II was a period of uninterrupted growth in the U.K., the national income increasing year by year, (although the rate of increase varied from one year to another). This period of growth came to an end in 1974 when national income fell, largely as a consequence of the increase in the price of oil, inspired by OPEC. National income also fell in the following year and again in 1980 and 1981. During the past decade, therefore, managers have no longer been able to plan their activities on the assumption that the total demand

3

for goods and services would increase.

This erratic pattern of change in total demand has been super-imposed on the changes in the pattern of demand between one product and another that characterize a mixed economy. (In a mixed economy production is undertaken by both private and public sector organizations, as shown in Chapter 3.)

The overall effect on producers of these changes in demand is illustrated in Table 1.1 below. It can be seen that between 1973 and 1980, while output increased in electrical engineering and chemicals, it was unchanged in food manufacturing, and fell substantially in metal manufacture, mechanical engineering, vehicles and textiles.

Table 1.1   Index of industrial production, selected industries (1975 = 100)

	1973	1980
Food	106	106
Metal manufacture	127	75
Chemical and allied industries	105	110
Mechanical engineering	97	86
Electrical engineering	92	107
Vehicles	113	89
Textiles	117	80

Source: *Monthly Digest of Statistics*

Changes in demand are reflected in changes in employment and unemployment. Figure 1.1 shows that the number of registered vacancies has fallen since 1973, and the number of unemployed has risen sharply. (The increase in unemployment is only partly due to a fall in demand; it also reflects a rise in labour productivity and an increase in the number of people available for work).

Changes in the pattern of demand are reflected in changes in the pattern of employment. Figure 1.2 shows the numbers employed in various sectors in 1978 and predicted employment in 1985. It can be seen that employment was expected to increase in, for example, services and construction, but to fall in manufacturing.

It would not be appropriate to give a detailed explanation of these economic changes, but it should be noted that they are the result of forces that operate on an international, rather than a purely national scale. Newspapers and television are constantly reporting on the activities of international companies, the progress of the European Economic Community, the behaviour of Eurodollar markets etc. Germany has replaced the U.S.A. as our major trading partner and the overall effect of

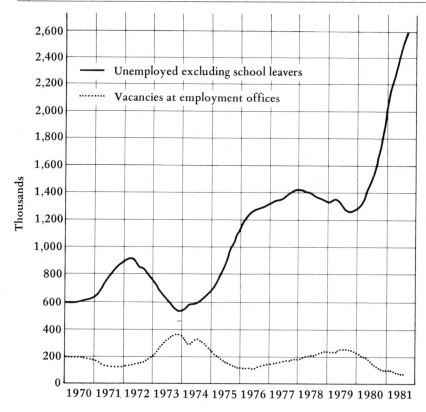

Figure 1.1 Number of unemployed and vacancies, U.K. Source: *Employment Gazette.*

Table 1.2 Shares of U.K. trade, by geographical area (%s)

	Exports			Imports		
	1970	1975	1980	1970	1975	1980
European Community	30	33	43	27	37	41
Rest of Western Europe	16	15	14	15	14	15
North America	15	12	11	21	14	15
Other developed countries	12	10	6	10	8	7
Oil-exporting countries	6	12	10	9	14	9
Other developing countries	17	15	12	15	11	11
Centrally planned economies	4	3	3	3	2	2
	100	100	100	100	100	100

Source: *British Business,* June 1981

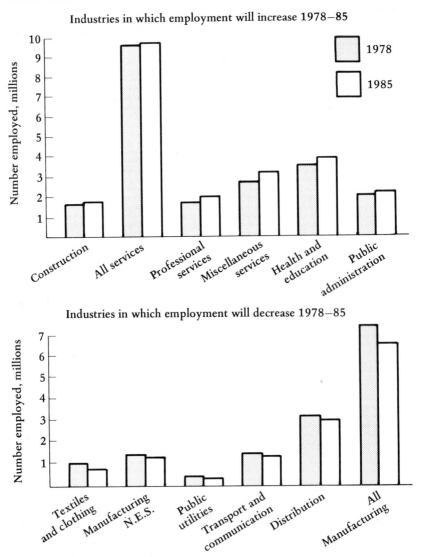

Figure 1.2   Predicted changes in employment. Source: *Employment News*, June 1981.

U.K. entry into the E.E.C. is a substantial increase in the proportion of U.K. trade accounted for by members of the European Community. This can clearly be seen in Table 1.2. This table also shows that, in the first half of the decade, the increase in oil prices caused an increase in the oil exporting countries' share of the U.K.'s imports and that their higher revenues allowed them to buy more of the U.K.'s exports.

These increases in the share of trade are, of course, reflected in a fall in the shares of other regions, including North America and other developed countries.

Foreign trade is more important to Britain than to most other industrialized countries, and British producers have often been criticized for failing to respond to changes in the international environment, such as the weakening of ties with Commonwealth countries and the growth of European markets. Such criticism is less justified today than in the past. We have shown that British producers have taken the opportunity provided by U.K. entry to the E.E.C., and Table 1.3 below shows the growing importance of exports in a wide range of industries.

Table 1.3 Import penetration and export sales ratio for products of manufacturing industries

	Ratio (sterling income) of imports to home demand		Ratio (sterling income) of exports to manufacturers' sales	
	1974	1980	1974	1980
Food and drink	21	14	5	6
Coal and petroleum products	16	14	14	16
Chemicals and allied industries	27	29	34	39
Metal manufacture	24	36	17	29
Mechanical engineering	28	32	40	46
Instrument engineering	50	61	52	63
Electrical engineering	29	37	29	38
Shipbuilding and marine engineering	57	26	25	32
Vehicles	23	39	39	42
Metal goods n.e.s.	10	15	14	18
Textiles	24	35	25	34
Leather and leather goods	27	41	28	33
Clothing and footwear	20	30	11	19
Bricks, pottery, cement, glass, etc.	9	9	13	14
Timber, furniture, etc.	32	27	5	7
Paper, printing and publishing	23	20	9	11
Other manufacturing industries	16	20	18	21
Total manufacturing	23.3	25.4	21.4	26.1

Source: *Economic Trends*

1.2.2 Technological

It is said that in the coming decades the application of technology will lead to changes comparable to those resulting from the industrial revolution.

Whether this prediction is fulfilled will depend largely on our ability and willingness to make the necessary social changes, e.g. to develop new patterns of work and leisure that will be required by a widespread introduction of 'micro-chip technology'. But even though social considerations are likely to moderate the pace of change, managers are going to be increasingly involved in decisions concerning, or resulting from, technological change. Indeed one can identify several areas in which technological change has already had a marked impact.

1.2.2.1 Materials and designs

New materials, particularly plastics, have revolutionized the design and construction of many of today's products. Many of the components of the modern car are now made from types of plastic which are cheap to produce, easy to replace and do not rust. These have replaced traditional materials such as steel. (The increase in the output of the chemical and allied industries, shown in Table 1.1, is partly due to the growth in the output of plastics and partly to increases in other chemically based products such as pharmaceuticals).

Electronic devices have replaced their mechanical counterparts in a wide range of machinery and equipment. (This is reflected in the different experiences of the electrical and mechanical engineering industries shown in Table 1.1.)

The incorporation of micro-chip technology in control systems has reduced the time spent by managers in this area of work, leaving more time for other areas such as change adaptation and the personnel problems of organizations. These new control systems are one aspect of the much heralded information and communications revolution. Other aspects include computerized data-banks with multiple access, the electronic transfer of financial assets, and facilities enabling conferences to be held with audio-visual links between numerous locations, thus saving the need for participants to assemble at a single site.

1.2.2.2 Transport

The post war period has seen a series of advances including Concorde, the Jump Jet, the High Speed Train, the Hovercraft and the Jumbo Jet. These developments have made it possible to transfer people and goods, often over long distances, more quickly and efficiently.

1.2.2.3 Health

Just as production and transport systems have benefitted from technological advance, so too have systems of health care. This has led to people living much longer. (In the U.S.A. there are whole communities based on sexagenarians and older people). This puts pressures on managers, particularly those in the public sector, who have to meet the greater need for health and welfare services arising from an increase in the number of senior citizens. At the same time these consumers open up new leisure markets for organizations which cater exclusively for the elderly, e.g. Saga which specializes in holidays for retired people.

1.2.3 Political

The general trend in the Western World in recent years has been for governments to increasingly influence the organizational and managerial environment by legislation, as part of their economic and social policies.

Despite attempts by the Thatcher Government in the U.K. and the Reagan administration in the U.S.A. to try to stem this tide of 'creeping bureaucracy' (by selling off government interests in certain organizations such as British Aerospace in the U.K., or by attempting to reduce the legislative control over companies in the U.S.A.), government still retains substantial influence and power. In the U.K. a Conservative government, ideologically in favour of 'disengagement' has continued to provide vast subsidies to B.L. Ltd., the steel industry (and in particular the British Steel Corporation), British Rail etc., rather than face the risk of even higher unemployment and a further erosion of the country's industrial base. This assistance did not however extend to providing financial aid to the 'champion of free enterprise', Sir Freddie Laker, when his airline faced financial problems and was forced into liquidation in February 1982.

Nor is the debate concerning the extent of central government control confined to the industrial sector of the economy. Within the public administration sector, the local authorities have lost a number of their functions. Moreover, their freedom to undertake their existing functions is limited by central government, not least by the restrictions on their powers to raise revenue. (The relationship between central and local government is considered at greater length in Chapter 3.)

1.2.4 Social/Environmental

1.2.4.1 Business morality

Seldom a year passes without an organization in the public or private sector receiving massive adverse publicity about the way it conducts its affairs. This might involve corruption (the Poulson affair), breaking the law (Watergate), tax avoidance schemes or the size of a 'golden handshake'. (At the time of writing it is proposed to give Mr. Jack Gill compensation of almost £¾ million at a time when the company from which he was dismissed, A.C.C., was losing money and had passed the interim dividend. This proposal was widely criticized, the critics including non-executive directors of the company and certain institutional investors which had substantial interests in the company.)

The idea that, in addition to pursuing efficiency and profit, managers should be socially responsible, goes back to the ideals of Robert Owen and his New Lanark factory. Today, the ability of the press and television to gather and broadcast information about organizations puts continual pressure on managers, especially in large 'visible' organizations, to maintain high standards of conduct in all their business dealings or face public wrath and retribution.

1.2.4.2 Business attitudes

Increased education and travel and the lowering of information barriers tend to cause an increase in people's work expectations. Class barriers ('blue' versus 'white' collar workers) are lessening. Employees now expect, as of right, longer holidays, sick pay, pension schemes, subsidized canteens etc. (At the beginning of 1982 the Ford Motor Company averted a strike, not by increasing its offer on pay, but by bringing the other conditions of manual workers closer to those already enjoyed by non-manual staff).

It is interesting to reflect that in Japan, which has perhaps the best economic performance of all industrialized nations in recent years, there is a system of almost total involvement by the organization in the lives of its employees. Many organizations provide housing, medical facilities, leisure activities, even holiday homes, in return for a lifetime of loyalty from their employees.

The rising unemployment of the late 1970s and early 1980s may affect business attitudes in ways that are not fully understood. On the one hand employees may press less hard in negotiations concerning pay and conditions; in this context it may be significant that the number of days lost through strikes in 1981 was the lowest for many years. On the other hand an increasing number of well-qualified, experienced and articulate people find themselves in the ranks of the unemployed; this may lead to a questioning of the traditional view of the work ethic. The widening gap between the 'haves' in employment and the 'have nots' in unemployment may well be the greatest challenge facing managers in the 1980s.

1.2.4.3 Environmental issues

The policies adopted by organizations with respect to pollution, noise, energy conservation, materials conservation and waste disposal are receiving increasing attention from organizations. In some instances this simply reflects managers' cost-consciousness and pursuit of efficiency; as the cost of energy has risen, organizations have found ways of reducing their energy needs. In other instances, organizations' policies are a response to the requirements of the law, e.g. not to discharge untreated effluent into rivers, or to the demands of pressure groups, e.g. to use a plastic which will be easily broken down when discarded by consumers. (Pressure groups are concerned with many issues other than those relating to the environment, e.g. the Consumers' Association has pressed for higher safety standards in domestic appliances and for the provision of more information to consumers).

The demands of pressure groups may be seen as part of the requirement, noted above, for organizations to be socially responsible. But it is not always clear what constitutes socially responsible behaviour. Although there are clear benefits in an unpolluted environment, there are also corresponding costs, which may be reflected in the prices of products. In the U.S.A. a study by the Environmental Protection Agency estimated that the consumer price index was 2.7 per cent higher than it would have been in the absence of federal anti-pollution laws, and that by 1986, the difference would be about 3.6 per cent.

The British government announced that lower limits for lead in petrol were to be brought into effect by the end of 1985 as part of a programme to reduce the dangers to health, particularly of young children from lead pollution. It was estimated that to meet the new requirements would cost the oil industry £200 million a year in additional crude oil and new equipment, and that the price of petrol would rise by up to 5p a gallon as a result.

1.3 Internal pressures

Having identified the major external pressures we now examine the pressures that arise within organizations. We shall see that many of these internal pressures become especially acute when the organization's environment changes quickly or becomes less predictable, an example of the interaction between external and internal pressures noted above.

1.3.1 Career expectations

The recession and high level of unemployment have considerably altered the career expectations of many managers and other employees. As organizations cut back, as people are made redundant, as vacancies remain frozen or posts disappear forever, so the opportunities for advancement up the managerial ladder are severely curtailed.

The reductions in staff have had particularly unfortunate consequences in the public sector because of the re-organization of local government, the health service and the water authorities in 1974. As part of this re-organization a large number of older employees took early retirement and their posts were filled by the new breed of professional managers, many in the thirty to forty age group. In normal circumstances these employees, with thirty or more years active service ahead of them, could look forward to expansion and the creation of new senior management positions for themselves and their subordinates. But the need to reduce staff, as part of the attempt to cut back government expenditure in the late 1970s and early 1980s, has meant that new posts are few and far between and that opportunities for promotion are reduced at all levels of the organization.

1.3.2 Organizational Change

As an organization's environment changes, the organization must also change if it is to continue to meet the needs of those it serves, be it consumers, Parliament or some other body. Managers have a responsibility to foresee the likely areas of change in relation to their organizations' activities, to make plans and decisions accordingly, and to smooth the path of change with their employees.

As noted above, changes in the environment have occurred more rapidly and have become less predictable during the last decade. Previously, managers were able to make many decisions in accordance with a regular procedure with fairly long time horizons. Today managers spend much more of their time reacting on a short-term basis to sudden shocks, such as a substantial increase in energy prices or a collapse of demand. (As an example of the difficulty of long-term planning we can quote the experience of our own institution. Changes in government policy mean that at the time of writing, early January 1982, the polytechnic still does not know the size of its budget for the financial year beginning in April, and hence cannot decide how many staff it will employ during that year).

1.3.3 Trade unions

Most managers have to deal with trade unions representing groups of employees within their organizations. The current level of unemployment and the general state of the economy have lessened the bargaining power of the unions, as people fear the loss not merely of fringe benefits but of their jobs with a consequent reduction in their living standards.

Nevertheless much of the legislation of recent years has considerably increased the status and negotiating position of the unions. (Legislation is discussed in greater detail in Chapter 15.) Moreover, most major unions can now afford to employ staff with expertise in the law , economics and financial matters. Briefed by these experts, union negotiators frequently know as much, if not more, about the organization as the management representatives with whom they are dealing.

1.3.4 Management style

The need to deal with union negotiators who are better equipped than previously is one example of a change in management style. The environmental and technological changes referred to above — a better educated work-force, the development of modern technological skills that transcend traditional boundaries within the organization, the substitution of new materials and products for old,—also call for a new managerial style. Managers are under increasing pressure to spend more of their (already scarce) time consulting with departments other than their own and with employees at all levels. Ironically, rapid change makes adequate consultation both more important and more difficult to secure. At the same time the rapid growth of communication and information systems (especially those based on the home T.V. set) have meant managers having to meet the needs of increasingly sophisticated consumers.

1.3.5 Women in management

The last twenty years have seen a revolution in the position and employment of women in organizations of all types. Women have constituted a steadily increasing proportion of the work force (at least until the steep rise in unemployment in the late 1970s). Moreover, as the gap between the average educational attainment of men and women has narrowed, more women have obtained managerial posts. At the national level the changing role of women is illustrated by the fact that Britain has both a female prime minister and leader of the House of Lords. There is no doubt that with a change in social arrangements and attitudes, e.g. the provision of more nurseries and creches, and a greater willingness on the part of men to share domestic duties, more women could hold down managerial positions. It is interesting to speculate whether these changes will be accelerated or inhibited by higher unemployment.

Incidentally, one of the issues that will have to be faced by all managers, men and women, is the greater impact of technological change on female employment. Many of the tasks traditionally undertaken by women in organizations — typing, filing, catering etc. — are the first to feel the effects of the micro-electronic revolution, as word processors, electronic document transmission systems, vending machines etc., replace manual operations.

One way of adjusting to this change may be to provide more opportunities for females in occupations reserved largely for men, e.g. bus drivers, joiners, electricians. Any manager who discriminates, in recruitment or in any other way, between males and females, may run foul of the law, the Equal Opportunities Commission or female pressure groups. If the manager is a man he may also incur the displeasure of his spouse and family!

1.4 Summary and conclusions

In this chapter we have introduced the reader to some of the wider issues and pressures facing managers. We have explored the major areas of change in the environment — economic, political, technological and social — and shown how these combine with the internal pressures that exist within organizations to challenge managers. We have suggested that the rapid rate of change that exists today is likely to persist, ensuring that the challenge to managers does not diminish.

Revision questions and exercises

1   Answer *briefly:*
A   What are the main external pressures facing managers?
B   In which industries is employment likely to increase over the next 20 years?
C   Which industries face a decline in the numbers employed?
D   List three technological changes affecting organizations.
E   Name three materials that have recently changed the 'make up' of products in everyday use.
F   Name two industries or firms that have recently received substantial government assistance.
G   What is meant by the social responsibility of business?
H   Give three examples of environmental issues facing managers.
I   Outline the major challenges managers face from within their organizations.
J   What is meant by organizational change?
K   What is meant by management style?
L   List three areas of female employment likely to be affected by micro-chip technology.
2   'The biggest challenge facing managers today is from within their organizations'. Discuss the validity of this statement with reference to public and private sector organizations.
3   If you were appointed economic advisor to the Government, what advice would you give in the light of the data contained in Figure 1.1?
4   What steps do you think the government should take to improve the trends in foreign trade shown in Table 1.3?
5   Discuss the major transport innovations in recent years and consider the benefits they have brought to organizations.
6   What will be the consequences of an increase in the number of old people?
7   What effects are social and environmental changes having on managers?
8   Discuss the effects of high unemployment on management career paths.
9   Is the work ethic still a valid concept in the 1980s?
10   'Women make good mothers and housewives but poor managers.' Discuss.
11   Should governments bail out inefficient organizations?
12   A meeting is called by the Department of Trade to discuss the causes and implications of increased imports into Britain. The participants at the meeting are: the Minister, (in the chair), senior civil servants, representatives

of the CBI and major British manufacturers, and representatives of Volkswagen, Sony, Datsun and Honda. Role play the various participants.

13 Role play a meeting between a consumer pressure group and the managers from a firm or industry (e.g. the electricity and nuclear power industries, a chemical firm, the oil industry). The consumer group is pressing for greater environmental safeguards in the products offered by the organizations concerned.

14 As a major employer in the public sector (e.g. Health, Water, Local Government) you are faced with the need to cut back the numbers of employees to meet budget restrictions. Your organization employs a large number of women in part-time positions. Your chief executive takes the view that women only work for 'pin money' and are obvious candidates for redundancy before the full time male employees. Role play a meeting between management and part-time female employees.

Further Reading

BELL, D. *The Coming of Post Industrial Society* (Heinemann: London, 1974).

CHILD, J. *The Business Enterprise in Modern Industrial Society* (Collier-Macmillan: London, 1969).

DRUCKER, P. *Towards the Next Economics* (Heinemann: London, 1981).

GLEW, M., WATTS, M. and WELLS, R. *The Business Organization and Its Environment* Heinemann: London, 1980).

HENNIG, M. and JARDIM, A. *The Managerial Woman* (Pan: London, 1979).

MANT, A. *The Rise and Fall of the British Manager* (Pan: London, 1979).

2

Management and The Manager

2.1 Introduction

In Chapter 1 we considered the increasingly difficult environment within which managers operate. In this chapter we look at the developing role of the manager and examine the major functions managers perform. (These functions are discussed in more detail in later chapters.)

2.2 The concept of management

Many definitions of 'management' exist. The Oxford English Dictionary describes management as,

'The application of skill or care in the manipulation, use, treatment or control (of things or persons) or in the conduct (of an enterprise, operations etc.).'

E. F. L. Brech (1976) defines management as,

'A social process entailing responsibility for the effective and economical planning and regulation of the operations of an enterprise, in fulfilment of a given purpose or task'.

Peter Drucker (1979), an American management expert, writes,

'Management is tasks. Management is a discipline. But management is also people'.

Despite all that has been written and despite the fact that increasing numbers of people aspire to be managers a clear, undisputable definition of 'management' or the term 'manager' still eludes us.

The situation is further complicated by the fact that in the public sector, (local government in particular), the term 'administrator' is often used to denote positions that would be termed 'managerial' in the private sector.

Despite these differences in definition, most managerial writers and theorists would agree that the concept of management involves three main elements: (1) the use of skills and techniques; (2) the control and co-ordination of people and resources; (3) responsibility for meeting the objectives of the organization.

The fascination of a managerial career is that despite all the written knowledge that is available, despite all the training courses and learning techniques with which the modern day manager is bombarded, there is no substitute for experience. The only way to become a good manager is to get out there and manage, learn by one's experiences and mistakes, and prove oneself in the eyes of colleagues and subordinates.

2.3 Managerial career paths

When someone asks, 'How do I become a manager?' the answer is often vague. If the reader wants to become a doctor or a dentist, then the training and career paths are fairly clearly defined. Having obtained the necessary 'A' levels you spend a period of training at an appropriate university. The academic training coincides with periods of practical work experience to develop the necessary diagnostic and medical treatment skills as well as the ability to deal with patients and develop a good 'bedside manner'. A series of examinations, testing the students' knowledge, skill, ability, have to be passed. Often the qualified doctor or dentist goes to work either in private practice or in some branch of the National Health Service. In most instances pay, working conditions and promotion patterns are settled on a national basis and well known and documented.

Not so in the case of an individual who wants to become a top manager in an organization such as I.C.I. or G.E.C. Instead of a single, clearly defined route there exists a multiplicity of possible ways to the top. Consequently, our budding manager is faced with a number of questions. Should he study law, accountancy, a science, engineering etc? In what type of company should he seek employment, and in which would he get the necessary experience? Is a period spent overseas useful or wasted time? How does he develop the right 'image' to impress the boards of major companies and demonstrate that he is the right man for the job?

If he looks, as an example to follow, to some of today's successful managers, the choice of a managerial career pattern becomes even more puzzling. Some of today's most successful managers have few, or no qualifications, having been 'flung in at the deep end', so as to speak, when they were demobbed from the services at the end of the Second World War. The most successful often built up their own businesses from small

savings accumulated with great difficulty over a period of years. Clive
Sinclair whose firm makes micro-computers is a good example of this
breed of independent businessman. All, if you asked them, would
probably admit that 'luck' played just as great a part in their success as
hard work and experience.

Nowadays those beginning a managerial career, many in middle and
some in senior management positions, belong to the so called 'new breed
of professional manager'. Armed with a variety of qualifications—
degrees, professional qualifications such as law, or accountancy, even
M.B.A.s — they are making their presence known in all types of
organization. Yet there is no guarantee that the possession of these
qualifications will make them any more successful than their unqualified
predecessors who still 'inhabit the corridors of power', albeit in reduced
numbers.

2.4 The developing role of the manager

In tracing the way the managerial role and function has developed three
main phases can be identified.

2.4.1 Pre-scientific management

The first phase covered the early years of the industrial revolution. One of
its greatest contributors was Adam Smith, whose book, 'The Wealth of
Nations,' was published in 1776. Adam Smith introduced certain
managerial concepts that are now generally accepted but which were, in
his day, quite revolutionary. These included the need for a division of
labour, i.e. organizing the production process so that each employee could
specialize in those things that he could do best. This would enable
employees to use their skills to the full, minimize lost time in passing from
one process to another, and utilize new machinery better. These concepts
are now embodied in the modern factory system with its assembly line and
specialized manufacturing units, and in the acceptance of management's
responsibility in co-ordinating the whole process rather than leaving it to
the individual whims of those involved.

The idea that people as well as machines were an important part of the
managerial function was pioneered by Robert Owen. In his textile factory
at New Lanark in Scotland, Owen, as well as seeking efficiency in
production methods and maximum machine utilization, also paid
attention to the human aspects of the industrial process. He tried to
improve the working conditions and he cared for the whole social
environment, at home as well as at the workplace, of his employees.
(These are still live issues today as indicated by frequent references in the
media to the 'boredom of the assembly line' and the squalor of our inner
cities.)

2.4.2 Scientific management

As the industrial revolution progressed, as the skills of controlling large numbers of people and machines within an overall process developed, so managers paid increasing attention to developing the most efficient methods of production. The key to the problem lay in management's co-ordinating and measuring role and one of the best-known managerial theorists in this area was Frederick W. Taylor, an American steel engineer.

In his two books, *Shop Management* (1906) and *The Principles of Scientific Management* (1911), Taylor developed his four main theories for management's role in the production process.

1 Breaking down each operation into elements, using observation and measurement techniques, (the forerunner of modern work study systems).
2 The recognition of the responsibility of managers by having a sub-division of all the duties within the organization between managers and employees.
3 Clear definition of the managerial responsibility to plan work.
4 Selection and training of all employees in the light of the necessary skills involved.

This recognition by Taylor of the need for management to achieve maximum efficiency in the production process was not without its critics. In particular, the new idea of observation and measurement of all processes — still the cause of many problems today — was often misunderstood, even in Taylor's lifetime, as being dehumanizing. But Taylor's major principle or concept, the application of scientifically based methods of work measurement by management, has been continuously developed and continues to flourish, aided by micro-chip technology.

2.4.3 Modern approaches to management

As the factory system became widespread, as the size and complexity of the industrial process grew, as more and more people began to work in large, often impersonal organizations (where they were often merely the brain on the end of a machine), so attention began to be focussed on the psychological and sociological aspects of the work process. Two individuals, Elton Mayo and Mary Parker Follet, made particularly important contributions to the understanding of this area of managerial responsibility.

Between 1927 and 1932 Elton Mayo, a sociologist at Harvard University, conducted some experiments at the Hawthorne (Illinois) plant of the Western Electric Company. At first it was thought that physical work factors such as lighting, heating, layout etc. were the main explanations for variations in productivity. As the experiments continued it became evident that psychological factors, i.e. job satisfaction, employee attitudes, were even more important influences. The very fact that someone was taking an interest in the employees and involving them in the conduct of the experiments, increased their productivity far more than putting in better lighting, for example. (These investigations are often referred to as the 'Hawthorne Experiments'.)

These experiments sparked off an interest that continues to the present day in the 'human side' of work. One manifestation of this interest is the development of an effective personnel policy in organizations, which we analyse in more detail in Chapter 15.

Mary Parker Follett, who lived in the same period as Elton Mayo, started to study human behaviour at the workplace, and she emphasized four main principles for management co-ordination, namely that it should:

1 Involve direct contact between those involved,
2 commence as early as possible,
3 be continuous,
4 be concerned with all the various elements in the work situation.

With the use of scientific and behavioural management principles now well developed, attention over the last few years has turned to looking at management within a total organizational context. The development of modern information systems and the growth, especially in the 1950s and 1960s, of large-scale organizations, multi-nationals in particular, has increased the complexity of the manager's role. It is now recognized that management cannot be studied in isolation from developments in the political, economic and technological spheres. Out of this recognition has arisen the 'systems approach to management' which is currently being pursued by management theorists, often using computers in an attempt to quantify all the factors which impinge on management.

The development of modern information systems, referred to above, has emphasized the need to consider the managerial concept in the light of changes in the area of communications. It is not surprising therefore, to find that 'Communications' is one of the central themes identified by the Business Education Council and developed in courses under their aegis. However, interest in communications and its relationship to management existed well before the advent of computers.

The modern manager operates with sophisticated computer technology to provide him with instant information to make decisions and control his job. He faces human issues such as demands from employees for participation and consultation. He operates in a world economy and so is affected by such issues as oil crises, swings in the exchange rates and political pressures of every kind. This may seem a far cry from the manager working in the comparative peace and quiet of Robert Owen's New Lanark factory. Yet both of these managers represent, in their own way, one step forward in the continuous advance and development of the managerial concept to meet the needs of the times. Perhaps this is the never ending fascination of management; it is always changing, always adapting and always requiring something new.

2.5 Managerial functions

Whatever type of organization a manager works in, be it big or small, in the public or the private sector, he will have to carry out a number of functions at one time or another. These functions are discussed in more detail in Chapters 4 to 10, but are introduced briefly now to assist the reader in more fully understanding the role of the manager and the concept of management. (Although we identify seven separate functions, there is in practice a considerable amount of overlap between them).

Every manager has to:

1 Communicate

All managers, as we saw in the definitions of Brech and Drucker, spend a large proportion of their time dealing with people. They do not spend their day 'sitting in ivory towers', or locked in a room without ever seeing, speaking or writing to anyone. Managers have to find out what people want, produce and sell the goods and services their customers need, and ensure that the organizations they work in, and the people they work with, adapt to change.

In troubled economic times like the present, managers are also fighting for their own and their organizations' survival, issues which are discussed in the next chapter.

2 Plan

A manager has to answer three basic questions:

What to do?	i.e. what are the aims and objectives of his organization? Having agreed upon these the manager then has to decide:
How to do it?	i.e. to translate the objectives into workable plans and determine the most effective way of implementing each plan. Finally he has to decide:
When to do it?	Good timing can make the difference between success and failure. For example a

new product can be introduced on to the
market too early, before consumers are
ready to change their purchasing habits, or
too late, after competitors have 'sewn up the
market'. Good timing will avoid both of
these dangers.

3 Make decisions

The concept of management implies that the manager holds a position of
authority, being expected to make decisions and, in making these
decisions, to be aware of their wide-ranging effects. Making decisions
implies having adequate information and this function is closely involved
with the communication function outlined above.

4 Organize

Having set the objectives and drawn up plans, a manager has to organize
his resources (people, plant, machinery, money, land, etc.) so as to
implement the plans efficiently.

5 Staff

Organizing human resources implies having the right people, in the right
place at the right time. This involves all aspects of the personnel function
and requires that attention shall be paid to the behavioural and social
aspects of work, as demonstrated by such people as Robert Owen, Elton
Mayo, and Mary Parker Follett.

6 Lead and direct

Making decisions is fairly easy; getting people to carry out the decisions
quickly, efficiently and with the minimum of fuss and bother involves
qualities of leadership and direction. All managers have to develop these
qualities and whilst they may not all be a Churchill or a Michael
Edwardes, they will be expected to take the lead, control their
subordinates, and take responsibility for their actions.

7 Control

To control implies: setting standards, measuring progress, taking
corrective action to minimize or avoid error, thus achieving the objectives.
This requires obtaining information in the right format at the right time.
This aspect of a manager's work has been greatly changed in recent years
with the advent of 'on line information systems'. Note, for example, the
Fiat Strada car, advertised as 'being built by robots', or the British
Leyland Metro assembly line where many 'people' jobs are replaced by

robots and practically the whole operation is controlled by computers utilizing the latest advances in micro-chip technology.

2.6 Summary and conclusions

In this chapter we have shown that the role of the manager is of fairly recent origin and that management, as a technique, draws heavily on practical experience as well as a well-developed field of knowledge for its effective operation. The modern manager is very much a 'professional' in every sense of the word, utilizing skills of communication, planning, organization, human relations, decision making, leadership and control. He or she operates within an organizational context, reacting to and overcoming the pressures and challenges we discussed in the last chapter.

Revision questions and exercises

1   Answer *briefly:*
A   What are the three main elements in the concept of management?
B   How does one describe a professional?
C   What is a managerial career path?
D   How did the industrial revolution change the concept of management?
E   Name two pioneers of pre-scientific management.
F   What is 'scientific management'?
G   To which areas of management did the following make an important contribution? (a) F. W. Taylor, (b) Morris L. Cooke, (c) Henry Gantt, (d) Harrington Emerson, (e) Henri Fayol, (f) Mary Parker Follet, (g) Chester Barnard.
H   What were the Hawthorne Experiments and why were they so important?
2   Is management an art or a science?
3   Explain why the development of scientific management was so important and discuss its relevance today.
4   What are the most important skills required by a manager in the 1980s?
5   Discuss the type of manager required in the 1990s.
6   Can one learn to be a manager from textbooks and courses, or is practical experience a necessity?
7   Plan your own managerial career path and discuss any difficulties you expect to experience in achieving your objectives.

Further Reading

BARNARD, C. I. *The Functions of the Executive* (Harvard University Press; London, 1938).
BRECH, E. F. L. *Management, the Nature and Significance* (Pitman: London, 1976).
BROWN, W. *Exploration in Management* (Penguin: London, 1976).
DRUCKER, P. *The Effective Executive* (Pan: London, 1970).

DRUCKER, P. *People and Performance: The Best of Peter Drucker on Management* (Heinemann: London, 1977).

DRUCKER, P. *Management* (Pan: London, 1979).

FOLLETT, MARY PARKER *Dynamic Administration, The Collected Papers of Mary Parker Follett*. (Metcalf, H. C. and Urwick, L. eds). (Pitman: London, 1965).

GALBRAITH, J. K. *The New Industrial State*. (Penguin: London, 1969).

McGREGOR, D. *The Professional Manager* (McGraw-Hill: New York, 1967).

PUGH, D. S., HICKSON, D. J. AND HININGS, C. R. *Writers on Organizations* (Penguin: London, 1977).

STEWART, R. *The Reality of Management* (Heinemann: London, 1963).

TAYLOR, F. W. *Shop Management* (Harper Bros: New York, 1906).

TAYLOR, F. W. *The Principles of Scientific Management* (Harper Bros: New York, 1911).

3

Organizations in the Private and Public Sectors

3.1 Introduction

Having acquainted the reader with the concept of management, the functions of managers and the environment within which managers operate, we now consider the types of organizations within which managers work.

Britain has a mixed economy, i.e. it has both a private and a public sector. Most private sector organizations supply goods and services with the aim of making a profit. Some public sector organizations supply goods and services, while others undertake purely administrative activities. We discuss both sectors in turn, beginning with the larger, private sector.

3.2 Private sector organizations

About two thirds of all workers (employees, self-employed and employers) are found in the private sector. This sector comprises several types of organizations. There are about 1¼ million unincorporated businesses — one man businesses and partnerships, making this the most important type numerically.

3.2.1 The one man business

By far the most popular type of organization is the one man business or sole trader. They are especially common in agriculture, retailing and the provision of local services such as building repairs, plumbing, window cleaning etc. Because the business is owned by one person, the management style is usually compact and personal and the owner is able to exercise his entrepreneurial skills to the full, e.g. by branching out into new lines of business.

In practice, most sole traders keep to the business they know well and remain small. For example, the typical small trader in retailing has one shop which he runs on his own or with the help of his immediate family. However, there are some outstanding exceptions to this rule. For example, David Quayle opened his first D.I.Y. shop on his own, built up a large chain of shops by 1981, before going public. Shortly afterwards the chain was bought by Woolworths for a considerable sum of money making David Quayle a very rich man indeed.

The main source of funds for the one man business are the owner's savings and ploughed back profits. These are often sufficient, but may well be inadequate if the owner wishes to expand rapidly. He may be able to obtain short-term credit from his suppliers, and equipment on hire purchase. He is also likely to approach a bank for a loan or overdraft facilities, but the bank will probably require what it considers to be adequate collateral (e.g. by means of a charge on equipment). The British banking system, (unlike its German counterpart), is not well known for its entrepreneurial spirit, although in recent years it has modified its 'safe is sure' attitude. (The financial problems facing small businesses, and the steps taken to counteract these problems, are considered in greater detail below).

The freedom to exercise the owner's entrepreneurial skills, noted above, may not be an unmixed blessing. In the early years of a business or when it is expanding, a wide range of managerial skills — financial, marketing, production etc. — may be required and these skills are seldom found to the same extent in one person. The danger is that in following his entrepreneurial nose, e.g. in finding new markets, the owner may disregard other areas that are equally vital to the health of the business, e.g. planning and controlling the cash flow. The successful owner-manager will recognize his weakness and obtain relevant advice—on a full or part-time basis — from others. (Sources of advice are also considered below.)

Even then the owner will probably have to work much longer hours — at least until the businesses is well established — than the average salaried manager. Shopkeepers often have to stock-take after the last customer has gone; farmers have to assess their needs for new machinery, fertiliser, seeds, and calculate the cost, after their 'working day' has ended.

Succession issues, i.e. what happens when the owner retires or dies, are also a cause for concern. Unless the business is to be sold as a going concern, future managers must be developed. It is sometimes said that a farmer should have sons or, if not, pretty daughters!

3.2.2 Partnerships

Partnerships are found mainly in the professions, e.g. doctors, dentists, lawyers, accountants. The partnership overcomes some of the problems faced by the one man business. First, capital is provided by all of the partners, who can be from two to twenty in number (except in the case of accountants, solicitors, members of a recognised stock exchange, patent agents, surveyors, land agents, valuers and estate agents). As providers of capital the partners share the financial risk.

Second, and probably more important, the partnership allows the spreading of the workload and the ability to draw on additional expertise; for example a legal partnership will try to ensure that at least one partner is expert in each of the major branches of the law.

The partners' salary and share of profits will be distributed on an agreed basis. In the event of insolvency, however, all of the partners are liable to contribute to the payment of the partnership's debts, and this means that great attention must be paid to the management of the business, including the choice and number of partners.

3.2.3 Limited companies

The term 'limited' refers to the fact that the owners' liability is limited to the capital subscribed in the company. (In contrast, partners can be obliged to use their private resources to pay the partnership's debts).

There are several types of company:

1 Registered companies

The most popular type, these companies are registered in accordance with the Companies Acts.

2 Chartered companies

These are charitable bodies and other institutions that are granted a royal charter.

3 Statutory companies

These companies are formed under a specific act of parliament.

Registered companies are by far the most important of the three types, there being almost 700,000 in Great Britain. They can be further divided into private companies (over 97% of the total) and public companies (not to be confused with public corporations) which are much more important in terms of their aggregate size.

The main reason for the small size of the average private company is

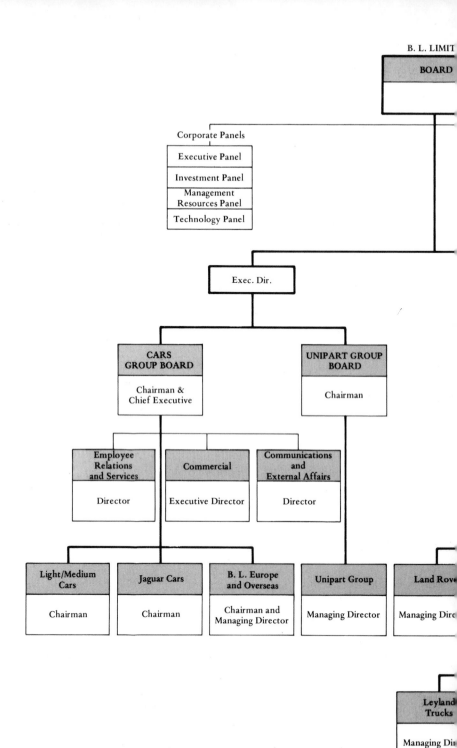

Figure 3.1   B.L. Ltd., 1982. Reproduced by courtesy of British Leyland, Ltd.

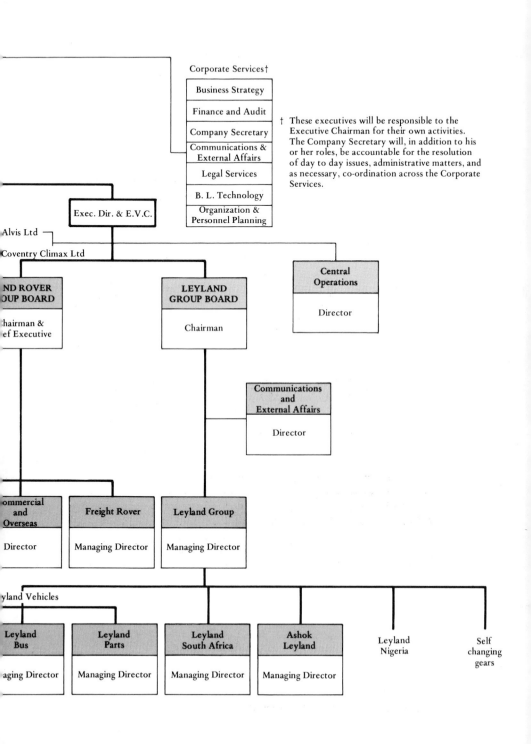

Corporate Services†

| Business Strategy |
| Finance and Audit |
| Company Secretary |
| Communications & External Affairs |
| Legal Services |
| B. L. Technology |
| Organization & Personnel Planning |

† These executives will be responsible to the Executive Chairman for their own activities. The Company Secretary will, in addition to his or her roles, be accountable for the resolution of day to day issues, administrative matters, and as necessary, co-ordination across the Corporate Services.

Exec. Dir. & E.V.C.

Alvis Ltd

Coventry Climax Ltd

ND ROVER
OUP BOARD

hairman &
ef Executive

LEYLAND
GROUP BOARD

Chairman

Central Operations

Director

Communications and External Affairs

Director

ommercial and Overseas

Director

Freight Rover

Managing Director

Leyland Group

Managing Director

yland Vehicles

Leyland Bus

aging Director

Leyland Parts

Managing Director

Leyland South Africa

Managing Director

Ashok Leyland

Managing Director

Leyland Nigeria

Self changing gears

LEYLAND TRUCKS

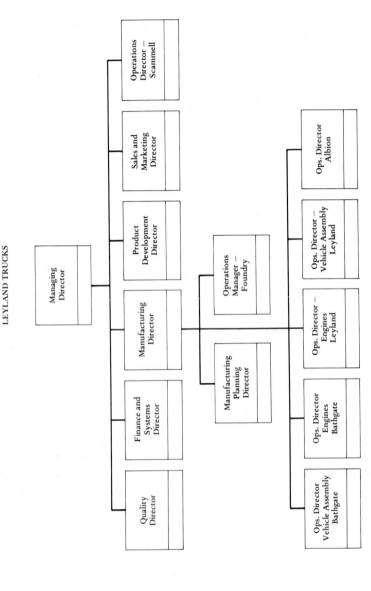

Figure 3.2 Leyland Trucks, 1982. Reproduced by courtesy of British Leyland.

that the maximum number of shareholders is limited by law to 50 (excluding employees). There is no limit to the number of shareholders in public companies. Moreover the securities of the larger public companies are quoted on the stock exchange, where they can be traded freely. This encourages small shareholders to buy shares, and companies such as I.C.I. and Marks and Spencer have many thousand shareholders. (However, an increasing proportion of shares is held by institutions such as insurance companies and pension funds, who are now the major shareholders in most large companies).

Public companies operate in a wide range of industries: manufacturing, construction, retailing etc. The biggest usually operate in several industries and in a large number of countries. This means that their revenue is very substantial. In fact, the turnover of General Motors (one of whose U.K. subsidiaries is Vauxhall Motors) is greater than the national income of many countries.

The management of these large companies or groups of companies is a very complex task, and a common way of making that task more manageable is to split the group into individual units (which may be companies or divisions) each of which is responsible for earning a profit. The main tasks of the central Board of Directors are to monitor the performance of the subsidiaries and to take strategic decisions, e.g. whether to supply export markets from domestic plants or whether to build plants overseas.

Within these units, whether independent or part of a large group, a wide variety of organizational forms may be adopted. Typical organizational structures are shown in Figures 3.1 and 3.2, which show the current structure of the British Leyland Group of Companies and Leyland Trucks.

3.2.4 Assistance to small companies

In our discussion of the one man business we referred to the financial and managerial problems that might be faced by small companies. In recent years, attempts have been made to provide more assistance to small businesses, including, of course, one man businesses. Among the measures introduced by the government were:

1 The Business Start-Up Scheme, introduced in 1981 for three years; designed to overcome the problems of raising equity at the start up stage of a business. In order to counteract the risks of investing in new businesses, the Scheme offers substantial tax reliefs for outside investors in 'qualifying' new businesses.

2 Loan Guarantee Scheme, also introduced in 1981 for three years; under this Scheme the government provides a guarantee for up to 80 per cent of a loan made by a bank.

Increasing public finance for small companies, especially in high technology industries, has also been made available through the National Enterprise Board (now part of the British Technology Group).

The clearing banks — Lloyds, Barclays, etc. — have also become more willing than previously to lend to firms for longer periods, and a number of financial institutions catering especially for small businesses have been established.

The government has also attempted to help small businesses by providing advice e.g. through the Small Firms Advisory Service, by giving tax concessions, and by exempting small firms from the provision of some legislation, e.g. the Equal Opportunities Act.

3.2.5 Collective Organizations

This final set of organizations straddles the private and public sectors, although in most instances the membership is to be found mainly in private sector organizations. The main aims of collective organizations are first to link members in a (professional, trade or other) group capable of exercising collective pressure, and second, to provide information, technical advice, training and other facilities that an individual member might not be able to afford on his own.

As we noted in the previous chapter some collective organizations, such as the Consumers' Association and Friends of the Earth, bring pressure to bear on business organizations. In this section we are *mainly* concerned with collective organizations that represent business organizations or their members (e.g. employees) in their dealings with other organizations and with government. There has been a considerable increase in the number and size of such collective organizations in recent years, for several reasons:

1 The tendency of governments to be more consultative in their approach to the private sector;
2 The growth and increased influence of public sector organizations at local level, calling for corresponding organized pressure from the private sector;
3 The need for greater technical advice and expertise, not within the financial resources of individual members.

Also, increased influence on the part of one collective organization may lead to the establishment or growth of an organization able to exert countervailing pressure, e.g. TUC and CBI (see below).

The collective institutions that we are concerned with in this chapter can be classified as follows:

3.2.5.1 Business groups

The largest business group, the Confederation of British Industry, is the management equivalent of the TUC, in that it advises and consults with the government on a wide range of issues affecting employers. Firms in particular industries have formed employers' associations (e.g. the Engineering Employers' Federation) to negotiate with trade unions on wages, conditions of employment etc. These or other associations (e.g. the Society of Motor Manufacturers and Agents) may also make representations to government concerning the level of imports, energy prices etc.

Chambers of Commerce and Chambers of Trade are particularly concerned with local issues. They deal with local and regional authorities with regard, for example, to planning applications or the provision of local road or sewage facilities. However, this local focus may involve activities over a wide geographical area, e.g. some Chambers arrange visits to export markets and entertain representatives of overseas companies which might build factories in the area.

3.2.5.2 Labour groups

The main objectives of unions are the protection and improvement of their members' positions, although they also enjoy a wider political interest. Unions may be organized on a 'craft' basis, e.g. ASLEF (the Associated Society of Locomotive Engineers and Firemen), an industry basis, e.g. the National Union of Mineworkers, or a more general basis, e.g. the Transport and General Workers Union. Most unions have officials on the shop floor (shop stewards) who are responsible for day-to-day negotiations with management (often involving the resolution of grievances relating to the individual factory or office). There are generally local and district committees, co-ordinated by a national excutive which usually has a paid secretariat. The executive deals with matters of policy.

Most unions are affiliated to the Trades Union Congress, a body representing some 50 per cent of the whole workforce of the country. Each year a Congress is held at which common policy aims are agreed. The Congress elects a Council which acts as its representative in consultations with the government and employers' associations.

3.2.5.3 Professional groups

These bodies control entry qualifications, lay down codes of conduct, provide advice and act as a pressure group for their members' interests. Because of their expertise professional groups are often consulted by government on relevant matters, e.g. one would expect the government to consult the British Medical Association on matters affecting the operation of the National Health Service, or the British Institute of Management on matters affecting managers in all types of organizations.

3.3 Public sector organizations

The public sector comprises many different types of organization, and these can be classified in several ways, two of which are considered here.

First, one can make a distinction between the trading and non-trading sectors. The trading sector consists of organizations which supply goods and services at prices designed to cover their costs. This sector, which mainly comprises the nationalized industries, accounts for around 10 per cent of the total employed labour force. The non-trading sector has organizations which provide goods and services free or at highly subsidized prices, or which are simply engaged in administrative activities. This sector accounts for over 20 per cent of the employed labour force, especially important areas of employment being health and personal social services, education and the armed forces.

An alternative classification follows what might be called the constitutional approach. It takes as its starting point the fact that all

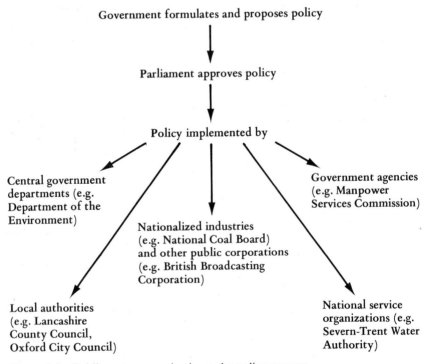

Figure 3.3   Public sector organizations: the policy process.

organizations in the public sector derive their authority from the Monarchy via Parliament. Parliament, as the supreme legislative authority, makes policy, largely by passing Bills introduced by the government. The government then has the responsibility for executing or implementing policy. It may decide that the implementation should be undertaken by central government departments, local authorities, nationalized industries, national service organizations or other government agencies.

We discuss each of these five sets of institutions in turn. We begin with the nationalized industries which, as suppliers of goods and services, come closest to the private sector organizations that we have already discussed.

3.3.1 The nationalized industries

The nationalized industries account for around one tenth of national income (GDP), almost one eighth of total employment and about one fifth of fixed investment (machinery, buildings etc.). Their assets are owned by the government, as representative of the public. Each industry is sponsored by a central government department, most often the Departments of Trade and Industry, and the chairman of the board of directors is appointed by the government. However, the employees are *not* civil servants. The nationalized industries obtain the bulk of their revenue by the sale of products at commercial prices. This means that, for example, the Post Office is a nationalized industry but the B.B.C., whose revenue is derived from licence fees, is not (although it is a public corporation).

In terms of employment, the most important nationalized industries are the National Coal Board (294,000 workforce), British Telecom (247,000), Electricity (231,000), British Rail (227,000), the Post Office (185,00), British Steel Corporation (110,000) and British Gas (106,000).

From this it will be evident that the state has a major stake in the industrial base of the country. The principle underlying nationalization was that while Parliament should have the right to monitor the progress of the industries, e.g. by questioning Ministers from sponsoring departments, the industries would be free from ministerial interference on a day-to-day basis. In fact, ministers and civil servants have intervened in the industries' activities to a much greater extent than originally envisaged. (This is probably partly due to the heavy reliance of many of the industries on public finance in one form or another).

Intervention has meant that decisions are often taken on non-commercial grounds. The Central Electricity Generating Board has bought domestically produced coal rather than cheaper coal from abroad and has built coal rather than oil-burning power stations that (at the time) were cheaper to run; British Airways has run unprofitable services to sparsely populated areas; the National Coal Board has kept open unprofitable pits in order to maintain employment.

This is not the place to discuss the merits of government intervention, (the identification and measurement of the related costs and benefits is extremely difficult). The main point we wish to make here is that government intervention, and a mix of commercial and non-commercial objectives, adds to the difficulties faced by managers in the nationalized industries. It also means that senior managers spend a great deal of time consulting with their counterparts in the civil service, and so have less time to devote to the process of forward planning than senior managers in private sector organizations.

One area in which governments have frequently intervened is the prices set by the nationalized industries. At times, the government has refused to allow the industries to increase prices as much as they wished. Subsequently, as financial losses have been incurred, controls have been lifted and prices have risen at a faster rate than in the private sector. This erratic pattern of price changes creates problems for the purchasers of the industries' products and adds to management's difficulties.

3.3.2 Central government departments

The Central Government plays an increasing role in the day to day lives of the citizens of most developed countries. Total government spending often amounts to nearly fifty per cent of the Gross National Product. In the U.K., despite recent attempts by the Thatcher Government to limit government involvement in the day-to-day operation of organizations (both large and small, public and private), the tide of central government influence shows little sign of retreating.

Although managers and organizations frequently seek more freedom to run their own affairs, they also demand government intervention; protection from cheap imports, or subsidies in difficult economic times, or government orders (as in the defence industry) to protect jobs. At the same time there are increasing demands for more social and welfare facilities, for minimum standards of health and safety in factories (the current asbestos scare is a case in point), for better job protection and minimum standards of training. These and many other demands lead to an expansion of government influence and involvement.

It would not be appropriate in a book of this nature to attempt a comprehensive account of the activities of the central government. (Moreover many readers will probably wish, in their further reading, to explore the impact of government on particular organizations or industries). But to aid the reader's understanding we present a classification of government departments and outline their main areas of

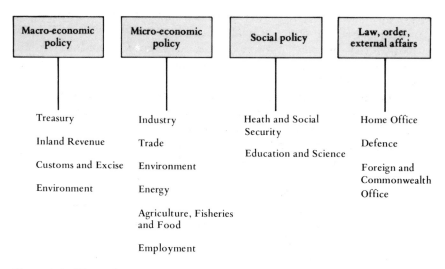

Figure 3.4   The main areas of responsibility of the major government departments.

responsibility. Four broad areas of policy can be identified as shown in Figure 3.4 (this figure relates to England only).

3.3.2.1 Departments responsible for macro-economic policy

Macro-economic policy is designed to influence the behaviour of the economy as a whole, e.g. the rate of inflation, the level of employment and unemployment. The Treasury is responsible for all aspects of macro-economic policy and its central role is recognized by the fact that the Prime Minister is its formal head, although the Chancellor of the Exchequer acts as its head on a day-to-day basis.

The basis of the Treasury's power is its responsibility for the raising of finance and government expenditure. (The Board of Inland Revenue and the Customs and Excise Departments, which also play an important role in the raising of finance, are both headed by Treasury Ministers).

The Treasury's responsibility for controlling expenditure frequently brings it into conflict with other departments which are anxious to maintain or increase their spending. This conflict becomes most acute when the government plans reductions in spending, as in the early 1980s.

The relationship between central government departments depends on the political strategies of the day. With the Thatcher government's reliance on monetary policies and the abandonment of prices and incomes policies, the influence and importance of the Treasury increased. The desire to operate strict spending limits on Local Government and the Health Service (to quote just two examples) led to bitter in-fighting between the central departments involved and the Treasury, and these conflicts were mirrored in Cabinet between the various Ministers on the one hand and the Chancellor on the other.

At the same time relationships between and within central departments were upset by pressures, from the Prime Minister in particular, to cut the number of civil servants and to shake up the civil service hierarchy.

The White Paper of 1982 'Efficiency and Effectiveness in the Civil Service, Government Observations on the Third Report from the Treasury and Civil Service Committee', called on all Whitehall departments to publish a detailed breakdown of their costs, responsibilities and staff numbers. The aim was to train a new type of civil service manager and to promote efficiency and financial control. It was proposed that the Treasury and Whitehall's Management and Personnel Office should co-ordinate the exercise and report progress within several months. However, the White Paper rejected the proposals made by many back bench M.P.s that the Comptroller and Auditor General should be able to carry out investigations at their request to ensure more open government and better access to the accounts of all public sector bodies and firms in receipt of private funds.

Nevertheless there is continuing pressure on all civil service departments to be more accountable and to introduce efficiency exercises and reduce numbers. (Mr Heseltine boasted that staff numbers in the Department of Environment had fallen by 20 per cent under his leadership. Whether it is wise for a Minister to reduce his power base so dramatically remains to be seen.)

The government announced in 1981 that control of pay and manpower in the civil service was to be transferred from the Civil Service Department (to be abolished) to the Treasury. The importance of this responsibility arises because the government is a major employer, so that the rates of pay and conditions of service that it negotiates have a considerable impact at the level of the economy as a whole.

We also include the Department of the Environment here since it oversees the spending of the local authorities, an important part of total government expenditure. (The relationship between central and local government is discussed in detail below.)

3.3.2.2 Departments responsible for micro-economic policy

Several departments are concerned with micro-economic policy, i.e. policy relating to particular markets, industries or sectors of the economy.

The Department of Industry is responsible for general industrial policy including overseeing the activities of the National Enterprise Board and government support for research and development, and for the industrial component of regional policy, including financial assistance to industry under the Industry Act. Although major decisions are taken at the Department's headquarters in London, it has a regional network based on eight regional offices in England. These offices represent the Department in its dealings with industry, local authorities and other organizations. They are also responsible for administering assistance to industry in Assisted Areas. In association with the Scottish Office and Welsh Office, the Department operates a chain of eleven Small Firms Information Centres. As noted in the previous chapter, these centres assist small firms in finding sources of help for financial, legal and technical problems. The department acts as sponsor for various industries, e.g. chemicals, textiles, and is responsible for several nationalized industries, including the British Steel Corporation and the Post Office.

The Department of Trade has four main areas of concern. First, it is responsible for commercial and economic policies that affect the U.K.'s international position. It promotes British exports and overseas commercial interests, and negotiates on tariffs and other barriers to international trade. Second, it is responsible for competition policy (monopolies and mergers, restrictive practices) and consumer affairs (consumer protection and information, consumer safety, consumer credit, trading standards, product liability and advertising). Third, the Department is the sponsor for the U.K. shipping and civil aviation industries, and is responsible for several nationalized industries. Finally, the Department has general responsibility for the basic legal framework which regulates industrial and commercial enterprises, and administers a number of statutes governing company affairs and insolvency.

The Department of the Environment is responsible, together with the local authorities, for housing policies. The Department of Energy is, of course, concerned with energy policy including the development of North Sea oil and gas. The responsibilities of the Ministry of Agriculture, Fisheries and Food have become more important in recent years on account of the negotiations concerning the E.E.C. Common Agricultural Policy. The Department of Transport is mainly concerned with land transport and in particular for motorways and major trunk roads. Many of the functions previously exercised by the Department of Employment were transferred in 1973 to the Manpower Services Commission, which now runs job centres and government skill centres and administers government financial assistance for training. But the Department of Employment retains responsibility for policy relating to the trade unions, and relationships between employer and employee.

3.3.2.3 Departments responsible for social policy

It is not always easy to make a distinction between economic and social policy and some departments are concerned with both. But social policy is the main concern of two departments. The responsibilities of the Department of Health and Social Security range from overseeing the operation of the National Health Service to the payment of social security benefits, such as child benefit and retirement pensions. These responsibilities are carried out through an extensive network of regional and local offices.

The Department of Education and Science is concerned with all aspects of education except the universities, which are funded by the Treasury via the University Grants Committee. Educational facilities are provided in conjunction with the local authorities, for whom education is the major item of expenditure (see below).

3.3.2.4 Departments responsible for law, order and external affairs

The Home Office is responsible for maintaining internal law and order and the administration of justice. It fulfils these responsibilities via the police, prison, probation, after-care and, perhaps surprisingly, the fire service. The external security of the U.K. is in the hands of the Ministry of Defence, which is responsible for all the armed services. Three separate ministries, the War Office, Admiralty and Air Ministry were merged in the early 1970s in an attempt to achieve a more co-ordinated defence policy.

The Foreign and Commonwealth Office is responsible for relationships between the.U.K. government and the governments of other countries, i.e. its role is primarily political. But it also engages in activities with an economic content, e.g. providing information and establishing contacts which aid British exporters.

The allocation of responsibilities discussed above is modified in various ways in Scotland, Wales and Northern Ireland. For example, certain regional industrial policy functions in Scotland and Wales are exercised by the Scottish and Welsh offices. Differences in the legal and educational systems of Scotland and England mean that the Scottish Office exercises responsibilities exercised in England by the Home Office and the Department of Education and Science. Internal security in Northern Ireland is the responsibility of the Northern Ireland Office.

3.3.2.5 The structure of central government departments

Differences in responsibilities mean that each department has its own organization and management structure. As we have seen, some departments are highly centralized while others have an extensive network of local offices; some departments operate in one country only, others in numerous countries within the U.K. and overseas.

In a department similar to that shown in Figure 3.5 political control would be firmly in the hand of the Secretary of State who would be assisted in the day-to-day running of the department by the ministers and parliamentary under-secretaries — all being political appointments. One

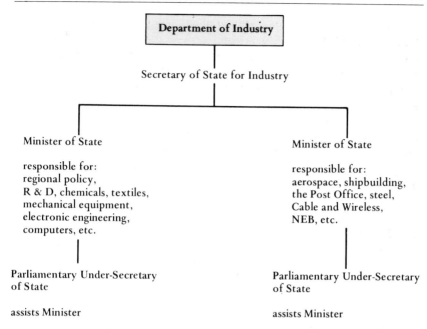

Figure 3.5   Department of Industry.

must not forget however, the tremendous influence wielded by the full-time civil servants who generally remain in their jobs, whereas Ministers come and go as their political standing changes. The well-known T.V. series 'Yes Minister' captured this relationship perfectly.

3.3.3 Local government

Local government was re-organized in 1974 on a two-tier basis (with an optional third tier, the Parish Council, in certain areas).

In England there are 6 (top tier) Metropolitan counties which cover the large urban conurbations: Tyne and Wear, West Midlands, Merseyside, Greater Manchester, West Yorkshire and South Yorkshire. Within these areas are 36 (second tier) Metropolitan districts (e.g. Stockport and Wigan in Greater Manchester) which vary in size and area.

The rest of England is divided into 39 (top tier) non-Metropolitan, or shire counties, (e.g., Lancashire, Cheshire) which are further divided into 296 (second tier) district councils (e.g., South Ribble and West Lancashire District Councils within Lancashire).

Wales has 8 (top tier) county and 37 (second tier) district councils and a number of smaller (third tier) community councils (the equivalent of the English Parish Council).

London has always had a separate organization from the rest of the country with the Greater London Council as the (top tier) authority, the City and 32 London Boroughs as (second tier) authorities.

In Scotland the re-organization led to the creation of 9 regional councils and 53 district councils. Orkney, Shetlands and the Western Isles became all-purpose authorities, mainly because of their geographic position.

Figure 3.6 shows this structure in diagrammatic form to assist readers in comparing the structure in different parts of the country, and Figure 3.7 shows the division of responsibilities between different types of authorities.

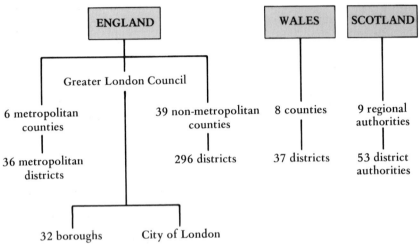

Figure 3.6   Structure of local government.

One of the main justifications given for the re-organization was that the creation of large (top tier) authorities would yield economies of scale in the provision of services, and would allow the same level of services to be provided throughout a wide area. However, re-organization is not generally considered a success. The division of functions still leads to confusion in the eyes of the general public. For example, in the Metropolitan areas education and social services are the responsibility of the local district council, whereas in the rest of the country they are the responsibility of the bigger and more remote county councils. Problems arising from the separation of refuse collection from disposal, arguments over local planning needs at district level compared with strategic issues at county level, arguments over recreation responsibility and current discussions on the need for the police to be more locally accountable, can only lead one to surmise that a further re-organization (possibly into smaller unitary authorities with total responsibility for all services within their area) will not be far away.

England:	Responsible for:
1. Metropolitan areas	
6 counties 36 districts	Overall planning, transport, police, fire, education, personal social services, housing, local planning, environmental health, leisure services.
2. Non-metropolitan areas	
39 counties	As metropolitan counties plus education and personal social services.
296 districts	As metropolitan districts, but excluding education and personal social services.
Over 8,000 local (i.e. parish and town) councils	Local amenities.
3. London	
Greater London Council Inner London Education Authority 32 London boroughs	Transport, overall planning, some housing. Education in Inner London. Housing, social services, leisure, public health, education (outside Inner London).

Wales:

8 county councils	Much the same as non-metropolitan England.
37 district councils	Much the same as non-metropolitan England.
About 500 community councils	Local amenities.

Scotland:

9 regions	Overall planning, education, social services, transport, police, fire services
53 districts	Housing, local planning.
Over 1,200 community councils	Local amenities.
3 Island areas	All regional and district powers.

Figure 3.7   The responsibilities of the local authorities.

The influence of local government has a tremendous effect on industry, commerce and the community as a whole. Educational standards and methods help to determine the quality of young people coming onto the job market and ultimately affect organizations' training policies. The planning process may influence an organization's growth and capital investment policies. Roads and refuse collection and disposal are needed by most organizations, as are the services of police and fire departments from time to time. In fact, it is at the local rather than the national government level that most organizations and managers have a direct interface with the public sector.

3.3.3.1 The organizational structure of a local authority

Just as there are elected M.P.s in central government, so local government has its elected councillors. Just as there is the Civil Service in central government so each local authority has its own full-time administrative and professional officers to manage its affairs.

There is no one organizational structure common to all local authorities. Prior to the 1974 re-organization, a committee looked at the organization and management structures of local authorities and the Bains

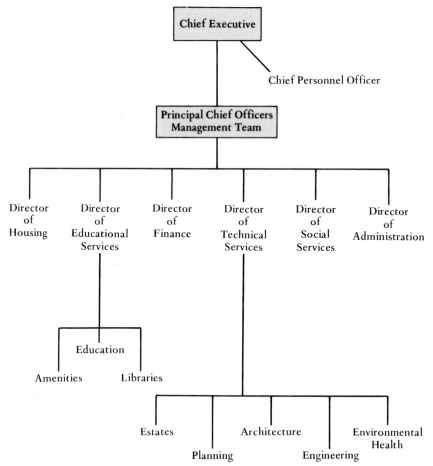

Figure 3.8 Organizational structure of a typical metropolitan district council.

Report on local authority management structures was the result. This report recommended various types of management structures for local authorities based on the concept of a chief executive to replace the old position of Clerk. A possible structure for a metropolitan district following the principles of the Bains report would be on the lines illustrated below.

Whereas the Civil Service relies on the 'generalist' administrator for its day-to-day running, local government is very much the preserve of the specialist professional officer — the Surveyor, the Architect, the Director of Education. This leads to management being concentrated on a strong departmental basis with strong departmental loyalties and few trans-departmental moves up the managerial ladder.

To offset this trend, the Bains report recommended the position of chief executive with overall responsibility for the whole of the running of the council's management, similar to that position in industry.

Many councils have appointed a chief executive and introduced the concept of a Management Team (composed of certain chief officers or directors) to give a corporate, rather than departmental, approach to issues. However, the personal experience of one of the authors of this book suggests that when 'the chips are down', when one is fighting for resources, when there is the opportunity to build up one's empire at the expense of someone else's, then departmental loyalties still predominate. It has always been so in local government and the pressures for professionals of similar background to stick together have never been greater than at present.

3.3.4 National service organizations

We next consider the health service and the water authorities, two sets of institutions that do not fit under either the central or local government heading, and which are perhaps best considered as being organized on a national basis.

3.3.4.1 The Health Service

The Health Service is big business. It employs over one million people, 20,000 being administrators and 70,000 clerical employees. This makes it the largest employer in Europe. In money terms, it is one of the largest consumers of public funds, over £8 billion in 1980/81, i.e. over £140 for every person in the United Kingdom, and 90% of its expenditure is funded through general taxation.

Until 1982, its structure comprised 14 regional health authorities, 90 area health authorities and 199 district authorities. But under the re-organization completed that year the area authorities disappeared and the number of district authorities was reduced. The membership of the district authorities was reduced from 32 to 16, the local authority representation being further cut from one third to one quarter of the total.

The aim of this re-organization was to get more doctors and nurses into clinical practice and out of administration. Previously, the area tier of management drew heavily on medical staff for its administrators, but critics have long argued that such staff do not usually make good administrators.

A second aim of the re-organization was to strengthen local autonomy. To quote the then minister responsible, Mr. Patrick Jenkin, 'The objective is to get decision making down to the hospital and the community level and to give authorities greater flexibility.'

It is also hoped to reduce costs. Savings of £30 million a year, i.e. 10% of the administrative and management costs, have been quoted. However, previous re-organizations in the public sector have been followed by cost increases, and it will be interesting to see whether these savings are in fact achieved.

3.3.4.2 The water industry

The 1973 Water Act re-organized the water industry, creating nine water authorities in England and one in Wales (the Welsh National Water Development Authority). Each authority is responsible for the conservation, supply and distribution of water, for land drainage, pollution prevention, sewage treatment and water recreation. The boundaries of these authorities do not coincide with local authority boundaries but are based on the river basins as natural water boundaries. This overlapping of boundaries has increased the complexity and cost of management.

In Scotland, the re-organization, which came into effect on the 16th May, 1975, led to the return to local authorities of responsibility for water supply, with responsibility being given to the nine regional councils and the councils of the Western Isles, Shetland and the Orkneys.

The National Water Council is the industry's controlling body. As well as providing technical and administrative advice to the government and the authorities, the N.W.C is also a member of the Union of the Water Supply Association of the European Community which liaises with other member nations of the E.E.C. on overall water resources.

3.3.5 Other government agencies

The nationalized industries and other public corporations can be considered as government agencies. In addition to these 'public sector producers' there are three other important categories of agency:

1 Executive bodies, e.g. the Manpower Services Commission, the Arts Council, which undertake a range of operational functions.
2 Advisory bodies, usually set up by government departments to provide expert advice, e.g. the Advisory Council for the Supply and Training of Teachers.
3 Bodies whose functions are regulatory or judicial, e.g. the Independent Broadcasting Authority.

These three types of agency are known as 'quangos' (quasi-autonomous non-governmental organizations), although it has been suggested that non-departmental would be a better phrase than non-governmental since they generally represent an extension of government. Quangos became an increasingly common form of institution in the 1970s and totalled more than 2,000 by the end of the decade. However, in 1980, the government decided to abolish more than 400, including the Location of Offices Bureau, the eight regional planning councils and the Supplementary Benefits Commission. But in April 1981 there were still in existence 1785 quangos, costing about £4,000 million to run.

The growth of quangos is not restricted to this country. The E.E.C. has experienced a massive growth in the numbers of quangos it employs with titles ranging from a Concerted Action Committee on Cellular Ageing and Decreased Functional Capacity of Organs to The Regulatory Commission on Duty-Free Arrangements and a Scientific Committee for Cosmetology.

Quangos are a symptom of the bureaucratic process and follow the old adage 'if in doubt set up a committee'. They also provide status for their members (as well as pay and allowances in most cases) and often number as many representatives of the trade unions as of management within their ranks. They provide a convenient, if costly way of bringing interested parties and advisors together and in this respect it would appear that quangos are here to stay despite government intentions to the contrary.

3.4 The relationship between central and local government

Relationships between central and local government have given rise to a series of conflicts, the most important relating to the financing of local government expenditure and to the allocation of responsibility for the implementation of policy.

In order to understand the debate between central and local government, it is necessary to say a little about the place in the economy of the government sector as a whole. There has been a long-term trend, which has continued in the post-war period, for the government sector to absorb an increasing share of the nation's resources. Government spending has risen as a proportion of total expenditure, and this has required an increase in the proportion of income taken by various forms of taxation. Corresponding to this increase in spending has been an increase in the share of employment accounted for by the government. During the period 1966 to 1975, while the total number of employees in employment fell by 2.3 per cent, the number in central or national government (excluding the Armed Forces) rose by 11 per cent and that in local government by 20 per cent.

People's views concerning the appropriate size of the government sector are influenced by political as well as economic considerations. On the whole the Labour party is more favourably disposed than the Conservative party towards an expansion of the government sector. But in

Table 3.1   Home Civil Service: staff in post[1]

United Kingdom		Numbers	
	1976	1979	1981
All non-industrial grades	557,363	559,025	536,213
Selected professional groups			
Accountants (Professional)	382	370	366
Actuaries	32	31	29
Economists	397	393	370
Factory Inspectorate	724	910	953
HM Inspectors of Schools	602	575	532
HM Inspectors of Taxes	5,922	6,616	6,531
Information Officers	1,480	1,275	1,217
Legal Category	861	874	890
Librarians	363	392	386
Medical Officers	699	677	650
Mines and Quarries Inspectorate	125	107	97
Professional and Technology Category[2]	44,216	42,695	41,361
Psychologists	247	255	257
Research Officers	446	432	423
Science Category[3]	18,624	17,418	16,879
Statisticians	516	537	498
Telecommunications Technical Officers	1,082	1,024	1,025
Valuers	2,956	2,566	2,298

[1] Full-time equivalents at 1 January each year. Part-time employees are counted as half units. Figures exclude casual or seasonal staff (normally recruited for short periods of not more than 12 months). Members of the Home Civil Service working in Northern Ireland are included, but the Diplomatic Service and the Northern Ireland Civil Service are not.

[2] Includes related Professional and Technology grades; there are architects, quantity surveyors, and engineers (mechanical, electrical, civil, electronics etc) in the category.

[3] Includes related Scientific Grades.

Source: *Civil Service Department.*

the mid-1970s there appeared to be consensus among people with differing political views that the expansion of the government sector should be halted and perhaps reversed. A Labour Chancellor, Mr Dennis Healey, introduced cuts in government expenditure and one of the planks in the platform of the Conservative government elected in 1979 was a further reduction in government activity.

Table 3.2 Local authority manpower: by service[1]

Great Britain		Thousands	
	1976	1979	1981
Education — lecturers and teachers	623.0	637.6	622.1
— others[2]	480.6	471.9	434.5
Construction	165.0	155.6	143.0
Transport	33.7	31.5	30.5
Social services	219.6	235.1	239.3
Public libraries and museums	35.8	36.6	35.9
Recreation, parks and baths	90.9	94.1	92.6
Environmental health	24.9	24.9	24.3
Refuse collection and disposal	60.3	60.7	58.1
Housing	48.7	53.7	56.5
Town and country planning	23.2	23.7	23.1
Fire service — regular	36.4	39.7	39.8
— others[2]	6.0	5.9	5.8
Miscellaneous services[3]	313.2	301.2	291.2
Sub-total	2,161.4	2,172.2	2,096.6
Police — all ranks	121.0	124.7	131.8
— cadets	4.4	3.4	2.7
— civilians	37.4	37.7	40.3
— traffic wardens	6.9	5.2	5.1
Agency staff[4]	0.3	0.5	0.4
Magistrates' courts/district courts[5]	7.4	8.1	8.9
Probation — officers	5.0	5.0	5.5
— others[2]	3.8	4.1	4.9
Total	2,347.6	2,360.8	2,296.3

[1] Full-time equivalents at June of each year, excluding the Job Creation Programme.

[2] Includes administrative, clerical and cleaning staff.

[3] Covers central services departments (e.g. engineers and treasurers) and others not included in listed departments or services, and also school-crossing patrols and staff on special functions, trading services, agriculture and fisheries.

[4] Staff working for local authorities from outside employment agencies.

[5] Support staff only in magistrates' courts (including coroners' courts) in England and Wales and in district courts in Scotland.

Source: *Joint Manpower Watch: Scottish Joint Manpower Watch.*

These policies obviously had an effect on the manpower employed in central and local government as can be seen from Tables 3.1 and 3.2 Table 3.1 shows the total number of non-industrial civil servants. The total number peaked at 562 thousand in 1977 but had fallen by 3.5 thousand by the beginning of 1979. From then on it fell even faster to reach 536 thousand at the beginning of 1981, a reduction of 4 per cent in two years. The general reduction in the number of white collar civil servants since the beginning of 1979 is reflected across most of the professional groups.

Table 3.2 shows that local authority manpower has also decreased considerably since 1979. The combined local authority manpower for Great Britain peaked in June 1979, but in line with present policies to contain public expenditure, the number had dropped by nearly 3 per cent by June 1981.

3.4.1 The financing of local government

It has become increasingly difficult to finance local government expenditure from local sources of revenue. In 1980 rates accounted for only 28 per cent of the local authorities' receipts as compared to the 46 per cent received in the form of government grants. (The remainder comprised rent, interest, borrowing etc.)

Although the detailed spending decisions are made by the local authorities, they have to operate within broad parameters established centrally. For example, the basic structure of the education service is determined by the Department of Education and Science, and the system for administering law and order by the Home Office.

The heavy involvement of the central government, both in the provision of finance and influencing the broad pattern of expenditure, has led to the suggestion that it should take full responsibility for some of the services currently provided by the local authorities, e.g. education, which accounts for almost a third of their total spending and 43 per cent of spending on goods and services. Such a change would also make it easier for central government to control spending on those services and therefore public spending as a whole.

On the other hand, it has been proposed that alternative forms of local finance should be developed so as to reduce the local authorities' dependence on central government. A stronger link between spending and payment would, it is claimed, increase interest in local political affairs and hence strengthen democracy.

A Green Paper issued in December 1981 suggested that local income and sales taxes or a poll tax would be the most promising alternatives. However, none of these was thought to be suitable as a single replacement for rates, and it was suggested that any solution would probably involve a combination of taxes, including domestic rates. This conclusion reflects the administrative problems associated with the various alternatives, e.g. when residential areas and areas of work are far apart it is not easy to determine appropriate boundaries for the authorities levying local income taxes.

Although the Conservative party is committed to the reform of local government financing, the government elected in 1979 has been mainly concerned with trying to improve the methods by which local authority spending can be controlled. Under legislation introduced in 1980 the government was empowered to issue spending guidelines to the local authorities and to reduce the rate support grant for any council whose spending exceeded the guidelines. Under further legislation proposed to operate from 1982 supplementary rate increases (introduced during the financial year) would be banned.

It was also announced that the percentage of current expenditure funded by central government grants would be reduced from 59 per cent in 1981 to 56 per cent in 1982, the largest cut since the reduction from 65½ per cent to 61 per cent in 1977.

3.4.2 Responsibility for the implementation of policy

No government of the country can afford in the long term to have its policies thwarted at local level by local government, and yet the very fact that local government is run by locally elected officials means that conflict has been inevitable. In many respects, this situation has been made worse by the trend in recent years for the local government elections to return control of councils to politicians from a different party to that in control of central government. This has meant clashes on various items of policy between central government and local authorities of a different political viewpoint. Example are, in education, whether or not to go comprehensive (the Tameside case being the best example), in transportation, the decision of the GLC to subsidize fares. In some instances, the conflict between central government and the local authorities involved has been resolved only by resorting to the courts, (in the case of the GLC and transportation to the House of Lords).

This conflict in policy formulation and implementation is not new and will no doubt continue as long as local government exists in its present form. How long this will be is open to debate and it is interesting to note that the Conservative party, the champions of democracy and freedom, mounted a concentrated attack on local democracy and accountability, led by the then Minister for the Environment, Mr. Michael Heseltine.

3.5 Summary and conclusions

In this chapter we examined the types of organizations in the public and private sectors of the economy. We started by examining the one-man business and we discussed the advantages and problems this form of organization brings. We looked at the larger business structures, partnerships, limited companies, registered, chartered and statutory companies and commented on the various sources of assistance available to these types of organizations. Collective organizations play an increasingly important role today and we commented on the three main types: business, labour, and professional. The public sector is very large in this country and is composed of a variety of differing organizations, the main ones being — the nationalized industries, central government departments, local authorities, the health and water services. We concluded our examination of organizations by looking at the numerous types of government agencies that exist and commented on the relationships that exist between central and local government. This relationship is somewhat strained at the present time and, like many other problems, has as its main area of friction the issue of financial control and accountability.

This chapter should enable the reader to fully understand the more detailed discussions on managerial functions in the next section, and to place these functions within the context of particular types of organization.

Revision questions and exercises.

1   Answer *briefly:*
A   List the various types of private sector organizations.
B   What is a partnership?
C   What are collective organizations?
D   What are main functions of professional groups?
E   What are nationalized industries?
F   List the main types of local authorities.
G   What was the format of the 1974 Health Service re-organization, and which tier was abolished in 1982?
H   What is a quango?
I   Give two alternatives to the rating system discussed in the 1981 Green Paper.
2   Discuss the possible consequences for local firms of a reduction in local authority expenditure.
3   Should local government remain local or should it merely be an agency of central government?
4   'Government intervention has hindered, not helped, the nationalized industries.' Discuss the validity of this statement.
5   Can civil servants be non-political?

6   'The private sector can provide certain government and other public sector services much more cheaply and efficiently.' Discuss with reference to (a) medical services, (b) refuse collection, and (c) direct labour organizations.

7   'Each year elderly people die because they cannot afford to heat their homes adequately. It follows that gas and electricity prices should be subsidized.' Discuss.

8   You are left £150,000 with the proviso that you set up your own business. What type would you choose? What organization structure would be required and what problems would you initially face?

9   A neighbour offers you a partnership in a small seaside amusement centre on Blackpool's 'Golden Mile.' The centre has a mixture of space invaders, video games and more traditional slot machines. A capital input of £5,000 is required.

What steps would you take before making up your mind whether to invest, and what terms would you require?

10   The National Coal Board proposes to close a number of pits which are running at a loss, but this is opposed by the National Union of Mineworkers. A meeting to discuss the proposal is attended by members of the N.U.M., the Department of Energy, the Department of Employment, the C.E.G.B., the British Steel Corporation and private sector users of coal and electricity. Role play these various participants.

Further Reading

ALEXANDER, A. *Local Government in Britain since re-organization* (George Allen and Unwin: London, 1982).

BANNOCK, G. *The Juggernauts: The Age of the Big Corporation* (Penguin: Harmondsworth, 1979).

BAYLEY, L. GORDON *Local Government—Is it Manageable?* (Pergamon: Oxford, 1979).

BLACKABY, F. *De-Industrialization* (Heinemann: London, 1979).

BOURN, J. *Management in Central and Local Government* (Pitman: London, 1979).

BROWN, R. G. S. and STEEL, D. R. *The Administrative Process in Britain* (Methuen: London, 1971).

BURNETT, D. NEWELL, M. J., RUTHERWOOD, L. A. and TODD, I.A. *The Organization* (Sweet and Maxwell: London, 1979).

DARKE, R. and WALKER, R. *Local Government and the Public* (Leonard Hill: London, 1977).

GERSHUNY, J. *After Industrial Society? The Emerging Self-Serving Economy* (Macmillan: London 1978).

HECLO, H. and WILDAVSKY, A. *The Private Government of Public Money* (Macmillan: London, 1978).

H.M.S.O. *The New Local Authorities, Management and Structures.* (The Bains Report, H.M.S.O. 1972).

Alternatives to Domestic Rates (H.M.S.O.: London, 1981).

HOOD, C. and WRIGHT, M. *Big Government in Hard Times* (Martin Robertson: Oxford, 1981).

KEMPNER, T., MACMILLAN, K. and HAWKINS, K. *Business and Society* (Penguin: Harmondsworth, 1976).

NICHOLS, T. *Ownership, Control and Ideology* (Allen and Unwin: London, 1969).

PRYKE, R. *The Nationalized Industries, Policies and Performance since 1968* (Martin Robertson: Oxford, 1981).

REDWOOD, J. *Public Enterprise in Crisis* (Blackwell: London, 1981).

RICHARDSON, J. and JORDON, A. *Governing under Pressure* (Martin Robertson: Oxford, 1979).

SALLIS, E. *The Machinery of Government* (Holt Business Texts: New York, 1982).

SCASE, R. and GOFFEE, R. *The Real World of the Small Business Owner* (Croom Helm: London, 1980).

STACEY, R. and OLIVER, J. *Public Administration: The Political Environment* (Macdonald and Evans: London, 1980).

STANYER, G. and SMITH, R. *Administering Britain* (Fontana: London, 1976).

Part Two
Communications and Management

In this part we demonstrate the importance of effective communication systems to organizations and managers. We then discuss in detail the basic functions managers carry out in the day-to-day operation of their organizations.

Chapter 4 examines the different types of communication systems with which managers are involved. Chapter 5 analyses three specific applications of communications: writing a report, chairing a meeting, and giving a speech, talk or lecture. Chapter 6 examines the planning function, one of the most important of all managerial functions and one which, by definition, precedes several other managerial functions. Chapter 7 analyses the way decisions are made and discusses the steps necessary for effective decision taking. Chapter 8 discusses the need for, and the methods of, organizing resources to achieve the objectives of an organization. Chapter 9 examines what is required to ensure harmonious and effective interpersonal relationships between managers and employees. Chapter 10 concludes this survey of the basic managerial functions by looking at the way managers control their resources within the organizational context.

4

Communications in Principle

4.1 Introduction

When we use the term communications in everyday life we refer to such things as stating opinions (History is bunk), asking questions (Do you come here often?), issuing warnings (Watch it!) and so forth. These everyday activities are, of course, part of the process of communication within organizations and are considered later in this and the following chapters. But first, we discuss two other closely linked aspects of communication that are part of the organizational setting: communication systems and communication channels.

4.2 Communication systems

A distinction can be made between internal and external communication systems and we discuss each in turn.

4.2.1 Internal systems

Communication systems link the various structural parts or units of the organization together. A very important element in this linkage is that between management and the various units for which it is responsible. Some of these are shown in Figure 4.1

4.2.1.1 The purposes of internal communications

From management's point of view communication fulfills three main purposes:
(i) To inform employees of management objectives and strategies.
    In these days of ever increasing competition, only the more efficient

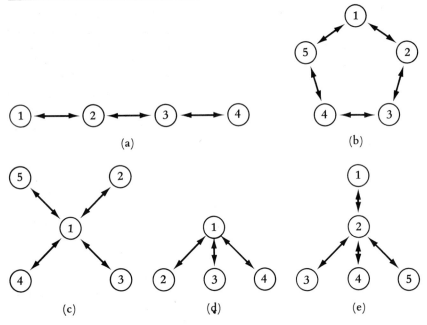

Figure 4.1   Types of communication system.
(a) Link or chain. This is a slow but effective method of communicating, with
information being passed up and down the chain by each participant in turn.
(b) Circular. This allows the individuals to choose a variety of communication
systems, within the overall circle. This type of communication system can give
rise to duplication and time wasting as messages are passed to and fro from the
various participants within the organization structure.
(c) Star-shaped. An effective method of communicating which places a lot of
power in the hands of the person in position 1, and which would only operate
in a very centralized organizational system.
(d) Direct. In this system all the power is with the holder of position 1.
(e) Bureaucratic (or hierarchical). In this type of structure, often used in such
organizations as local government, position 1 is the Chief Officer post, position
2 the Deputy Chief Officer post and 3, 4 and 5 Assistant Chief Officer or
Section Head posts. This system can have the disadvantage of isolating the
Chief Officer, who has to rely on the Deputy, or can lead to the Deputy being
by-passed by the Chief Officer, who makes direct contact with those in positions
3, 4 and 5.

organizations survive and prosper. One of the key aspects of efficiency is
that every member of the organization should work towards the same
objectives. This is possible only if these objectives are clearly defined by
management and communicated throughout the organization.
(ii) To enable these objectives to be attained with the expenditure of the
minimum time and effort.

This follows from the previous point, but it also implies that management should be open to communications from other members of the organization i.e. honest two-way communication. However much thought is given to defining objectives and formulating policies, management cannot hope to identify in detail how these policies should be implemented. On the one hand unanticipated problems may arise, on the other hand better methods of operation may be discovered. The communication system should allow information on these matters to flow. (This is the aim of so-called suggestion schemes in many organizations).

(iii) To facilitate control.

Once the best methods of operation have been identified and the required procedures established, management must ensure that these procedures are followed. A simple control system is illustrated in Figure 4.2.

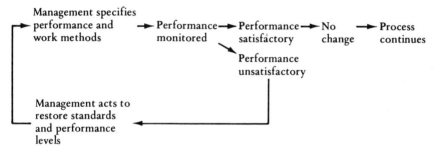

Figure 4.2   Information control.

It can be seen that the monitoring of performance is central to the control system. The results of this monitoring are communicated to management. If management finds performance is up to standard it takes no action. On the other hand, if it finds that performance is unsatisfactory it will take steps to improve the performance; this may also involve setting new standards and work methods and so the process begins again. This improvement may also take the form of, for example, a reduction in cost, an increase in output, a smoother flow of work; points which are discussed in other chapters.

There are many ways of monitoring and modifying performance. In some instances these involve detailed scrutiny by individuals. For example, when a new worker is learning to operate a machine, he may in the initial stages be watched by a supervisor who tells him whenever he does something wrong. In other instances instructions are given via machines. A well-known example is the bar traffic light. When a vehicle hits the bar, or sensor, its presence is recorded by the control box. The control box in turn transmits information — a green light — to the driver of the vehicle, and other information — a red light — to drivers of vehicles travelling in a contrary direction.

In this instance the modification of performance or behaviour — stopping at a red light, going through a green—remains the responsibility of the individual. In other instances, a machine both monitors and modifies performance. A simple example is a thermostat which turns a valve which then controls the heating in order to maintain a constant temperature. A more complex example of monitoring by machine is the stock control system such as the one introduced by Mothercare, the retailer of baby, infant and children's goods. Sales made at all Mothercare branches are recorded by a central computer, which then calculates what goods remain in stock. When stock levels fall to a pre-determined level the computer prints out orders for despatch to the manufacturer.

The use of machines reduces the frequency and extent of intervention by individuals. But however much managers delegate to machines, they continue to receive information on performance and retain the ultimate responsibility and right of control.

Internal communication systems also link different functional areas of the organization. For example, marketing strategies are communicated to the sales force, the results of sales drives are fed to the production department so that the required output can be produced and orders fulfilled, the production department liaises with the distribution department to ensure that vehicles are available when required.

4.2.1.2 Communication and the individual

In the previous section we showed that good communication enables people to perform well and that this benefits the organization. But good performance is also of direct benefit to the individual in that it increases his or her job satisfaction, can influence earning capacity and may improve an individual's chance of promotion.

Good communication also helps to improve the social element which has been shown to be an important aspect of work. Having information about what is happening in the organization often, although not always, helps to reduce suspicion and conflict and thus contributes to a happier working environment.

4.2.2 External systems

'No man is an island.' Nor is any organization. The business organization has to be aware of the behaviour and attitudes of the consumers, or potential consumers, of the goods and services it provides. It must also remain alert to the activities of competitors. This implies constant feedback from the market place and this may require the organization to set up its own external communication network. As part of this it can make use of other networks, such as the statistics provided by various government departments, information appearing in the press and on television, etc.

The non-business organization, such as a central or local government department, has to take account of the opinions and attitudes of the general public, as clients, tax payers or electors, and of the views of their elected representatives, i.e. M.P.s and councillors.

In addition, the external communication system of both business and non-business organizations can be used to convey information about the organization. This information can include advertising, lobbying of M.P.s, making representations to government departments and presenting financial results to shareholders.

4.3 Communication channels

Just as water flows through a channel from one point to another, so information flows through communication channels. A further analogy can be drawn: water channels are sometimes the result of a formal planning process — as when a canal is built to link two towns — and sometimes accidental as when a river bursts its banks. So too, formal channels of communication are deliberately established whereas informal channels develop spontaneously.

4.3.1 Formal channels

There is a close link between formal channels of communication and communication systems. In fact, we can see the system established by management as comprising a variety of formal channels. These channels might include negotiations between industrial relations officers and trade union representatives on issues of pay and conditions of work. When agreement is reached the results will be communicated to the wages office which will in turn transmit the actual money wages to the employees. When we consider later the method of communication used in formal channels, we shall see that there is a strong emphasis on written communication.

4.3.2 Informal channels

No matter how well developed formal channels of communication may be, informal channels will also spring up. The 'office grape-vine', 'typing pool gossip', 'board room leaks' and 'cabinet leaks' are to be found in many organizations.

These informal channels can be so effective that on occasions they may be used by management in preference to formal channels. A strategically made 'leak' can smooth the path for a future change in policy that it would be premature to announce formally. For example, consider a bus company which decided that, because of a shortage of male drivers, it will be necessary to conduct a recruitment drive aimed at women. If it was felt that some male drivers would not take kindly to the idea, their attitude could be improved by making it known that delays and cancelled services were causing the public to be hostile towards existing staff.

The use of informal channels can also increase the flexibility of the organization. If it was subsequently decided that improved recruitment of male drivers meant that it was not necessary to try to recruit females, no further action need be taken. Whereas if a policy decision had been formally announced, this would subsequently have to be retracted, with a possible loss of credibility on the part of management.

In some circumstances information travels more rapidly through informal then formal channels, since the latter may involve calling meetings, preparing agenda etc. Furthermore informal channels may be more effective. Employees may believe the 'real facts of the situation', as related by Doris the tea lady or George the chauffeur who just happened to hear two executives talking, than an official statement or memo. This is most likely to happen when employees perceive the communication system and style as secretive, or inadequate in some other way, and this may indicate that improvements in the system are required.

Information received through informal channels may result in a great deal of stress and anxiety being generated within an organization and this may eventually force management to make a formal communication earlier than they had planned. For example, in times of economic recession rumours abound concerning redundancies, cutbacks, closures, etc. These rumours — even if completely unfounded — can lead to poor morale, a lack of co-operation among the workforce and lower standards of performance. To clear the air, management may feel obliged to provide more regular detailed information on orders received, production plans, etc. In other words the formal communication arrangements are determined by the informal ones.

When information is fed through formal channels management can be fairly certain as to who will receive that information. Informal channels are much less predictable and this unpredictability can give rise to serious problems. Some employees will receive this information before others and this may give them a considerable advantage. For example, if a factory is likely to close and there are few alternative jobs in the locality, prior knowledge of the closure will enable those in possession of the information to snap up these jobs before the employment market becomes flooded following the formal announcement of closure.

Quite often those in junior and middle management are the last to know in these situations. Senior management is, of course, aware because they are involved in the decision. People like typists and the executive canteen staff are often the first to hear by chance in the course of their work; their informal grape-vine often extends to the shop floor and supervisory level, who are often relatives and friends. A middle manager may only find out when a shop steward knocks at his door and asks him to comment on the rumour about the firm closing down.

At a different level of the organization, people receiving unofficial or informal information about the financial performance of a company have been able to buy or sell the shares of the company. When this information becomes generally known and the share price changes, the person who has bought or sold earlier is able to realise a profit or avoid a loss. The unfairness of this situation has led to such 'insider trading' being declared illegal.

We can see then that informal communication channels, based in the main on personal relationships between individuals, can give rise to both desirable and undesirable consequences. Managers may sometimes encourage the development of such channels and indeed may use them themselves. But they must also remain aware of the dangers of mis-use.

4.4 The art of communicating

So far in this chapter we have considered communication mainly from the viewpoint of the organization as a whole. We have looked at the procedures that might be adopted by management, as a group, in order to ensure that the organization achieves its objectives.

In this section we narrow the focus to consider how the individual can improve his communication ability. The discussion in this section can, in principle, be applied to all members of the organization and indeed to people who are not members of an organization. But in line with the main theme of the book, we draw most of our illustrations from situations in which the individual manager might find himself.

We should stress that there is no single correct way to communicate; each situation must be treated on its merits. What follows, then, is a series of ground rules which experience suggests will contribute to a successful outcome in most situations.

4.4.1 Make adequate preparation

In formal meetings this may require the preparation of a check list, on paper or mentally, with thought being given to each point on the check list before the meeting begins. In other situations, preparation may comprise a few moments thought before speaking. But even this limited amount of preparation may make a tremendous difference. The result of a lack of preparation may be a bad start or aggressive words when a sense of calm and reassurance is required. This may make it impossible to put across the intended message no matter how much smooth talk follows. People expect managers to show qualities of leadership, control and calmness. This presumption that they will think before they act, rather than giving voice to their immediate impulses, is expected of managers at all levels. Moreover a smooth, polished performance will often reinforce the manager's status and standing among his colleagues.

4.4.2 Ensure the accuracy of the communication

Adequate preparation implies making oneself familiar with the situation. The next step is to pass on one's knowledge as accurately as possible. This implies giving a straightforward answer to a question or admitting your ignorance if you do not know the answer. If anyone tries to cover up and the real facts of the situation eventually come to light, that person's credibility and future ability to communicate will be impaired. This is a particularly serious matter for managers who, because of their position of authority, are held responsible for what they say. If a manager says something, people assume he means it.

Managers are sometimes asked to provide information which they think it would be premature to reveal. For example, if a company is negotiating for an important contract it may wish to keep this secret from competitors. In such situations, managers must retain the right not to divulge information. However, the good manager will 'come clean,' he will make it known that he is exercising his right to control the timing of the release of information and will indicate why he believes release at that time would not be appropriate.

4.4.3 Strive for simplicity

People can absorb only a limited amount of information at one time. This amount of intake is likely to be especially small during periods of stress or major change. Keeping the presentation and the facts simple, restricted to a small number of major issues or points, goes a long way to ensuring the comprehension of the communication.

4.4.4 Learn and practise

Although some people are inherently less fluent than others, there is no one who cannot develop his natural ability. A manager's life is a constant learning process and it is in the communications arena that a manager has to learn as quickly as he can.

Learning is sometimes informal, as when a manager makes a mistake, recognizes that he has done so and takes steps to ensure that he does not repeat the mistake in the future. In other instances learning is formalized, as when managers take part in mock interviews in a television studio. Managers and trade union leaders are often called upon to explain and defend their views on television and radio, and practice in this particular medium helps to ensure that their views are expressed as effectively as possible. (However the benefits of such training need not be confined to people in positions of authority.) In the institution in which the writers work, students who are about to seek work are given the opportunity to practise their communication skills. They take part in mock interviews, with a skilled interviewer playing the part of the employer. These are video-recorded and subsequently played back. In this way, the students can identify and rectify faults or weaknesses in the way they present themselves.

Finally, learning may be partly informal and partly formal. Communication is more effective when the speaker is aware of, and hence is able to take account of, difficulties that might be faced by listeners. The effective communicator will learn from experience, but it is sometimes useful to supplement experience by examining communication problems in a formal, structured, manner. In this way, the communicator will be better prepared to cope with a problem that he has not previously encountered; even better, he may be able to ensure that the problem never arises.

To conclude this chapter then, we consider the communication problems that occur most frequently.

4.5 Communication problems

4.5.1 Lack of attention or interest

This is particularly likely to occur if external circumstances are unfavourable e.g. if the listener has to sit through a long and boring speech, if he is tired at the end of a busy day, or if the crucial communication occurs in the middle of other items in which the listener may have no interest.

4.5.2 Inflexibility

Where the recipient has fixed ideas and the communication cuts across these ideas, the chances of its being accepted are slim. For example, if a person who has worked for the organization for twenty years and has been a very loyal employee, hears on the grape-vine that he is going to be made redundant along with other people, he may dismiss the rumour as pure gossip. On the other hand, a worker who believes that managers have not the slightest concern for the welfare of other employees may refuse to accept official assurances that the company is chasing orders in order to stave off redundancies.

The temptation to disbelieve information is particularly strong when good news is expected but the reverse occurs. For example, if sales have been booming, management may refuse at first to believe figures that show a downturn. Even if they believe this particular set of figures they may not take the appropriate action, such as reducing prices, preferring to treat the downturn as a chance occurrence or temporary aberration from the long-term trend. There are many examples of companies that have refused to heed warning signs such as falling sales and profits until bankruptcy was imminent.

4.5.3 Source credibility

If the person making the communication is not trusted the communication itself is less likely to be believed (see the earlier section on the accuracy of communication).

4.5.4 Language difficulties

When the source of the communication is a machine, the recipient may not fully understand the language used, which may involve combinations of sounds, colours, shapes, etc. A great deal of effort has been put into compiling computer languages which correspond as closely as possible to the language of everyday use. The aim is to enable people to communicate freely with computers either by writing and reading or, looking ahead, by talking and listening.

If communication is between individuals, understanding can be impeded by the use of technical jargon, accents and by difficulties in the interpretation of foreign languages. This problem is growing in importance as business becomes more technical and international and is very difficult to overcome.

4.5.5 Organizational climate

A sudden change in organizational climate or management style can lead to a breakdown in communication. A change in senior management, a change of shop stewards, or the unionization of a previously non-unionized organization can all have a major impact on communication.

4.6 Management's response to communication problems

As we said before, the more aware managers are of communication problems, the better equipped they will be to prevent such problems arising in their own organization. The prevention of such problems — including those which may partly be the fault of the listener — is management's responsibility.

Such problems are least likely to arise if managers create the right organizational climate and a management style appropriate to the situation. They should also reinforce each communication as soon as possible (actions speak louder than words), try to put themselves in the situation of those receiving the communication, and always provide for sufficient feedback.

This involves paying attention to all the aspects of communication considered earlier: communication systems, communication channels and the art of communication.

4.7 Summary and conclusions

In this chapter we have discussed communication from various points of view. We showed that management establishes communication systems in order to help it achieve its objectives. We explored the relationships between these systems and communication channels. We examined the role of formal and informal channels and suggested that the good manager would use both. We showed how managers and other employees might improve their ability to communicate and outlined the problems that can reduce the effectiveness of communication.

Although we illustrated our discussions with a variety of examples, we have mainly been concerned in this chapter with the principles of communication within an organizational setting. In the next chapter we demonstrate at greater length how these principles can be applied to specific situations.

Revision questions and exercises

1   Answer *briefly:*
A   What are the three main purposes of communication?
B   List two of the steps in the information control process.
C   Give two examples of information monitoring.
D   Why is communication important to individuals in organizations?
E   Why are external communication systems important?
F   Give an example of a formal communication.
G   Give an example of an informal communication.
H   List two of the ground rules that can assist more effective communication.

1   What is meant by source credibility?
2   'Successful communication is a major factor in business and organizational success'. Discuss.
3   Discuss the view that communication is an art and can be learned only by experience.
4   'Formal communications are fine but if you really want to know what is going on then you must pay attention to the informal communication network of an organization'. Discuss.
5   You are asked to give a talk to students at your polytechnic/college on 'Preparations for good communications'. What would you say?
6   Outline the major problems in communications and discuss the steps you would take to overcome them.
7   Communication exercise. Pass a message of not more than thirty words verbally from one member of the group to another, (using a tape recorder if possible). See what mistakes occur between the original and final versions.
8   Communication exercise. Take some current contentious issue and try to convince someone with opposing views to yourself of the validity of your viewpoint. Use a variety of communications media. Students should operate on a 'one-to-one' or small group basis, discussing opposing views.

Further Reading

ARGYLE, M. *Social Interaction* (Methuen: London, 1969).
ARGYLE, M.   *The   Psychology   of   Interpersonal   Behaviour*   (Penguin: Harmondsworth, 1972).
BERNE, E. *Games People Play* (Penguin: Harmondsworth, 1977).
FAST, J. *Body Language* (Pan: London, 1971).
HARRIS, T. A. *I'm O.K. — You're O.K.* (Pan: London, 1976).
MORRIS, D. *Manwatching* (Jonathan Cape: London, 1977).
POTTER, S. *The Complete Upmanship* (Rupert Hart-Davis: London, 1970).
WILSON, M. *Face Values* (BBC Publications: London, 1978).

5

Communications in Action

5.1 Introduction

Having demonstrated in the previous chapter the importance of good communication we now consider in detail three practical applications: writing a report; attending and chairing a meeting; giving a speech, talk or lecture.

5.2 Writing a report

Report writing is one of the most common communication activities undertaken by many employees, including managers. Reports are fundamental to the communication system within most organizations. Because they are formal, written and often available for wide circulation, it is worthwhile taking care over their content and presentation. Many an employee's promotion prospects have been enhanced by a particularly well-presented report at a crucial stage in his career.

In preparing a report the original writer has to bear in mind (a) What to say, i.e. the terms of reference and content; (b) How to say it, i.e. the style and phraseology; (c) Who is going to read the report. These three issues are inter-related. For example, a highly technical report aimed at technically qualified readers can utilize technical jargon. On the other hand, if the report is aimed at non-technical readers the amount of technical jargon will be minimized and indeed the whole approach will be different.

A report differs from other forms of communication by the fact that it is a permanent record of the author's thoughts, available for people to see over a long period of time. It can be referred to again and again and, as many politicians have found to their cost, it can be embarrassing to be confronted by a report, written some time previously, showing a completely different viewpoint from that held at the present time.

For certain types of communication a report may be the only acceptable format. For instance, all companies are obliged by law to prepare an annual report, giving specified details of the past year's operations. (However even in the absence of this legal obligation, most companies would no doubt feel it essential to produce such a document as a record of past activities and a reference point for future operations.)

The terms of reference of a report are often given to the writer by a senior manager, and in this respect the content is to some extent pre-determined. But it may be useful, before starting work on the report, to check the terms of reference to ensure that they cover all the relevant issues and to clarify the purpose of the finished document, since this will also influence the content and presentation. For instance, a report describing a new product might be phrased in one way if the objective is to provide information to the company's salesmen, or in a slightly different way if the objective is to persuade distributors to stock the product, and in yet another way if the report is to serve as the basis of a briefing for the company's advertising agency.

Being sure of the terms of reference helps the writer at the next stage, 'How to say it'. The style of a report is determined by a number of factors, such as the position, inside or outside the organization, of the people who will read it, the nature of the organization's communication channels, and finally the intended effect or impact of the report.

The readership also determines the format of the report's recommendations and conclusions. For instance, if the report is to be read by senior management, terms like 'recommend' or 'strongly advise' would be used. If the report has to be acted upon by more junior employees, a more direct approach would be used. It is far more difficult to write a report for a wide audience composed of people in different positions, with different educational backgrounds, ages and experience, than it is to aim at a more selective group. The danger in writing for a wide audience is that the writer may play it safe and use a civil service type of terminology, which may be widely acceptable but which removes much of the 'fire' and reduces the impact of the finished document.

5.2.1 Guidelines

Assuming that the writer has clarified the situation with regard to the factors discussed above, then following the guidelines set out below will go a long way to ensuring that the report receives a sympathetic response.

1 Research thoroughly

Make sure that any facts and figures quoted are correct; mistakes will discredit the whole report. Moreover, if it is felt that the mistakes are due to a lack of attention or, even worse, are deliberate, the credibility of the writer may be permanently damaged. Information can be obtained from a large number of sources: surveys, government statistics, files of clippings from newspapers and journals, personal research. In fact, one of the secrets of good report writing is often the ability to select the most salient pieces of information from the mass that is available.

2 Identify sections and headings

A report has a beginning or introduction, a middle section which usually examines the various alternatives or options and a final section with conclusions and recommendations. Each of these parts, especially the middle section, may be sub-divided. The various sections should be planned so that a busy reader can get the gist of the report by quickly skimming through it.

3 Write the first draft 'as it comes'

All but the simplest reports normally require several drafts. This means that the writer can allow the words to flow naturally in preparing the first draft, the niceties of style (discussed below) being attended to subsequently. This allows the real character of the writer to show in the report. If the writer can draw on his own experience this will help to show his personality in the report. However, he should include only those experiences that are appropriate, given his terms of reference.

4 Be practical and specific

Words have been described as 'ideas in print' and even though at first draft stage the writer can probably afford to disregard the finer stylistic points, he should try to ensure that the ideas are formulated in a logical, easily understandable style. Moreover, the ideas should be practicable since, if the report is accepted by senior management, the ideas will be put into practice.

It follows that the writer should attempt to be as specific as possible. He should state the terms of reference and objectives. He should examine each option in turn and he should clearly state his conclusions. A report should only be as long as is required to state what the writer wishes to say and to convince the reader of the necessary course of action.

5 Put aside

If time allows, it is useful to put the first draft on one side for a few hours or perhaps even a few days. This allows the writer to give further thought to the issues without the distraction of writing. Furthermore, reading after an interval is more likely to show some matters in a different light and suggest the need for modification.

6 Re-draft, modifying content and style

It was suggested above that re-reading is likely to suggest a need for modification. If the report has been researched thoroughly in the first place, the content is unlikely to require much modification although the writer may feel it advisable to change the balance, playing down one point and giving more emphasis to another.

More modification to the style is likely to be needed and the points listed below should receive particular attention.

7 Engage the attention of the reader

A long introduction should be avoided so that the reader can get to the main point as quickly as possible. The opening paragraphs should be used to impress on the reader the importance of the issues to the organization as a whole and to the reader in particular. (However, superlatives should be used sparingly, both in this and other sections.) The originator should also seek to put the reader in a frame of mind in which he is receptive to the conclusions to be presented later.

Varying the length of paragraphs and sentences also helps to retain the attention of the reader and reduces the risk of monotony. It also enables the writer to emphasize particular points.

The use of appropriate illustrations and examples can also be helpful in this context. Even the most technical reports can benefit from the use of illustrations, both visual and verbal. These should, of course, be chosen to match the readership.

Finally, it may be useful to consult guidebooks or manuals such as Roget's Thesaurus which can help with the choice of appropriate phrases.

8 Review

When these modifications have been made, the redrafted report should be reviewed, so that the writer can satisfy himself that the piece as a whole is acceptable. It may also be useful at this point to ask a colleague, who is familiar with the framework, to read the report and comment on readability, presentation, logic, accuracy, etc. If there are points on which the writer is not an expert, but on which he wishes to be doubly sure, he may wish to consult someone who is an expert.

9 Final draft into finished document

The preparation of a further draft gives the opportunity to make any final modifications suggested by the review. Also at this stage the writer prepares the final instructions to the typist or whoever is responsible for the production of the finished article. Previous drafts might already have been typed and if the report is long, an automatic typewriter or word processor that can store and edit texts has its merits!

A long report may also require binding, and care should be taken that the first impression of the reader will be favourable. A shoddy binding or dog-eared pages can reduce the impact of the report.

10 Despatch

In some cases the writer will have been given instructions as to who is to receive the report. It may, for example, be only his immediate superiors. In these circumstances the only task is to ensure that it is despatched to these persons.

In other instances, however, the writer may be required to send additional copies to other interested parties and this can provide the opportunity to create additional benefits for the writer and perhaps for the organization. For example, if the writer is a member of a professional institute such as the Institute of Personnel Management or the Institute of Marketing, the judicious dissemination of non-confidential reports may add to his status within the profession.

5.3 Attending and chairing a meeting

5.3.1 Introduction

Most managers spend a considerable amount of time in meetings of one kind or another. In the public sector, meetings (and committee meetings in particular) are the cornerstone of the whole operation of managing, for example, a local authority. Because of the importance of meetings and their cost, especially in terms of managerial time, it is essential that they are properly planned and run so that they achieve their objectives as a communication medium without undue time wasting.

5.3.2 Advantages of meetings as a means of communication

From the communications viewpoint, a meeting of several individuals, be it a committee meeting or a less formal meeting e.g. a weekly progress meeting, has several advantages.

1 It provides a means of instant communication with those present, minimizing the risk of errors in the communication chain.

2 Instant feedback, reactions, explanations, etc., can be given at one time to all interested parties.

3 A number of differing viewpoints can be put forward and tested.

4 Decisions will be shared. This has the advantage of obtaining commitment from all those present and makes future implementation much easier. (A good example at the national level is the doctrine of 'collective responsibility' which must be accepted by members of the Cabinet).

5 Young managers, trainees, outside researchers, can attend meetings in an observer's role. They can see the actual decision-making process in action and watch the various participants put their viewpoints, without being an interloper or an obstacle to the decision-making process.

6 Meetings can perform a variety of managerial functions: advisory, decision taking, forward planning, financial, etc. They are therefore a very flexible communication method.

7 Senior managers are provided with a forum in which to demonstrate their managerial skills; this is particularly true of the position of chairman of a meeting, about which more is said later.

5.3.3 Disadvantages of Meetings

1 Any method of communication that involves a number of people spending a period of time together will inevitably be costly, particularly if the participants are senior managers.

2 Meetings often require considerable additional communication time and effort, e.g. the preparation of agendas, minutes, research, etc.

3 Shared responsibility for the decisions taken may mean that no one individual can be responsible or relied upon to get things done; (although a good chairman will ensure that responsibility for the implementation of decisions is agreed).

4 A strong chairman will often get his or her way irrespective of the wishes of the meeting. An individual decision may be presented as a collective decision even though the majority do not really agree with it. This is a form of 'corporate dishonesty' and can be very bad for morale.

5 Friction between departments and individuals may come to the surface in meetings. This is not always a bad thing but it requires skilful chairmanship to overcome the problems and make progress towards an agreed solution.

5.3.4 The importance of the chairman

The skill of the chairman can determine whether a meeting is a success or failure. All a manager's communication skills are tested to the full when he or she takes on the role of chairman and these general, as opposed to professional management, skills are not necessarily present in all managers. Consequently care must be exercised in the choice of chairman.

Ideally the chairman should possess the following skills:

1 The ability to manage a meeting to ensure it achieves its objectives.
2 The capability of smoothing over differences between individuals and departments and obtaining a consensus whenever possible.
3 The skill of 'getting the feel' of the meeting.
4 Independence, combined with the ability to inject some sense of status into the position of chairman.
5 Being able to communicate the results of the meeting to outsiders, and having the ability to fight to get recommendations implemented.

5.3.5 Chairing a meeting

As each meeting is, in one way or another, unique (e.g. the mood of the meeting may be different from the last meeting, there may be different people present), a chairman must have a flexible approach. He will set the tone of the meeting by his opening remarks, explaining the purpose, and outlining the agenda items. He should make sure that the overall objectives of the meeting are clearly understood and should pay attention, in particular, to the following points:

1 Preparing the agenda

In preparing the agenda the chairman should ensure that the items are placed in the correct order so that the main issues are considered before subsidiary ones. An experienced chairman knows that the strategic placing of items on the agenda can influence their success or failure. For example, early items often receive extensive discussion because time is not pressing. As the end of the meeting approaches, or as lunch or tea looms nearer, items may pass through almost 'on the nod' as people rush to get through the remaining items. A very controversial item placed early on the agenda can allow everyone to 'let off steam'; they may then be more prepared to be co-operative on later agenda items. The reverse could happen of course and the chairman should carefully weigh the benefits against the risks involved.

It is another function of the chairman to find out what issues other people may wish to raise and be prepared for them to be raised on the agenda or under 'any other business'. All relevant information relating to the agenda should be sent out to everyone concerned so that they can come to the meeting fully briefed.

2   Running the meeting

The chairman has the following responsibilities:
(a) Keeping to the agenda unless there is a very good reason to do otherwise.
(b) Controlling time, i.e. keeping the participants' discussion to the points on the agenda and stopping people going off on tangents or taking too much of the meeting's time at the expense of other people who may want to participate.
(c) Steering the meeting to a decision and obtaining a commitment from a specific person or persons to implement that decision.
(d) Ensuring that all decisions and any major points of discussion are faithfully recorded. The chairman must check the minutes, ensure that they are a fair and reasonable record of the meeting's deliberations and distribute them to all interested parties.

5.3.6 Committees in the public and private sectors

Committees in the public and private sectors have a great deal in common; all of what has been said above applies to both. But there are also important differences. For instance, the chairman of a local government committee often requires skills that are not needed by private sector counterparts. He may have to help the committee to reach agreement on issues concerned with intangibles that cannot easily be measured, e.g. the output of a social worker, the worth of a home help, the value of education.

Moreover, problems can arise from the mix of members; many committees comprise elected representatives, probably of differing political persuasions, advised by full time professional officers. The chairman must try to maintain harmonious relations in the committee so that the differing skills and experience of the various members can be fully utilized. Perhaps the most difficult task is to reconcile the aspirations of the elected members with the realities of what can be achieved, given available resources.

In organizations in the private sector the issues to be resolved in committees are normally more clear-cut. Although there may be different views as to how a particular objective is to be attained, the objectives will be more clearly defined e.g. an increase in output and sales or a reduction in costs. Moreover, although the membership of committees change, there is seldom such a radical shift in membership as when an election leads to a change in political parties.

5.4 Giving a speech, talk or lecture

5.4.1 Introduction

Those readers who are fortunate (or unfortunate) enough to spend time at lectures, speeches, or more social addresses, know the difficulty in trying to recall all the speaker said. In a one hour lecture, for example, the listening or attention pattern would be roughly as follows. For the first five minutes the audience is settling in and adjusting to the speaker. The next twenty to thirty minutes is the main period of fairly concentrated attention, this being followed by a period during which attention wanders as the listeners consider the speaker's mannerisms, the architecture of the lecture theatre, or the essay that must be completed that evening. The final five or ten minutes are normally fairly attentive as the audience gears itself to a final listening effort, secure in the knowledge that the end is in sight.

From this not untypical breakdown one can see that the speaker has the listener's undivided attention for only about half the scheduled hour. But the problem does not end there. Some of the information absorbed during this half hour will be forgotten before the listener leaves the room, and most of the remainder will be forgotten over the next few days. It is a rare individual who can recall five or six main points made in a speech or a lecture two weeks ago. Is it any wonder that skilled, experienced lecturers often insist on their audience taking notes, or make use of copious handouts?

The less experienced person who is called upon to address meetings only occasionally, is likely to face similar problems and he may be less well equipped to deal with them. But whatever a person's inherent ability as a lecturer or speaker, he can expect to improve his performance, i.e. the audience is more likely to absorb and retain what he has to say, if he pays careful attention to the following points.

5.4.2 Topic

In most cases, the broad area to be covered will be self-evident. The sales director addressing a sales convention will be expected to deal with past sales performance, factors affecting future sales, new products in the pipeline, future advertising campaigns, etc. The personnel officer, addressing a group of newly recruited management trainees, will no doubt describe the main features of the organization — number of employees, location of offices and factories, employee conditions, etc. and give an outline of the management training programme.

But the speaker will often have some discretion as to what areas he covers and he should choose only those areas in which he is an expert. If there are areas on which he feels his audience would like to have information, but on which he is not competent to speak, he should clearly identify these areas and indicate where his listeners could obtain the required information.

5.4.3 Audience

It follows from the previous points that the speaker must try to identify in advance the composition of his audience. It may not be sufficient for the managing director to know that he is to address a group of branch or departmental managers. He should know which branches or departments will be represented, so that he can deal with topics of particular interest to them.

If the audience is external to the organization it may be helpful to be informed about their political bias, their views on current economic issues and the aims and objectives of the professional bodies or societies to which they belong. Thus informed, the speaker is less likely to offend the audience with adverse consequences for the organization he represents.

5.4.4 Audio-visual aids

Audio-visual aids have two main advantages. First, they enable information to be presented in such a way that it can be easily and quickly absorbed by the listeners. Second, when the speaker introduces, say, a tape-slide sequence, the change in the method of presentation helps to avoid monotony or boredom and helps to maintain the listener's attention.

However, there are some risks attached to the use of audio-visual aids. One of the present writers remembers being asked to address a group of students in a school where he was assured a projector would be available. He planned his talk around a series of slides — most unwisely as it turned out, since the low-powered projector was completely inadequate given the bright sun pouring through the windows! Failures occur even in the best organized institutions, as shown by the blank screen that occasionally faces millions of viewers in the middle of a television news programme.

5.4.5 Notes

Few speakers feel confident enough to appear without any notes, but these may range from a few headings scribbled on the back of an envelope, to a transcript of the entire speech. The former has the advantage of giving scope for spontaneity. The latter ensures that no important point is missed out. The final choice will depend partly on the speaker's preferred style and partly upon the nature of the address. An after-dinner speech, marking a colleague's retirement, is quite different from the chairman's address to the shareholders' Annual General Meeting.

5.4.6 Presentation

In some instances, such as the announcement of where redundancies are to fall, the content of the address will be of such interest that the audience will listen carefully however bad the presentation may be. But in most instances the presentation is important and the speaker should seek to attract and retain the audience's attention. It has been suggested that a teacher should tell his pupils what he is about to say, say it, and tell them that he has said it. Even with more mature audiences this is sound advice: a preview helps to gain attention and a summary helps to reinforce the message.

It also helps to retain the audience's attention if the speaker varies the tone, pitch and speed of his delivery. He should also avoid mannerisms, such as extreme gesticulations and constantly patrolling the platform, which distract attention from what he is saying. The language, e.g. technical and non-technical, should obviously be appropriate to the audience, and anecdotes and illustrations can help to enliven the presentation.

On a more personal note, the dress of the speaker can also play a major part in determining the audience's reaction to the content of the speech. Care should always be taken to ensure that this area of personal presentation is appropriate to the tone and setting of the event.

An experienced speaker is often able to judge his impact from the reactions of the audience and, if appropriate, to modify his presentation accordingly. If he feels that he has failed to put across an important point then he should re-state it in a different way. If he feels that audience participation would be useful, he might break off and invite questions.

5.5 Summary and conclusions

We have examined three common and important forms of communication and we have seen that they all require a variety of skills if their objectives are to be achieved. The mix of skills varies from one form to another but several requirements are common to all: adequate preparation, identification of the audience, clarity in presentation and reinforcement of the message. The report writer, the chairman of a meeting and the lecturer neglects these at his peril.

Revision questions and exercises

1   Answer *briefly:*
A   To what factors should the writer of a report pay particular attention?
B   Give an example of a communication for which a report format has to be used.
C   What are the objectives of the draft stage of the report process?
D   List two ways of retaining the attention of the report reader.
E   List three advantages of a meeting as a means of communication.
F   List three disadvantages of a meeting as a means of communication.
G   List the main rules to be followed in running a meeting.
H   What are the main advantages of audio-visual aids?
I   Why do speakers use notes?
J   Why is 'dress' so important?
2   You have been asked to improve your organization's arrangements and procedures for running meetings. Discuss the steps you would take.
3   Dicuss the advantages and disadvantages of television as a communication medium.
4   You are asked to make arrangements for a one day conference that involves several outside speakers on 'The role of micro-technology in communications'.
A   List the possible facilities required for the speakers.
B   Write out the briefing note for the speakers.
C   Draft your conference vote of thanks.
5   *British Leyland Case Study*
     You are appointed managing director of the above company at a difficult time. The sales of the bus and truck division are falling. In cars, the Metro is maintaining its success but the overall market share is falling in the face of increased competition from imports and despite collaboration with certain Japanese producers.
     You are advised by your marketing organization that the group needs another 'Buy British' communications and publicity campaign to persuade the public to buy your products.
     Discuss the various methods of communicating this message to the public and other organizations, and outline the methods and media you would use.
6   *Government Advisory Board Case Study*
     As President of the Students Union you are invited to become a member of the newly constituted North East Regional Advisory Council, which comprises representatives of central government, local government, industry and commerce.
     The aim of the Council is to promote a communications forum for all the interested parties in the local economy and prepare reports for central government to act on. At the first meeting the chairman states that he has received a request from the Secretary of State for Employment that the Council prepare, urgently, a report on the methods to deal with:
     1 Unemployment in general;
     2 Unemployment amongst school leavers and young people.

Role play the different parties involved in the Council. Try to reach agreement on a consensus viewpoint on the two issues, and prepare the reports.

7   *Nuclear Power Station Case Study*
      You are the chief publicity officer of the United Kingdom Atomic Energy Authority at a time when the Government is considering a rapid expansion of the fast breeder nuclear reactor building programme. The industry has recently been criticized in the press because of the possible inadequacies of safety systems of this type of reactor and because of the loss of plutonium fuel pins at Dounray. You are asked to prepare a report justifying the investment in a larger nuclear generating programme demonstrating the advantages of nuclear, as opposed to conventional, fuels.

A   Outline the contents of the report.
B   As the publicity officer of a newly formed anti-nuclear pressure group, prepare a report to convince the Central Electricity Generating Board of the dangers of nuclear power and the need to develop other energy resources.
C   Role play a meeting between the U.K.A.E.A. and the anti-nuclear group.

8   *Planning Inquiry Case-Study*
      The local county council intends to build an inner city ring road which will involve demolishing the old public hall. This has been little used since a new civic centre was built, but it is a building of great historic interest and has great sentimental value for a large number of the older inhabitants of the town.
      Role play the following in a public inquiry meeting:
      1 Present the case for the new inner ring road as an aid to industry and transport in the town.
      2 Present the case against the inner ring road on the grounds that it is a waste of public money, that the use of public transport is falling due to exhorbitant costs and charges, and that the new road building programme is impossible to justify in the present economic climate. Use any other arguments available.

Further Reading

ANSTEY, E. *Committees: How they work and How to work Them* (Allen and Unwin: London, 1965).

ARDREY, R. *Hunting Hypothesis* (Fontana: London, 1977).

FUST, J. *Body Language* (Pan: London, 1970).

LAWRENCE, R. S. *A Guide to Public Speaking* (Pan: London, 1979).

LOCKE, M. *How to Run Committees and Meetings* (Macmillan: London, 1980).

MARKS, W. *How to Give a Speech* (IPM: London, 1980).

MORRIS, D. *Gestures* (Stein and Day, London, 1979).

PARKINSON, C., NORTHCOTE AND ROWE, N. *Communicate* (Pan: London, 1979).

POTTER, S. *The Complete Upmanship* (Rupert Hart-Davis: London, 1970).

TORRINGTON, D. *Face to Face* (Gower: London, 1972).

6

The Planning Function

6.1 Introduction

In this chapter we examine the importance of planning to managers and organizations. As shown in Chapter 2, the current rapid rate of change in the environment within which organizations operate makes planning difficult. But even in such periods of rapid change it is necessary for managers to look ahead and formulate plans for their own organizational development and survival.

6.2 The importance of the planning function

All organizations, big or small, are faced by a number of questions. How can we best use our resources? What is the most favourable time for branching out in a new direction? Which way of meeting a particular objective should we choose of the several that are available? In formulating answers to such questions, managers are operating some form of planning system. Planning systems are tailored to the needs of individual organizations, and reflect differences in management style and in the number of managers involved. But most medium- and large-scale organizations (especially in the private sector) employ systems which embody the various steps or elements shown in Figure 6.1.

Although Figure 6.1 shows the planning process as a series of discrete steps, with one leading to another, it should be emphasized that in practice there may be overlap between two steps, and that a considerable amount of feedback may be built into the system. For example the organization's objectives will be heavily influenced by the opportunities that it perceives; similarly some of these opportunities may be identified only when alternatives are being evaluated.

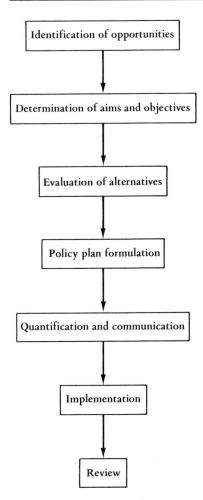

Figure 6.1   Steps in the planning process.

We now examine each of the steps in detail, considering its position within the system as a whole, and the people within the organization who are most involved at each stage.

6.3 Steps in the planning process

6.3.1 Identification of opportunities

The board of directors and other senior managers are involved at this stage of the planning system. As noted in Chapter 2, most directors have responsibility for a specific area of the organization's activities, e.g.

marketing director, personnel director. But many organizations employ, on a part-time basis, some directors who do not have specific responsibilities. Such non-executive directors often have wide industrial and commercial experience, and are well placed to draw attention to opportunities that the full-time members of the organization would not be aware of.

However, many other people are also likely to be involved in the identification of opportunities. Sometimes this will be a by-product of their main function, as when salesmen report that the organization is not meeting all of its customers' current needs. In other instances the identification of opportunities is the person's or unit's primary concern, e.g. when market research, economic analysis and financial appraisals are undertaken. In large organizations these activities are frequently undertaken by a specialist unit or department and, in addition, studies are often commissioned from outside specialists.

6.3.2 Determination of aims and objectives

In the light of the information gathered during the identification of opportunities open to the organization, the next stage in the process is that of objective setting, i.e. deciding on the aims and purposes of the organization and the targets which must be reached. This task is the responsibility of the board of directors and other senior managers.

In setting these objectives, attention should be paid to the following points:

1 Objectives must be definite and specific when possible. For example, 'an expansion of output by 10 per cent' rather than 'to become bigger'.
2 It should be possible to translate objectives into policies and plans for execution, e.g. to achieve higher sales by heavier advertising and by spending more on research and development.
3 The timescale should be clear, and often have a series of short-term objectives which are part of, or steps towards, a longer-term objective, e.g. 6 months, 1 year, 5 years, 10 years.
4 The various objectives must be compatible; this requires that the constraints that one objective creates for others must be identified.
5 Flexibility and scope for the revision of objectives and policies must be maintained. For example, if economic conditions deteriorate it may be necessary to lower the planned rate of growth; alternatively new policies may have to be adopted if the initial objective is to be fulfilled.

Most organizations set objectives for some or all of the following areas:

1 Profitability;
2 Market standing and position;

3 Innovation;
4 Productivity;
5 Resources required;
6 Management performance and development;
7 Employee performance and attitude to the organization;
8 Public and social responsibility.

Another way of looking at organizations' objectives is in terms of the relationship between the organization and the individual. If they are to be successful, organizations must meet the needs of the following four groups of people; (the numbers in brackets relate to the objectives listed above and indicate which objectives are particularly important with respect to each group):

(a) *Customers* (2, 3). Goods and services are provided to meet the demands of customers. As consumers' tastes become more sophisticated, shoddy goods and poor service become less acceptable.

(b) *Employees* (4, 5, 6, 7). The most obvious need of employees is for the money that enables them to meet their requirements as consumers. But other needs are also important, especially when choosing between one employer or occupation and another. The other needs include job security, job satisfaction, a socially acceptable working atmosphere and good working conditions. The satisfaction of these needs is becoming seen as the norm rather than the standard to be reached in the distant future.

(c) *Shareholders* (1). Organizations that have shareholders are expected to safeguard their investment and to provide a return that adequately compensates for the risks undertaken.

(d) *Community* (8). In addition to meeting the needs of these three specific groups, organizations are often deemed to have a more general responsibility to the community in general. All organizations must now reconcile their own objectives with those of the local community. These objectives range from providing employment by using local suppliers, to ensuring they do not pollute the environment. This responsibility involves maintaining contacts with local authorities, helping voluntary organizations, reacting to the views of local pressure groups, and encouraging managers and employees to contribute to local community needs (e.g., serving on governing bodies of schools).

6.3.3 Evaluation of alternatives

The main purpose of this step is to consider how a given objective might best be met or how a given opportunity might best be exploited. At this stage a point mentioned in connection with the setting of objectives assumes importance again, namely that one objective may create a constraint for other objectives. To take an obvious example, there would be no point in reducing price in order to meet an objective of an increased sales volume, if this caused the firm to fall short of its profits objective. Consequently, alternatives have to be evaluated in the light of all the organization's objectives.

In many instances the question is whether the policy implemented hitherto should be continued or modified. Modification may be required because the initial policy proved to be mis-judged, because alternative policies have since emerged as possibilities, or because circumstances have changed.

The change in circumstances may arise in the external environment, e.g. it may be decided to modify the design of a truck so that it can be sold more cheaply to third world countries where demand is expanding. In other instances a change in policy may follow from a change in internal circumstances, e.g. a local authority may introduce a system of leasing rather than purchasing for its vehicles in the car pool in order to avoid the increased maintenance costs that would result from a wage award to mechanics.

The need to regularly evaluate alternative ways of achieving given objectives is generally most keenly felt by private sector organizations whose market is under constant threat from competitors. But the need also exists in the public sector, especially today when budget cut-backs require all managers to make the most efficient use of the resources under their control.

Although we have concentrated the discussion in this section on the evaluation of alternative ways of meeting objectives, we must remember the point made earlier, that this evaluation can lead to changes in those objectives, Consider the policies of the clearing banks. For the past few years, they have been considering how they could best meet the needs of their customers in order to counteract the increasing competition from foreign banks and other financial institutions such as the building societies. Several banks have changed their structure in such a way as to make a clearer distinction between those parts concerned with firms and other organizations on the one hand, and those concerned with personal business on the other. This clearer identification of a personal market is one of the reasons that has led the clearing banks to offer an increased range of services to this sector, the most notable recently being the huge expansion in loans for house purchase.

6.3.4 Policy/plan formulation

We now reach the stage at which objectives are translated into detailed policies and plans. This is usually undertaken by an ad hoc team comprising personnel seconded from their usual operational roles. At this stage the broad implications for the various parts of the organization — divisions, departments or, in large groups, companies — are made clear. Targets for each manager are laid down, perhaps with an indication of the reasons for any changes from the current targets, and the available resources may be specified.

The degree of detail contained in these policy documents varies considerably from one organization to another. At one extreme are private sector groups such as GEC which lay down financial targets for each company within the group and give each company considerable freedom as to the policies that it adopts in an attempt to reach that target. At the other extreme, public sector organizations tend to be much more specific about the policies to be adopted and the resources available, with detailed budgets being established for equipment, materials, staff of various kinds etc.

6.3.5 Quantification and communication

We have noted that some degree of quantification and communication is involved at the policy/plan formulation stage. The reason for distinguishing this as a separate stage is to denote that a different group of personnel now became involved in the planning process. Accountants, engineers, work study officers, sales managers, and production managers all use their specialist skills to further quantify the plans, and to set departmental and individual work targets. These targets must then be communicated to the people concerned.

The principles underlying successful communication were outlined in the previous chapter. The plan must be well written, capable of being understood by all those who need to use it. (Some organizations have made the mistake of introducing massive corporate plans, comprising several volumes. While these are comprehensive, few managers read them). At one time it was thought desirable to present targets that were unattainable since this would make people try harder. It is now generally accepted that this is counter-productive, and that it is preferable to establish targets that are realistic in terms of both 'quantity' and time-scale; in this way people's commitment is more likely to be retained.

6.3.6 Implementation

The activities involved in implementing plans are discussed at length in later chapters, and there is therefore no need to discuss them here. It is sufficient to note that the more changes are made from current policies, the more problems in implementation will need to be overcome (unless, of course, the changes are designed to remedy existing problems in implementation).

6.3.7 Review

Do the policies and plans work in practice? Line managers, supervisors, administrators and financial staff assemble data and compare performance with target, outcome with prediction (often utilizing computers). This information is then passed to senior managers for their consideration.

It is at this stage that the full benefits of having a proper management structure for planning are realized. If departmental managers make progress reports (implying a commitment on their part to the planning process), and if the top management structure ensures that these reports will be received, the system has a good chance of working. But any departmental jealousies, personal rivalries and power struggles are likely to inhibit the flow of information and cause the planning system, or total managerial system, to fail.

At the end of planning cycle, usually yearly to coincide with the annual budget, most organizations incorporate the results of the planning exercise in their annual report. Management must then ask whether, given the time and cost involved, the exercise has proved worthwhile. If the answer appears to be no, then the planning system should itself be evaluated and an attempt made to remedy deficiencies.

6.4 Planning in action

6.4.1 Corporate planning

In Section 6.3 we discussed the steps taken in the policy/plan formulation process. Some organizations, particularly those in the public sector, have developed this process to a high degree of sophistication and introduced a system of total or corporate planning to cover all the activities of their organization.

Corporate planning may be regarded as the planning process at its most sophisticated stage of development. Corporate planning makes use of the total information and communication resources of an organization, relates these to the decision-making processes and introduces a systematic approach to planning and management for all the resources of an organization. It implies the willingness of some managers and departments to subjugate their own particular plans to the overall requirement for the organization. To achieve this a central unit to control and monitor the developing situation is often essential.

There are a number of reasons for introducing a corporate planning system.

1 Many organizations need to think out their objectives and identify gaps that exist between their current supply of goods and services and what the market actually wants.
2 The larger the organization, the more likely there is to be a competing need for scarce resources. To achieve maximum benefit this implies the need for central planning and control as opposed to planning by individual departments or managers.
3 The pace of change is quickening and organizations have to adapt and react to changes corporately, rather than on an individual departmental basis.
4 Modern computer-based information systems provide an overall, as well as departmental, viewpoint and this aids overall planning to a degree that was impossible several years ago.

One of the major decisions senior management have to face when introducing a corporate planning system is, who is to gather the information and formulate the corporate plan. In many organizations corporate planning will involve changes in the existing management and organizational structures (e.g. in the public sector, changes in the committee structure, alterations to the membership of the management team). In some cases the answers to this preparation and control problem have been resolved by having a large central planning unit which gathers the information, formulates plans and then monitors the total process. In other cases, planners may be seconded to work with individual departments or managers, and a small central unit merely acts as a co-ordinator to the planning process.

Whichever system is chosen, corporate planning involves time and money, particularly the time of senior managers. It is essential therefore that a 'quick pay off' for all this time and effort is realized. If members of the organization have to wait several months or even two or three years before they reap any of the benefits of the corporate planning system, then they are likely to revert to their own individual, unco-ordinated planning systems.

Corporate planning can be very effective when operated properly. But it does involve time and effort in the setting up process, an acceptance of change and a realization by managers that the corporate need may be more important than their own individual needs and ambitions. Many organizations are now counting the heavy costs of corporate planning systems in the light of rapid changes in their operational environment, and comparing these costs with the benefits of a total approach against an unco-ordinated and individualist approach. This dilemma has faced managers and organizations for many years and is likely to continue to do so for the foreseeable future.

6.4.2 Management by objectives

In the 1960s a technique of planning by objective setting on a total organizational and individual basis was developed, in the main by J. Humble of Urwick Orr and Partners. The system was called Management by objectives (MBO). This system was used to assess managerial performance (see Chapter 15), but it was in the area of planning that the system made its greatest impact.

The system rested on the setting of

1 Quantifiable objectives i.e. How much?
2 Qualitative objectives i.e. How well?
3 Verifiable objectives i.e. With what result?

It was hoped that involving staff in the setting of their own objectives, in consultation with their managers, would lead to better and more committed performance by individuals, i.e. agreed plans and objectives = agreed performance.

The system was developed in the growth era of the 1960s and adopted by numerous organizations. However, in the recession-riddled 1970s the system fell into disrepute. Many organizations questioned whether the time and money involved in setting up the system really paid off when the pace of change quickened and the future was so uncertain. For example, during the three day working week era, 1973/74, organizations were re-assessing their objectives on an almost daily basis.

The advocates of MBO claim the following advantages for this system of planning and appraisal:

1 It results in better management as it clarifies and commits managers to agreed objectives.
2 The organizational structure is questioned and as a result anomalies and problems sorted out.
3 The system increases commitment on a total organizational basis to the organization's objectives.
4 Effective controls over departments and individuals are developed.
5 The discussions at all levels of the organization lead to better overall objectives and plans as everyone makes an input to the total process, not just senior managers or specialist planners.

Various problems in applying the system have been experienced, including:

1 Failure by senior management in many organizations to spend sufficient time teaching the philosophy of the system and selling it properly.
2 Failure to give proper guidelines to the setters of objectives.
3 Setting too optimistic objectives that in practice were difficult to meet.

4 The objectives and goals had too short a time scale.

5 Setting up an inflexible system that could not adapt to rapid changes within and from outside the organization.

6 The system sometimes proved unable to accommodate rapid environmental changes.

6.5 Why planning systems fail

Experience shows that there are many reasons why the results of planning may not appear to justify the costs so that planning is regarded as having failed:

1 Lack of commitment by the people concerned, particularly senior management. This has been found to be the single most important reason for the 'failure' of planning within organizations. The effectiveness of corporate planning departments has been found to depend crucially upon the degree of support received from the board of directors or management team.

2 Other personal deficiencies: resistance to change, a reluctance to delegate, a failure to recognize the total scope and all-encompassing nature of the planning function and system.

3 Operational deficiencies: a failure to establish meaningful objectives and policies, a confusion between the preliminary study stages of planning and operational plans, over-reliance on past experience or hunch, insufficient quantification, poor and inflexible control techniques.

4 A hostile environment: a period of change so rapid as to require constant planning adjustments without it ever being possible to achieve identifiable results.

6.6 Summary and conclusions

In this chapter we have examined the importance of the planning process within the total managerial function. We examined the steps to be taken in setting up a planning process, discussed the need for proper objective setting, discussed management's role in the planning function and looked at two planning systems, corporate planning and management by objectives. Finally, we outlined some of the common causes of failure in planning systems.

Revision questions and exercises

1   Answer *briefly:*
A   What is the first step in the planning process?
B   Why are non-executive directors useful in the planning process?

C   Who decides the aims and objectives of an organization?
D   List four areas for which objectives are set.
E   Why are policies that have been implemented often changed?
F   Why is the review process so important in the total planning system?
G   What is corporate planning?
H   What is MBO?
I   What is meant by 'operational deficiencies' with reference to corporate planning?
J   Name two areas of 'personal deficiency' that can affect the success of corporate planning.
2   Explain why the planning function is so important.
3   Outline the main steps in the planning process.
4   What key areas should be considered in setting objectives for an organization? Which of these areas do you consider to be the most important?
5   Outline the main advantages of the system of management by objectives, and the reasons why it might fail.
6   Discuss the issues to be considered in introducing a system of corporate planning.
7   'All planning systems are doomed to failure in the end'. Discuss this statement with reference to organizations in the public and private sectors.
8   Draw up a career plan for yourself for the next five years and discuss with other members of your group the constraints and problems that are likely to affect your chosen path.

Further Reading

ARGENTI, J. *Corporate Planning* (Allen and Unwin: London, 1968).

BRECH, E. F. L. *The Principles and Practice of Management* (Longmans, Green and Co: London, 1963).

DRUCKER, P. *Managing for Results* (Heinemann: London, 1964).

EDDISON, T. *Local Government Management and Corporate Planning* (Leonard Hill: Leighton Buzzard, 1975).

GREENWOOD, R. and STEWART, J. D. *Corporate Planning in English Local Government* (Charles Knight: London, 1974).

HUMBLE, J. W. *Improving Business Results* (McGraw-Hill: London, 1968).

HUSSEY, D. E. *Introducing Corporate Planning* (Pergamon: Oxford, 1971).

STEINER, G. *Top Management Planning* (Macmillan: New York, 1969).

7

Decision Making

7.1 Introduction

In the previous chapter we examined the planning process within organizations. We saw that planning involves a series of decisions about the (desired) future activities of the organization. In the present chapter, although we again refer to the planning process, we are much more concerned with decisions that arise during the implementation of plans and policies. We are therefore extending the argument in time. The focus is also widened in the sense that all managers, whether involved in planning or not, are involved in decision making.

7.2 Stages in the decision-making process

7.2.1 Defining the problem

It may seem strange, in the light of the introduction to the chapter, to begin with 'defining the problem'. If the problem arises because of a failure to fulfil plans, surely it will be obvious what the problem is? Unfortunately, this is by no means always the case. The issue that first comes to the manager's attention may only be a manifestation of a much bigger problem, and the manager must delve below the surface to discover whether this is so. Otherwise the wrong decision may be taken.

For example a firm may experience a cash flow problem because sales fall below the target. One way to overcome the problem might be to obtain a bank loan, and this solution might be satisfactory if the fall in sales is due to special circumstances, e.g. a spell of unusually cold weather, and is soon reversed. On the other hand the fall in sales may reflect a more permanent change, e.g. a loss of custom to a competitor who has recently introduced a new product. In these circumstances spending borrowed money might constitute 'throwing good money after bad', and a better alternative would be to try to re-allocate the firm's resources into the making of other products. It is clearly important that the cause of the decline in sales should be identified.

Let us take an example from the personnel area, an increase in employee absences on the grounds of sickness. If the manager simply reacts to the immediate issue, he might authorize the spending of more money on company medical facilities, or introduce more extensive medical checks for applicants. Before taking these steps, however, it would be sensible to ensure that the increased absences were not, in fact, symptoms of a deeper problem, e.g. a loss of job satisfaction because of changed working methods, or personal conflicts due to staff changes.

It follows that managers should ensure that they give adequate attention to all the elements that impinge on the area of decision. However, having done so, they should then decide which of the various issues are the most important. An experienced manager is able to isolate the critical factors and concentrate his attention on them.

7.2.2 Determine the decision process to be followed

Several important issues arise under this heading. First, who should take the decision? The person who first becomes aware of a problem (or at least of the symptom) may not be in a position, or have the authority, to provide the solution. For example, the sales manager may first become aware of a short-fall in sales, but this may be due to a failure on the part of the production department to provide the quality of products required by the customers. Even when the person who first identifies the problem is involved in the solution the organization's style of management may require that the decision be taken jointly with other managers.

In the public sector decisions are often made by committees of several individuals (see below). Even in organizations with a large amount of delegated responsibility, decisions are often shared between several managers or departments; only the really crucial issues are ultimately decided by one person and that is often someone very senior in the organization.

If a decision ultimately gives rise to a number of more minor decisions the responsibility for these minor decisions may be delegated to junior managers or even supervisors. For example, a decision may be taken at a senior level to introduce a work sharing scheme. In some of these schemes the actual design and production methods are pre-ordained, but it is left to the employees to allocate various functions amongst themselves so as to avoid boredom or undue fatigue.

Public sector organizations, especially those in the non-market sector, frequently take decisions on the basis of precedent, i.e. 'What did we do last time in a similar situation?'. This may involve getting out the relevant files and going through all the previous correspondence and minutes relating to similar issues, and using these as the basis for the present decision. Alternatively, reference may be made to manuals in specifying the course of action to be taken.

There are two justifications for proceeding in this way. First, by 'routinizing' decisions it is possible to push responsibility to lower levels in the organization. Second, it ensures consistency in decision making, a factor that is particularly important in organizations implementing government policy, e.g. in paying social security benefits to individuals or granting financial assistance to firms.

On the other hand such a system would not be appropriate in organizations using new technologies or in other innovatory situations. Previous 'case histories' are unlikely to exist and even if they did they might inhibit rather than encourage change.

7.2.3 Choosing the time scale

Two separate issues arise here: the time period within which the decision must be taken, and the period within which the decision's consequences will be felt. We have stressed the importance of carefully defining the problem and of considering all the relevant factors. However, there is often a trade-off between information and cost. The more information is sought the greater the cost involved, in terms of employees' time (which could otherwise be devoted to doing other things), and also, perhaps, in commissioning special studies. Moreover, delaying the decision may also increase the cost of implementing the solution, especially in inflationary conditions when costs rise over time. For example, if a firm has to buy new machinery to improve product quality, that machinery is likely to cost more next year or even next month than today. Consequently, it is often necessary to have a cut-off point, by which time the decision must be taken, even though it might be possible to obtain more information.

If the decision is a particularly difficult one to make or is likely to have wide-ranging effects that cannot be immediately ascertained, it may be better to make a temporary decision on the issue so as to postpone a final solution until the situation becomes clearer or until more favourable times, e.g. in the hope of an upturn in the market or lower interest rates. The building societies often operate in this way, delaying a change in their mortgage rate following a change in other interest rates. They make a temporary decision to leave the rate unchanged, knowing that subsequently they may have to change this decision.

The effects of some decisions are felt over a longer period of time than others. Changes in fiscal or monetary policy may take a long time to work their way through all sectors of the economy and their initial impact may be slight. This may be a good thing from a producer's point of view since sudden changes in economic conditions make it difficult to plan their operations efficiently. On the other hand it is obviously undesirable if the government is faced with a crisis requiring an immediate change in conditions.

The use of computer simulation techniques now allows managers to achieve, what a few years ago was almost impossible, a fairly accurate estimate of the total impact of a decision, over a given timescale, on all sections of their organization or, in the case of government, on individual sectors and the total economy.

This facility may also be available to critics of the decision maker. When the Government or the Chancellor announces a change in economic policy, the effects of the policy can be predicted by simulation using the Treasury economic model, which is now made available to the public, or other models, e.g. that of the London Business School. This allows the critics not only to comment on the chances of the outcome predicted by the Government coming to pass, but also to work out the assumptions on which policy is based, e.g. changes in wage rates. This has made government economic decision making much more of an 'open event' than in the past.

As noted in the previous chapter, managers have to weigh up their long- and short-term objectives. These may sometimes conflict, e.g. a decision to cut the price of a product may keep the cash coming in and maintain production and employment for a few weeks. But in the long term such a price may be impossible to maintain. One of the advantages of planning is that is enables the effects of the decision on the total organization to be estimated and reduces the chance of taking decisions that are not in accordance with the long-term objectives of the organization.

7.2.4 Gathering information

As noted in the previous chapter, organizations generate a great deal of information in formulating and reviewing plans. Consequently, when a problem arises much of the information required for the solution may already be to hand. If, for example, a decision has to be made concerning a change in the level of output, the managers involved ought to be able to 'call up', perhaps from a central computer file or from the records of individual departments, data showing the effect of the change on production costs, materials requirements, the number of workers needed etc.

In current circumstances, when private sector firms are facing keen national and even keener international competition, when the public sector is being requested to give even greater value for money, information on costs is vital. The growth in importance of the accountancy profession in recent years mirrors the vital role financial information now plays in all managerial decisions (see Chapter 11). Increasing competition has also led to more information being gathered on a regular basis on the markets served by producers. This information relates to trends in demand and to the activities of competitors — prices, advertising, changes in product quality etc. (see Chapter 12). Much of this data is quantitative but decisions are also made on more 'qualitative'grounds, including people's past experience. There are still managers who have a distrust of figures ('There are lies, damn lies and statistics') and prefer to manage 'by the seat of their pants'. But a good manager will combine both these approaches in his decision-making process. He will use quantitative data, but will be aware of the potential deficiences and will interpret the data in the light of his own experience.

If the necessary information is not available within the organization then it may be necessary to use outside resources. Specialist consultants in, say, the engineering or marketing areas can undertake surveys and provide information, and make recommendations for management to act upon. External statistics, particularly those produced by government agencies, can also help, and 'on line' computer systems and document and data transmission systems enable organizations to draw on statistics from all over the world, e.g. the use banks make of international financial data, stock market data etc.

Managers have to sure that the format in which information is gathered and presented is understandable, not only by themselves, but also by other people who may wish to check the basis of the decision at a later date. Managers have to be confident about the reliability of the information and of its source.

When all the available information has been examined managers must return to stage one and consider whether, in the light of this increased knowledge, the problem still appears to be the same as it did initially and whether the original aims of the decision are still valid.

7.2.5 Examining the alternatives

As noted in Chapter 10, many decisions, especially in the control area, are in effect taken by computers, the role of the manager being confined to decisions relating to the introduction and design of the system. However, as noted in our discussion of planning, managers are seldom presented with information that leads to only one possible decision or course of action. (If this were so there would be no real need for managers, as people would merely act according to the dictates of the information). In choosing from the alternative courses of action the manager will be aware that he will have to live with the consequences of the decision. Indeed if the decision is a major one his future career may depend upon the outcome. Choosing the right alternative, far from being a matter of simply following the direction indicated by the statistics, becomes a very personal decision.

7.2.6 Implementation

Unless the manager is running a one man business every decision will require the assistance of someone else to carry it out. This means that to complete the decision-making process a manager must:

1 Ascertain who takes what action and at what time;
2 Ascertain the time each part of the decision will take to implement;
3 Decide on the methods of communicating the decision;
4 Consider what effect the decision is going to have on other people and take steps to counteract any adverse reactions;
5 Set up a system of information feedback so that he can modify his decision in the light of experience, if necessary.

7.3 Decision making by committee

So far our comments on the decision-making process have been mainly concerned with individual management decision making, although the steps to be taken are common to all decisions. Readers who work in, or are familiar with, the public sector will know that committee or group, rather than individual, decision making is the norm. It may be useful to outline the advantages and disadvantages of this type of decision-making process.

7.3.1 Advantages of committees as a decision-making medium

1 A committee allows differing viewpoints to be brought together in the same place and at the same time. Differences can be aired, alternatives hammered out, all the relevant information being available for all to see.
2 The committee, as every good politician realizes, is a good co-ordinating medium. Having all the relevant parties to the decision in one room is a far better and easier way of co-ordinating progress, than relying on memos or telephone calls. (This benefit is felt mainly by the manager who would otherwise have to write the memos or make the telephone calls. There are, however, corresponding costs, as pointed out below).

3 Individuals feel better motivated if they have been involved in making the decision and have personally followed the arguments and discussions over the alternatives. By involving everyone concerned, by obtaining a consensus, a committee can achieve a higher level of motivation than most other decision-making methods.

4 Committee procedure is useful for training purposes. Newcomers, e.g. management trainees, can 'sit in' on committees and gain experience at first hand. They see the personalities in action, learn about the power play and observe the operations of pressure groups.

5 Creativity, it is argued, is improved in a committee environment. People bounce ideas around and follow the various threads of an argument. The clash of trained minds can spark off new ideas that may not occur to an individual sitting alone pondering a set of alternatives on a computer-print out.

6 The committee system provides work for a large number of people — committee clerks, typists, reprographics staff, information gatherers and disseminators. It is, perhaps, not surprising that the committee system is so popular in the public sector where 'size is might', where the bigger your committee, the more important a chief officer or a chairman you are. (Again there are corresponding costs, as noted below.)

7.3.2 Disadvantages of committees as a decision-taking medium

1 People may hide behind committee decisions. No one person can be held responsible: 'It was the committee's decision, I was against it, but....'. This can lead to 'buck passing' and delays if further decisions are required or if the original decision proves to be wrong. The bureaucratic process thrives on the 'vagueness' of the committee system.

2 Committees take time. Time is money, and if one works out the costs of the committee system of a local authority, for instance, the result can be frightening. To the salaries of the committee members have to be added the costs of typing the minutes, printing the agendas etc.

3 Committees lead to compromise. In some circumstances the 'good old British compromise' can be beneficial. In other situations it leads to a 'second-best situation' and merely glosses over the real divisions between those involved. In effect the real decision is postponed.

7.4 Effective participation

Whenever decision making involves two or more people meeting face to face, certain factors can contribute to effective participation.

1 *Room Layout*

Informal layouts, easy chairs, lack of undue distance between those involved, even a round rather than a straight table (so that no one has to be at the head and thus have greater status), are things that can help.

2 *Threat reduction*

A 'them and us attitude', should be avoided. Uniforms, personal attitudes, the way the meeting is conducted should all 'open up' the decision process.

3 *Leadership*

There is much to be said for a shifting pattern of leadership.* In really successful decision-making meetings the chairman says very little, merely guiding the meeting to its conclusion and allowing the discussion to move from one group or individual to another so that everyone leads the process at some time or another.

4 *Agenda*

The agenda should be clear, understandable and cover all points participants want to raise.

5 *Consensus agreement*

Wherever possible the discussions should continue until a consensus has been reached (although the costs of prolonging the discussion must be borne in mind). The chairman should ensure that the consensus can be expressed as clearly defined goals and objectives.

6 *Status or elitism*

As indicated above, status or elitism should be avoided. People should be valued for their contribution rather than their rank or salary level.

These points demonstrate that senior managers can do a great deal to create the right environment for participation in the decision process and this is an area that is very much their responsibility.

7.5 Decision making and accountability

As sources of information multiply, availability and access improve, and educational standards rise, several issues concerning decision making and accountability have received greater attention.

7.5.1 Use of information

There is general public disquiet at present about 'hidden information' held on individuals on computer files compiled by government departments, the police, or various private sector organizations. This issue was examined by the Lindop Committee.

In Sweden the 1776 Freedom of the Press Act, re-affirmed in 1810 and 1949 gives every Swedish citizen free access to official documents. In practice even foreigners are not excluded and 'documents' include punch cards, computer tapes and memory banks. Norway and Denmark also allow access to documents providing a security risk is not involved and the searcher specifies the documents required. In America, there is much more freedom of information than in Great Britain and the trend to more open government is now well established (overseas that is, but not in this country).

7.5.2 Public participation in decision making

Decisions taken, or about to be taken, by organizations ranging from governments to multinational companies, are increasingly subject to public scrutiny and debate. The spread of television has been of paramount importance here, as noted in our discussion of communications. Although this may not, strictly speaking, amount to public participation in decision-making, the decision makers themselves are often influenced by the public debate.

7.5.3 The factors influencing decisions

Extending public discussion of decisions almost inevitably means that decision makers take into account factors that otherwise they would not have done. A good example is the debate concerning the siting of a third London airport. There seems little doubt that the committees that have examined the issues have been influenced by the opinions expressed by the inhabitants of the various possible locations. Furthermore when the government made the decision not to build another airport, at least for the time being, it was also influenced by public opinion.

7.6 Summary and conclusions

Decision making is important to all managers, a successful career often depending on the manager's ability to choose the best course of action from the various alternatives open to him. The decision-making process involves defining the problem, determining the decision process to be followed, choosing the appropriate time scale, gathering information, examining the alternatives, making and implementing the decision. As part of the move to a more participative management style, more decisions are being taken in open committees. This requires senior managers spending considerable time and effort creating an environment which will encourage participation by each member of the committee. Managers are also having to give greater attention than previously to issues raised during public discussion of their decisions.

Revision qustions and exercises

1   Answer *briefly:*
A   What is the first stage in the decision process?
B   Name two methods of decision-making aids used by public sector organizations.
C   What is meant by the time scale of decisions?
D   Differentiate between quantitative and qualitative information.
E   Outline the steps in the implementation stage of decision making.
F   How is a committee system useful for decision training?
G   What is meant by collective decision making?
H   List four factors that can assist participative decision making.
I   What is meant by 'threat reduction'?
J   Give an example of public participation in the decision-making process.
2   Outline the steps to be taken in the decison-making process and explain which you think are the most important.
3   Are committees a good medium for making decisions?
4   'The vast majority of the general public do not want to get involved in local government decisions. They are happy to leave matters to their elected representatives'. Discuss the validity of this statement.
5   'The police computer system gives instant information to aid decision making at the expense of individual liberty'. Discuss.
6   This exercise should be undertaken in groups and each group should arrive at a single, agreed answer. Rank the following categories of people in order of their importance in helping to restore the economic prosperity of this country; trade unionists, academics, car workers, politicians, designers, social workers, farmers, police, hairdressers, coalminers, electricity employees, civil servants, insurance brokers, transport employees, salesmen, computer specialists, T.V. and radio staff, North Sea oil employees, shipbuilders, British Telecom employees, tax inspectors.
7   As individuals, record the ways the latest advances of microtechnology can aid decision making, giving as many examples as you can think of. Compare your answers with the other members of your group.

Further Reading

ADAIR, J. *Training for Decisions* (Macdonald: London, 1971).

AUDLEY, R. *Decision Making* (BBC publications: London, 1967).

DRUCKER, P. *The Practice of Management* (Pan: London, 1968).

DRUCKER, P. *Managing for Results* (Heinemann: London, 1964).

JENKINS, D. *Job, Power, Blue and White Collar Democracy* (Heinemann: London, 1974).

HEBDEN, J. and SHAW, G. *Pathways to Participation* (Associated Business Programmes: London, 1977).

H.M.S.O. *Committee of Inquiry on Industrial Democracy* (The Bullock Report, 1977).

REDDIN, W. J. *Managerial Effectiveness* (McGraw-Hill: New York, 1970).

SEDDON, V. J. and BUTEL, J. *A First Course in Business Analysis* (Holt, Rinehart and Winston: New York, 1981).

TAFFLER, R. *Using Operational Research* (Prentice Hall: New York, 1979).

WHITE, D. J. *Decision Theory* (Allen and Unwin: London, 1969).

YEWDALL, G. A. *Management Decision-Making* (Pan: London, 1969).

8

Organizing

8.1 Introduction

Having agreed on their plans and objectives and having made decisions in the light of all the known information, managers must then organize the resources under their control to achieve their objectives as efficiently as possible. In this chapter we examine the factors that influence a manager's choice of organizational structure and we consider some of the problems this 'organizing' function can lead to.

8.2 Why organize?

Any grouping or collection of people who are trying to work together to achieve a given objective, be it a number of soldiers trying to win a battle or a number of building operatives and craftsmen trying to build a house, work more effectively and quickly and have more chance of achieving their objective, if they are organized correctly.

Without organizations, modern day life would quickly degenerate into near chaos. We depend on organizations to bring our food to the local supermarket, to supply petrol to the pumps at the local garage, to educate our children and to look after us when we are sick. We are part of an organization in our working lives, while at home the family, that oldest organization of all, has stood the test of time and change and still survives, loved and cherished by most of us.

Organizations and organizing are so much part and parcel of our lives that we accept the concept of organizing without a second thought. Organizing means utilizing whatever resources are available — people, time, money, equipment, services etc. — to achieve objectives. For some people this may not mean much more than organizing their time throughout the day. Managers, however, control substantial resources, and they have to learn how to organize employees and organizations.

For managers the organizing function is made more difficult by the fact that much of their time is spent organizing people, and people change, daily, hourly, even by the minute. Managers are therefore constantly making adjustments to their organizations to cater for such things as the sickness of a key employee, an unexpected resignation, or the shortage of some key component because of a strike in a supplier's factory.

Some of the advantages of organizations were considered during our discussion of types of organizations in Chapter 3. We noted, for example, that a partnership could draw on a wider range of expertise and greater financial resources than a one man business. Organizations are also social units; help and advice are provided to the members of the group, worries are shared, and the chances of success are improved when people from different backgrounds, ages and skills work in unison towards an agreed objective.

It is this basic need for human contact, to relate to other people and to have a greater chance of achieving success in any activity, that gives rise to the desire to organize and be organized. We may all be 'loners' occasionally, but we only reach our full potential as part of an organization, however small. Management is about maximizing potential and management is therefore about organizing.

8.3 Principles of organization

8.3.1 Spans of control

There will always be a limit to the number of people a manager can effectively control. Some management experts feel that six to eight people is the maximum; others have suggested a smaller number. The appropriate span of control will depend on a variety of factors. First, are the subordinates qualified to make decisions without having to constantly refer upwards to the manager? Have they the skills and experience required to take the right course of action and see it through? Second, is the manager concerned prepared to delegate authority to his subordinates? Is this desirable for the manager's own career progression, or is it possible he might delegate himself out of a job? Third, a manager can supervise more people if the organization has a well-defined planning function and agreed set of objectives, than if the objectives are vague or not widely understood. (On the other hand when, in a period of rapid change, decisions of a vital nature have to be taken on an almost daily basis, managers may become involved in the detailed running of the organization in order to keep control of all aspects of the situation, thus reducing the effective span of control.)

Similarly, where an organization has well developed, tried and tested communication systems that feed information quickly, to and from senior management, each manager is able to control a larger number of people. Indeed this may be the primary benefit of the modern communications and information systems discussed in Chapter 4.

Finally, some organizations, particularly those in the public sector, depend a great deal on personal contact to operate effectively. These types of organizations will inevitably have small spans of control and involve many levels of subordinates and co-ordinates, the hallmark of a bureaucratic type of organization.

8.3.2 Unity of objectives

Whatever the organization structure finally decided upon, all parts of the organization should work towards common objectives. In these days of international competition and scarce resources no manager can afford the luxury of parts of the organization 'doing their own thing'. This is particularly true of labour-intensive organizations in the public sector and the service industries in the private sector, where the human resource plays such a key (and very expensive) role.

As noted above, people are more likely to pursue the organization's objectives rather than their personal interests if these objectives are clearly defined and widely understood. Unfortunately, experience shows that in public sector organizations 'politics' often leads to objectives being blurred or constantly changed, with consequential loss of efficiency.

8.3.3 Delegation

As noted during our discussion of the span of control, delegation implies that a senior manager gives discretion to a subordinate. Successful delegation requires that attention should be given to the following factors. First, adequate authority must be given to the subordinate to carry out the task. If a junior manager is given the job of running the mailroom, it should be made clear that he has authority over the mailroom staff and can specify the timing of the collection and delivery of the mail.

In situations like this, specifying the limits of authority is often easy. It is much more difficult where a senior manager has only a vague idea of what he wants and gives only broad and general instructions to a subordinate. In this situation there is much more likely to be a dispute later on as to whether the junior manager has exceeded his authority. Consider the situation in which a senior manager asks a subordinate to prepare a report on the feasibility of a proposed new product. The manager feels that a satisfactory report could be prepared as the basis of internal discussions with the production manager, personnel director etc. But the subordinate feels it necessary to obtain information about competitors' products and therefore asks the market research department to undertake a survey. Two obvious sources of conflict arise. First, the market research staff may refuse to do what the junior manager requests. Second, if they do accept his authority and undertake the work, the senior manager may complain because of the costs involved.

Second, and following from the previous point, tasks being delegated must be properly assigned, i.e. the subordinate must understand what is involved, accept the delegated discretion and know that his position and authority are not duplicated elsewhere in the organization.

Finally, responsibility for the discretion delegated cannot be greater than the authority delegated, e.g. if a manager gives a subordinate the authority to sell certain items, that subordinate cannot be held responsible for high rates of breakages and customer complaints due to a bad design or faulty manufacturing.

Most successful managers are happy to delegate. They see it as being helpful to themselves and their organizations for a variety of reasons:

1 By delegating one can see which subordinates are likely to be 'high flyers', suitable for promotion, and which have reached the limit of their competence.

2 Delegation can provide a useful training tool, in that it enables managers to develop their potential. This may mean that junior managers are given discretion even though they do not perform as well as their seniors in the early stages. As they learn from experience and gain confidence, their performance is likely to improve, and senior managers are often pleasantly surprised at how successful subordinates can be, given time and encouragement in undertaking tasks previously thought to be the preserve of the senior manager or 'the boss'.

3 All managers and individuals do some things better than others. If a subordinate is particularly skilled in some tasks it makes sense for a senior manager who may see these tasks as a 'bit of a chore', to let the junior manager do it. The tasks are likely to be performed more effectively and the senior manager will be able to spend more time on tasks for which he is better fitted.

4 Where an organization is spread out geographically, e.g. with a headquarters and a number of area offices, it may be wise to delegate certain functions to junior managers in the area offices who are in closer touch with customers and the general public.

Whatever degree of discretion a senior manager eventually decides to give to his subordinates the general principle is clear cut. Senior managers should concentrate their time and effort on the major issues facing their organizations. Most senior managers are overworked, with more calls on their time than the working day allows for. Delegation of tasks to subordinates wherever possible makes good business and managerial sense. The tasks will often be done more cheaply, employee job satisfaction will be increased, and senior managers will be more effective.

8.3.4 The 'scalar' principle

In any organization some individual must take ultimate authority and responsibility for the actions of that organization. The more clear-cut is the line of authority between this individual and all the subordinate positions within the organization, the more effective will be the decision-making process and the greater the organization's efficiency. This unbroken line of responsibility between all individuals in an organization is known as the 'scalar' principle. Unless the chain of command is clear-cut, people will not 'know where they stand', i.e. to whom they are responsible and to whom they refer matters beyond their own authority.

8.3.5 Unity of command

Where an individual has responsibility to one clearly defined superior, the less likely it is that he will receive conflicting instructions. He is also likely to obtain more job satisfaction and a greater sense of purpose and responsibility in carrying out instructions, than if he is responsible to two or more superiors. The bigger the organization, the more specialists it employs, the more difficult it is to observe this 'unity of command' principle, with consequent adverse effects on morale and efficiency. For example a personnel officer may be asked by the production manager to provide additional workers; to meet this instruction may conflict with recruitment and induction procedures laid down by the personnel manager.

8.4 Types of organization structure

There are two types of organization structure, which exist side by side.

8.4.1 The formal organization

This is the organization structure designed by senior management to achieve the objectives of the organization. It is the network of communication, reponsibilities and groupings of individuals, that is seen by senior management as being the most effective. This network is often depicted in an organization chart, as shown in Chapter 3.

As mentioned previously, formal organization structures are constantly modified by managers in response to a variety of pressures. Nevertheless it takes time for a new structure to become fully operational, for all the relevant parts of the formal organization to be re-organized, and for all the relationships to be modified.

8.4.2 The informal organization

Within every organization, alongside the formal organization structure there exists the informal structure. This is based on relationships between individuals and groups and as such is much more dynamic and less easily definable than the more rigid formal structure. The 'old boy network', the 'office grapevine'; a temporary liaison between two sections to gain a working advantage over a third, e.g. sales and marketing versus production, are all examples of informal relationships.

In many ways, these informal organizations, because they reflect the present, real world situation, rather than what managers think the situation is, are more powerful than the formal organizational links. If the two structures seriously diverge, it may become necessary to formalize at least some of the informal relationships; otherwise communication channels may break down and managers' freedom of action become curtailed. However, it is usually undesirable to try to suppress all informal relationships, since they can sometimes help to lubricate the formal machinery and make the organization a more interesting place in which to work.

8.5 Levels within an organization

Each organization has its own individual number of levels, determined by an amalgamation of all the issues discussed in this chapter. But most organizations contain certain levels within the hierarchical structure, with clearly defined functions. At the top there are a few senior managers making policy decisions. At the bottom there are a much larger number of employees carrying out the detailed work of the organization at the 'sharp end' so to speak. In the middle are the co-ordinators, planners and section heads controlling their particular functions, referring issues to senior management and receiving instructions back. The organizational hierarchies of typical public and private sector organizations are depicted in Figures 8.1 and 8.2.

It will be seen that the hierarchy at the top of the public sector organization is more complex because of the political element involved. Ratepayers and politicians take a much keener interest in the running of a local authority and are much more likely to change their views — with

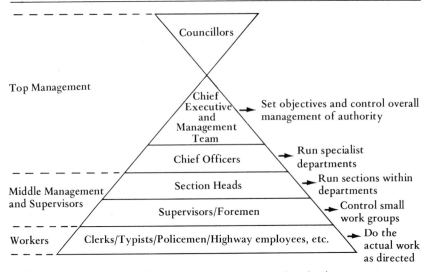

Figure 8.1   Organization hierarchy/pyramid of a local authority.

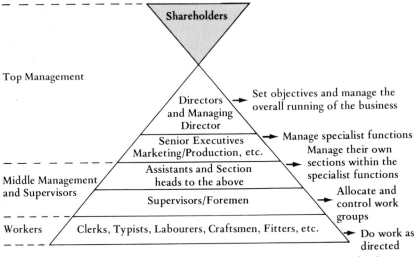

Figure 8.2   Organization hierarchy/pyramid of a private sector organization.

consequent effects on the organization — than the shareholders of a private company. The bureaucratic organizational and management structure tends to operate so as to deaden and soften the impact of political change in order to aid the organization's survival and facilitate its management.

Private sector organizations reflect the impact of external changes more quickly and more fully, mainly because the implications of a change are less extreme. Although a loss of sales is a serious matter, it would usually lead to fewer changes in policy than would a change from Conservative to Labour control of a large county council, especially if the political views of the council were not tempered by the advice of permanent officers.

8.6 Centralization versus de-centralization

Many large organizations have to decide whether all major decisions, responsibility and authority, should be concentrated at head office or whether there should be wider 'power sharing' with, for example, some decisions being made in area offices. There is obviously a connection with delegation, but we are concerned here with the structure of an organization as a whole, whereas delegation refers to the style of individual managers.

Centralization has a number of advantages:

1 Communication systems of all types are made easier by having people and departments alongside one another.
2 Services such as mail, photocopying, plan printing, filing, reception, telephone, canteen, car parking and other support services can be provided on an overall, rather than departmental, basis. This will produce savings in staff and enable costs to be more closely controlled.
3 The corporate image of an organization is improved when the organization is situated in one location. We are all familiar with the Town Hall or County Hall as symbolizing the centre of administration in a town. The large new civic centres and old Victorian 'gothic-style' town halls add a touch of grandeur and dignity to the operation of local services in a way several smaller buildings scattered throughout an area would not.
4 Various aspects of security can be improved in a centralized location, although against this has to be offset the dangers inherent in 'having all one's eggs in one basket', e.g. all the organization's records could be destroyed in one fire or robbery.
5 It is easier to manage the operation and people when everything is under one roof.

De-centralization has the advantage that it places decision making 'where the action is'. The sales office on site at a housing estate, the social services area office, the local clinic and the local police station are all examples of de-centralization. These out-stations provide a local link with the people they serve and ease of access for consumers. They enable a local approach to problem solving to be combined with help and advice from a headquarters organization.

De-centralization only works if the people in the various locations are given adequate authority to make decisions, and responsibility proportional to the decision-making power of each individual is agreed and exercised at all levels of the organization.

De-centralization works best when the headquarters provides advice or some specialist support or research activity and this is coupled with good communication systems, widely understood objectives, and control systems which are followed by all concerned.

'On-line' computer systems now allow constant contact between a network of area or branch office and the main information files at headquarters, and thus help to overcome one of the main problems associated with de-centralization. Previously if you went into your bank, building society or the gas showroom, and wanted detailed information about your finances or accounts, a long wait frequently ensued. Now the answer is immediately available on a visual display screen with print out.

The most advanced example of this is the police national computer linked to the DVLC at Swansea. When a car's registration number is fed into the computer, details of the car, and its owner, can be given in seconds to the patrolling policeman on the beat.

There is no right answer to the question : 'should one centralize or de-centralize?' Each case must be treated on its merits and in the light of local circumstances. However, it would appear that more and more larger organizations in both the public and the private sectors are taking heed of the maxim 'small is beautiful' associated with the late E.F. Schumacher and are running their operations with local offices, linked by modern communication systems to a small headquarters organization that provides policy guidance and advice and specialist help when required. In this way modern advances in electronic communications enable organizations to satisfy the increasing demand by consumers for the personal touch in their dealings with businesses and the public sector.

8.7 Departmentation

Having decided, or even before making the decision, on centralization or de-centralization every senior manager has to decide how to group the various activities and individuals within his organization. This organizing function is known as departmentation, and the main forms of departmentation are outlined below. (Note that within one organization different forms may be used for different activities; moreover there may be some overlap between one form and another).

8.7.1 By customer

Where an organization has a very important customer who requires a particular type of product or standard of service, it makes sense to have a group which can concentrate on the needs of this customer. Advertising agencies have 'account executives' whose job it is to look after the interests of a particularly valuable client and co-ordinate their agencies' approach to the client. Many food manufacturers have 'key account executives' who negotiate terms with the chief buyers of the large grocery multiples.

8.7.2 By advertising channel

The use of the various media now requires specialist skills if they are to be fully utilized to the advantage of an organization. The high cost of advertising time or space makes it worth an organization's while to develop a co-ordinated approach to the media concerned in order to obtain the preferential rates available to bulk buyers.

8.7.3 By process or equipment

Organizing under one head or section the computer operations of an organization, or a particular type of production process that requires specialist skills, makes for organizational as well as managerial efficiency. Maintenance is made easier and the relevant trade and management 'know how' can be concentrated in one area.

8.7.4 By service or product

The establishment of a group to provide specialist recruitment advice, or to oversee the development of an engine would be examples of this form of departmentation. This should result in the more efficient use of specialized resources and a more co-ordinated approach to outside individuals and pressures.

8.7.5 By function

Organizing the total resources of an organization by specialist functions — sales, production, accounts — is common practice in most organizations and does not really require further comment here. Suffice it to say that the more numerous and more specialized the various departments are, the more difficult is the task of senior management to co-ordinate and manage.

8.7.6 By geographical area

Most readers will be familiar with this type of departmentation. It is particularly common in dividing up an organization's sales or marketing forces into say the Scottish region, Wales, Northern England, the Midlands and the Home Counties. (There may then be a subsidiary form of departmentation with a split by function). Regional and local tastes and differences can be catered for in this way, and it also aids overall managerial control in very large organizations that have national or international markets.

8.7.7 By time

Organizing according to time scales, e.g. day and night shifts, makes sense where round the clock production, service, or monitoring systems are in operation, and where, over long time periods, the human response is limited in its operational capability.

8.7.8 By actual numbers

The armed forces departmentalize themselves on these lines, e.g. a platoon has 30–33 men in it, a brigade 3,000. Whether in the private sector or the public sector there often exists an optimum number of people to do a particular job; too few and the job folds up, too many and people are 'falling over one another'. Dividing the workforce up by numbers on the basis of the 'span of control', discussed earlier, takes account of the need for people to identify within a group.

8.8 Organizational relationships

Whatever span of control is chosen, whatever the number of departments or groupings eventually decided upon, management has the choice of certain tried and tested organizational relationships within the organizational structure they finally decide upon.

8.8.1 Line relationships

This refers to the direct working relationships between the vertical levels of an organization structure. This is the most common type of working relationship where authority flows from the departmental head to the deputy, to the section head and eventually to the person who actually does the job of work. The communication channels are clear, authority is agreed, and instructions and information flow down and up between the individuals concerned.

8.8.2 Staff relationships

Most textbooks refer to a 'staff' relationship as an advisory function in either a specialist or assistant type of position. This is true insofar as the personnel manager or a management services officer may be regarded as 'advisors' to line managers (e.g. the production manager). But in many large organizations the difference between the 'line' and 'staff' function is often less clear cut. In such organizations one often finds staff specialists who also have line responsibility over their own staff. For example the personnel manager or director would have a 'staff' relationship or advisory role to the managing director on personnel policy, but line responsibility over staff in the training, employment, recruitment and safety sections of his own personnel section.

The best guide to the reader in attempting to assess whether a position is 'line' or 'staff' is to remember that the ultimate test is based on the personal relationships, especially in terms of authority, between the individuals concerned and not by purely departmental or sectional activities.

In systems of 'corporate planning' or the 'management team' concept in local government, the two roles are often combined, e.g. the director of education will be acting as a 'line' manager when he comes to speak on educational matters to the other members of the management team, but will act in a 'staff' capacity or advisory role when, as a member of the corporate management team of authority, he criticizes some service aspect of the corporate plan or budget.

8.8.3 Functional relationships

This relationship occurs where a line manager delegates to an individual or section the authority to carry out particular processes, policies, operations etc. The function can be delegated to either other 'line' managers or 'staff' advisors and specialists. This form of delegation is especially common in situations which require a grouping of people and activities to do a particular job, e.g. the move to a new office building, the installation of a new computer or the setting up of a new grievance procedure. Once the job is completed the functional authority often ends and the staff concerned return to their normal work.

8.8.4 Committee relationships

We have already made reference to committees as a system of managing. Suffice it to say here that committees play a large part in organizational structures in both the public and private sectors. Indeed it is often said that they are part of the British way of life; if in doubt then set up a committee. Viewed as part of the organizing function, committees can either be formal, i.e. have written remit and authority to carry out a specific function, or informal or ad hoc, i.e. set up for some temporary purpose to act as a pressure release valve or as a 'sounding board' for management.

Figure 8.3   Organization charts.
(a) Vertical.
(b) Horizontal (This type is often a vertical chart shown on its side for
convenience or fashion).
(c) Circular or concentric.
(d) Flow.

(a)

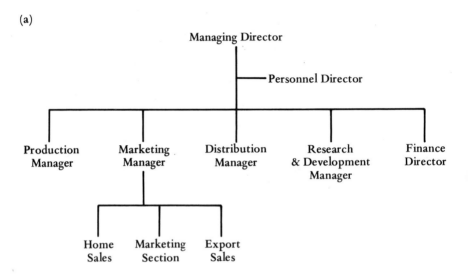

(b)

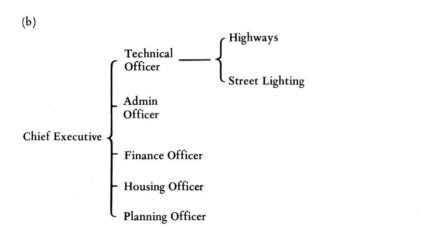

(c)

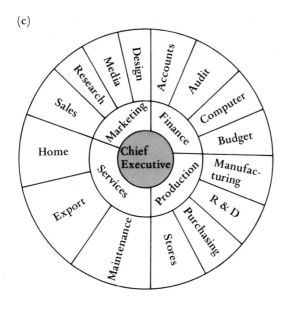

(d)

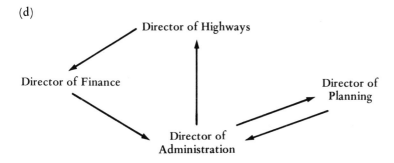

8.8.5 Working parties

In recent years the increasing need for participation and specialist advice has led to the setting up, particularly in the public sector, of a variant of the committee system, i.e. the working party.

The aim of a working party is to co-ordinate the specialist knowledge of various interested parties to solve a particular problem. (The need to reconcile these differing viewpoints often throws a heavy burden on the chairman). This means that the relationships in a working party differ slightly from those in a committee. In principle in a working party the members contribute from their own specialist viewpoint and not as equal participants able to criticize everyone and everything as in a committee. (In practice the members of a working party often behave as if they were members of a committee, as those readers who have served on working parties will know to their cost).

8.8.6 Matrix relationships

This type of organizational relationship was pioneered by the Americans in their space programme in the 1960s. It combines many of the relationships we have discussed and involves staff having a dual responsibility. First, they have a responsibility to their immediate superior. Second, they have a relationship to the specialist working group and the project team of which they are members. The aim of this structure is to obtain the benefits of multi-discipline project teams at middle management level and below, whilst allowing line managers at senior level control of their specific responsibilities, even though these may be spread over several projects.

8.8.7 Organization charts

There are four main types of charts that are commonly used to depict the relationships in organizations. These are shown in Figure 8.3 on p. 116.

8.9 Problems managers face when organizing

Organizing the resources under their control is one of the most difficult functions managers have to undertake and, whatever the solution ultimately chosen, most managers will experience one, or a combination, of the following problems.

1 The plans laid down by senior management are translated into imprecise, unachievable objectives that have not gained the commitment of the employees concerned.
2 Working relationships within the organization are ill-defined, vague and exist only on an informal or very personal basis.
3 The degree of delegation is inadequate and inadequate authority is given to those to whom responsibility is delegated.
4 Communication systems are inadequate with the result that management does not really know what is going on or is unaware of the true feelings of the workforce.
5 A breakdown occurs in the chain of command, such as the mixing up of line and staff relationships, the granting of functional authority

without responsibility, bad supervision.

6 A period of rapid change leads to constant re-organizations so that the whole structure is in a state of flux, and no one has time to adapt to and fully implement organizational changes.

Experienced managers will recognize the above symptoms and take steps to rectify the situation. In many cases the above issues are the results of 'people problems' and can only be solved by re-training and management development, or at the worst, removal of the individual concerned.

8.10 Summary and conclusions

In this chapter we have looked at some of the issues raised by perhaps the most important management function of all, that of organizing the total resources at a manager's command to achieve the objectives of the organization efficiently and effectively. We started off by asking the question, 'Why organize?'. We looked at some principles of sound organizational design, followed this by looking at the main types of organization structures, the levels within organizations, the issues of centralization or de-centralization, departmentation, organizational relationships, organization charts, and concluded by discussing some of the major problems managers face in organizing.

In the next chapter we look at the problem of getting people to work effectively and efficiently within an organizational framework, i.e., the management functions of leading and directing.

Revision questions and exercises

1   Answer *briefly;*
A   Why should managers organize?
B   What is the meaning of the term span of control?
C   What is meant by unity of objective?
D   Explain the meaning of delegation.
E   What is meant by the term scalar principle?
F   What is meant by the term unity of command?
G   Explain the difference between formal and informal organization structures.
H   List four ways of organizing by departmentation.
I   What is the difference between a line and a staff relationship?
J   What is a matrix organization?.
2   A friend who is setting up a business to manufacture double glazing systems, asks you to advise him on the type of organization structure he should adopt.
     (i) Write your advisory report.
     (ii) Role play a meeting between yourself, your friend, and his other advisors (banker, lawyer etc).

3   Discuss the main principles of organization and state which you think is the most important.
4   'The family is the only type of organization structure that really works'. Discuss the relevance and validity of this statement.
5   A colleague at work never delegates and is obviously suffering the strains and stresses of overwork. You are asked to try to persuade him to delegate more in order to avoid a coronary or nervous breakdown. What would you say to him?
6   Discuss the benefits and disadvantages of centralization and of decentralization.
7   'Small may be beautiful but big it best'. Discuss the validity of this statement with reference to a public sector organization.
8   What organizational relationships should be taken into account by senior managers when deciding on their organizational structure?
9   Outline the major problems managers face when organizing resources under their control, and explain which you think is the most important.

Further Reading

ACKOFF, R. *The Systems Age* (Wiley: New York, 1974).

BARNARD, C. I. *The Functions of the Executive* (Harvard: Boston, 1938).

BRECH, E. F. L. *Organization: The Framework of Management* (Longmans: London, 1965).

CLARK, P. A. *Organizational Design and Planned Change* (Tavistock: London, 1971).

CHILD, J. *Management and Organization* (Allen and Unwin: London, 1973).

DRUCKER, P. *The Practice of Management* (Heinemann: London, 1961).

FAYOL, H. *General and Industrial Management* (Pitman: London, 1967).

H.M.S.O. *The New Local Authorities Management and Structure* (London, 1972).

MARCH, J. and SIMON, H. *Organizations* (Wiley: New York, 1958).

SAYLES, L. and CHANDLER, M. *Managing Large Systems Organizations for the Future* (Harper Row: New York, 1971).

TOWNSEND, R. *Up the Organization* (Michael Joseph: London, 1970).

9

Leading and Directing

9.1 Introduction

We showed in the previous chapter that there are various ways of structuring an organization in order to utilize resources effectively. But an organization's effectiveness also depends upon the leadership provided by its managers, whatever the structure adopted. Successful leadership means getting people to 'give of their best', often in adverse circumstances. In this chapter we examine the nature of this interpersonal relationship between managers and employees, and outline some of the theories that have been propounded to assist managers in their leadership role.

9.2 The leadership role

By the very nature of the management role and function, managers are responsible for people within their organization, for their work and for their working environment. In order to fulfil this responsibility managers must employ a range of communication and leadership skills. It is sometimes said that leaders are born and not made, and some people are undoubtedly better equipped with the skills than other people. But these skills can be developed and deployed more effectively through constant practice. In fact a careful study of 'natural leaders' usually reveals that they have very thoroughly practised the skills that now appear to come so naturally to them.

9.3 Motivation

Of these skills none is more important than the ability to motivate people. In order to motivate people, managers must understand what their needs are, what 'makes them tick'. We consider below the theories of motivation advanced by a number of writers, theories that have added to our understanding, and have helped to increase managers' efficiency. But we must emphasize that when seeking to apply any theory to his own organization, a manager must be sensitive to the current needs and attitudes of *his* colleagues. This is not as easy as it may sound. Each individual has a unique set of needs and attitudes; moreover these needs and attitudes change over time. A worker's attitude on a wet Monday morning after his car has suffered a puncture on the way to work will differ from that on a warm sunny Friday afternoon, with a long weekend ahead. A more widespread difference in attitudes will occur in times of economic recession as compared to an economic boom.

The challenge to the manager is to obtain a high level of commitment and good performance from the employees despite these changes in circumstances. In meeting this challenge managers utilize a range of motivators, which fall into two broad categories, 'rewards' e.g. holidays, company car, increased salary, and 'punishments' e.g. demotion, redundancy, transfer to another section. The ability to identify the appropriate mix of rewards and punishments (carrot and stick) is one of the most important managerial skills. With this in mind let us see what light is thrown on this matter by other writers.

9.4 Theories of motivation

9.4.1 Maslow and the hierarchy of needs theory

Abraham Maslow, psychologist, saw an individual as having certain needs that required satisfying in the following order of importance.

1 Physiological needs

These needs — food, water, shelter, clothing, sexual satisfaction — must be met if human life is to continue. Maslow stated that until these basic requirements had been met, people would not progress or be motivated by any of the other needs outlined below. (In many ways this was recognized by Robert Owen at his New Lanark factory where he tried to provide these basic needs for his employees, as mentioned in Chapter 2.)

2 Security and safety needs

These include such things as freedom from physical danger, loss of job or home and property.

3 Affiliation needs

The basic physiological needs and the need for security and safety having been satisfied, attention can be given to the needs that people feel as social beings. We like to be accepted by other people, and one way of gaining this acceptance is to become affiliated to others, by joining a club (e.g. golf, tennis, working men's club, or that great British unofficial club, the local pub). When people are asked to say what they enjoy about their work, they often mention inter-personal relationships ('getting on well with the other lads', 'working together as a team') indications that their affiliation needs are being met at their workplace.

4 Esteem needs

People want to be recognized as important and this often leads them to seek power, prestige and status. Some people achieve this by becoming a senior manager, some by having a big house and a swimming pool, and some in both ways. For most people, however, this need has to be met in other but still very important ways; for the worker on the factory floor it may be the chance to talk to managers during a tour of the factory, or the presentation of a gold watch after twenty-five years service.

5 Self-actualization

This is the highest point in Maslow's hierarchy, denoting the situation in which one realises one's maximum potential or maximum self-satisfaction. For some this may mean becoming a prominent politician or the chairman of a merchant bank. For others it may mean being a social worker or living in a hippie commune in California. This implies, of course, that financial success is not all important, but is incidental to achieving what one really wants to be.

If managers agree with Maslow they must try to ensure that their employees have at least a living wage, reasonable job security, pleasant colleagues and working conditions, recognition of their worth as individuals, and promotion prospects.

These benefits to individuals are likely to be reflected in high morale and low labour turnover. There will doubtless be some employees whose ambitions cannot be met by a particular organization and who will move elsewhere to find bigger challenges and rewards. Although no organization likes to lose a good man, managerial mobility can make an important contribution to the efficient functioning of the economy.

9.4.2 Herzberg's two factor theory

Frederick Herzberg in his book *Work and the Nature of Man* (1966) proposed a two factor theory of motivation. He listed a group of factors such as working conditions, job security, salary, quality of supervision and interpersonal relations which he called 'maintenance' or 'hygeine factors'. These factors do not positively motivate people, but if they are unsatisfactory or inadequate people become dissatisfied with their work. The second group of factors, called 'motivators' by Herzberg, included aspects of work personal to an individual, such as the development of his or her job, responsibility, a sense of achievement and the challenge of the work. This second group were said to be the job specifications and the success each individual perceives he has achieved in meeting these.

Herzberg's work has been criticized on two grounds, the method of enquiry by which he obtained his results, and the fact that by concentrating on the satisfaction and dissatisfaction elements of the job, he ignored the wider behavioural aspects. Nevertheless his theories provide useful insights for managers, in drawing attention to the contribution of 'job enlargement' and 'job enrichment' (Herzberg's motivators) to job satisfaction.

9.4.3 Vroom and expectancy theory

Victor Vroom, in his book *Work and Motivation* (1964) argued that people follow certain courses of action, or react to certain instructions from managers, if they believe or expect that their actions will help them achieve desired goals or objectives. For example if money is a motivator and if people expect that more money (e.g. in the form of an incentive payment) will follow effective performance, then they will perform effectively.

This theory highlights the fact that differing individuals have different needs and motivators and that these differ from those of the organization an individual works for. A skilful manager will offer the inducements needed to ensure that satisfying these needs benefits both the individual and the organization, e.g. an incentive payments system, if correctly designed, can give the employee a higher income and give the organization, via a higher output, higher profits.

9.4.4 Porter and Lawler's model

L. W. Porter and E. E. Lawler in their book *Managerial Attitudes and Performance* (1968) expanded Vroom's theory. They emphasized the importance of intrinsic rewards (e.g. accomplishment) in the performance process arguing that performance in a job is determined in the main by the amount of effort an individual puts into that job, and his ability and his knowledge of what is required to do the job successfully.

For managers this points the way to training, delegation, the setting of clear objectives, careful job specification and an adequate reward system, i.e. a total management system is required to ensure that employees are confident that they can do jobs assigned to them, and are satisfied that the rewards match the effort involved.

Other behavioural scientists have also carried out research into motivation needs. For example, D. McClelland identified three types of motivation needs: for power, affiliation, and achievement. A. Patton carried out research into the motivation of senior management and found a variety of motivators, among the most important being money, competition, fear, status seeking, the challenge of the job and the need to achieve leadership.

In this section we have presented only a sample of the large amount of research that has been, and is being, carried out into the subject of motivation. Some of this work is very theoretical and may not reflect the real world of business, and much of it is certainly a simplification of that world. However even 'unrealistic' theories can provide useful insights as we have shown. Whichever of these ideas or insights is adopted by the individual manager in establishing a system of motivation, that system must:

1 be accepted by employees, implying that it should be seen to be fair and reasonable.
2 be flexible.
3 be comprehensive and cover all the employees and departments within the organization.
4 fit in with the political and economic climate of the day.

In addition the system will often have to incorporate both monetary and non-monetary rewards such as status, security and responsibility. Such a system can make a big contribution towards meeting the organization's objective of creating an effective and efficient work-force.

9.5 Management style

'Style' is something all managers have to develop. The actual style chosen will depend on a variety of circumstances but will, in the main, be determined by how the manager perceives his role within the organization and his view of the employees for whom he is responsible.

Douglas McGregor in his book *The Human Side of Enterprise* (1960) highlighted the dilemma facing attitudes to employees. The 'theory X' manager assumes that:

1 His employees dislike work and will try to avoid it wherever possible.
2 Employees have therefore to be coerced, controlled, directed and threatened with punishment if they are to achieve the objectives set for them.

3 Most people dislike responsibility, have little ambition, and value security above all else.

The 'theory Y' type of manager, on the other hand, assumes that:

1 Physical and mental effort in work is as natural as play and rest.
2 If people are committed to objectives they will exercise self-direction and control, eliminating or reducing the need for threats and external control.
3 Commitment to objectives is a function of the rewards associated with their achievement.
4 Given proper working conditions people can learn to seek responsibility.
5 Imagination and creative thinking are widely, not narrowly, distributed among the population.
6 The intellectual potential of the average person in industrial life is only partially realized.

The theory Y assumptions are attractive to the participative and more democratic type of management required in most organizations today. But experience has shown that adopting theory Y assumptions is no more of a guarantee that a manager will be a personal success, than adopting theory X assumptions. There are many managers who are aggressive towards their colleagues and drive their subordinates hard, who nevertheless have achieved, and perform well in, senior management positions.

In practice an organization is unlikely to have managers who conform entirely to either of the models presented by McGregor, but the managers will combine, in one proportion or another, characteristics of each model. Moreover, the appropriate combination will differ as between organizations. In a company facing rapid technological change the theory Y style is likely to predominate, whereas the theory X style will be called for in a company in which most operations have become routinized and profits are being squeezed by vigorous competition from rivals. Furthermore, organizations may need to modify their management style in the light of changing circumstances. Although many changes in the post-war period have favoured the adoption of the theory Y approach, as noted above, theory X may be more appropriate in the current difficult economic circumstances, when decisions concerning redundancies etc., have to be made.

9.5.1 Leading and directing

Blake and Mouton (1964) developed a two-tier framework for analysing managerial style. They used the dimensions 'concern for people' and 'concern for production' on a nine point scale or grid. They used their 'managerial grid' system in training programmes designed to develop the 'ideal managerial style'. (The ideal is that of a manager high on the nine-point scale, on each of the two dimensions, i.e. caring for people and efficiency.

Blake and Mouton (1967) later added a third dimension of 'effectiveness' based on managers' ability to maintain a given style under pressure. However, later theorists have tended to take the view that what is needed under pressure is a degree of flexibility. This is particularly true in the present-day industrial relations climate where fast-changing situations require managers to adapt to a variety of pressures. Flexibility, not rigidity, would appear to be the key attribute of successful leaders of the future.

Whatever style is eventually followed, successful managers realize that there is no one single correct style. They will adapt their management style to the situation and the organizational environment, and pay particular attention to the human issues involved, including the need to: deal with people on an individual as well as group basis; accept that people vary from time to time; see that employees obtain job satisfaction; try to get employee commitment to the organization's objectives. Managing is not an easy task, it has to be carried out in the bad times (such as a depression) as well as the good times (such as when the firm has gained an important export order). In the end all managers realize that whatever style is developed, it will have to accept the fact that in any organization 'people matter most of all'. That is why today's modern manager spends over half of his or her time on 'people problems'.

9.6 Summary and conclusions

In this chapter we have examined the importance of the manager's role in leading and directing the employees for whom he is responsible. We discussed the meaning of leadership and examined some of the better known theories of motivation propounded by Maslow, Herzberg, Vroom and Porter and Lawler. We concluded by looking at the issue of 'management style', high-lighting the work done on this subject by Douglas McGregor and Blake and Mouton.

Revision questions and exercises

1   Answer *briefly*
 A   What is the aim of successful leadership?
 B   Why do managers need to motivate their employees?
 C   Give two examples of Maslow's physiological needs.
 D   Give examples of Herzberg's maintenance factors.

E   What is meant by management style?

2   'There is no such thing as one correct leadership style for all individuals in all
     situations'. Examine this statement, drawing on your knowledge of some of
     the theories of management style that have been propounded.

3   How would you lead and direct the people in each of the following types of
     organization, and what type of management style would you adopt?
     (a) A prison, (b) a car assembly plant (c) a university or polytechnic, (d) a
     charitable organization such as 'Help the Aged'.

4   What is meant by the theory X and theory Y styles of management? Describe
     their relevance to the management of modern organizations.

5   'The modern requirement for participative management takes away a
     manager's right to manage.' Discuss.

6   'Motivation is fine, but you cannot be efficient in this day and age and still
     care for your employees'. Do you agree with this statement?

Further Reading

ARGYRIS, C. *Executive Leadership* (Harper: New York, 1953).

BINDRA, D. and STEWART, J. S. *Motivation* (Penguin: London, 1971).

BLAKE, R. R. and MOUTON, J. S. *The Managerial Grid* (Gulf: London, 1964).

BLAKE, R. R. and MOUTON, J. S. *The Managerial Grid in Three Dimensions (ASTD
     Journal:* January 1967, pp. 2–5).

DALTON, M. *Men Who Manage* (Wiley: New York, 1959).

FIELDER, F. E. *A Theory of Leadership Effectiveness* (McGraw-Hill: New York,
     1967).

FOX, A. *Man Mismanagement* (Hutchinson: London, 1974).

HERZBERG, F. *Work and the Nature of Man* (World Books: Cleveland, 1961).

LIKERT, R. *The Human Organization: Its Management and Value* (McGraw Hill:
     New York, 1967).

McGREGOR, D. *The Human Side of Enterprise* (McGraw-Hill: New York, 1960).

PIGORS, P. and MYERS, C. A. *Management of Human Resources* (McGraw-Hill: New
     York, 1964).

PORTER, L. W. and LAWLER, E. E. *Managerial Attitudes and Performance* (Richard
     D. Irwin, Inc.: Homewood, 1968).

REDDIN, W. J. *Managerial Effectiveness* (McGraw-Hill: New York, 1970).

TANNEHILL, R. E. *Motivation and Management Development* (Butterworths:
     London, 1970).

VROOM, V. *Work and Motivation* (J. Wiley & Sons: New York, 1964).

VROOM, V. H. and DECI, E. L. *Management and Motivation* (Penguin:
     Harmondsworth, 1975).

10

Controlling

10.1 Introduction

In previous chapters we have shown how important it is that managers
should plan the activities and operations of the organization, agree its
objectives and ensure that these are communicated to all employees,
organize the resources (physical, human and financial) required to meet
these objectives, and establish systems to motivate employees to work
towards these objectives.

In this chapter we conclude our discussion of the functions of managers
by examining the control process. We show that the essence of control is
the setting of performance targets, the measurement of actual
performance, and the correction of any deviations from the targets. This
implies that control is not an end in itself; rather it is a means of ensuring
that the end (the organization's objectives) is attained.

10.2 Control as a managerial function

Senior managers are concerned with the establishment of control systems.
Thereafter their involvement tends to be very limited, being confined to
major decisions, relating, for example, to widespread changes in working
practices that might be required if costs exceeded the target. Control is
mainly exercised at lower points in the managerial hierarchy. At the level
of first line supervisor, section head or departmental manager, the control
process accounts for a major proportion of a manager's time and effort.
In fact many first line supervisors spend nearly all their time controlling
the workers in their section.

Whatever the level at which control is exercised, the process will involve
a number of steps or stages:

10.2.1 Setting or agreeing objectives

This has been extensively discussed in Chapter 6, and no further comment is required.

10.2.2 Translating those objectives into plans

This is done on an organization-wide, departmental group and individual basis. This has also been discussed in Chapter 6.

10.2.3 Communicating these plans to all concerned

For control purposes it is usual to express the plans in terms of targets. At one time it was common practice to set targets that were virtually impossible to meet, the argument being that the more difficult the target the harder people would try to achieve it. More recently, research into motivation (see Chapter 9) has suggested that this is most unlikely to be so; targets that are widely accepted as attainable are now seen as the best motivators. Moreover, an unobtainable target is certainly unsuitable as a basis for control. What is required for this purpose is a target that is expected to be achieved given satisfactory (not super-human) performance.

Many targets relate to the output that an individual or group is expected to produce. In manufacturing organizations output will often be expressed in terms of the quantity of goods. Output can also be measured quantitatively in some service organizations, e.g. a television engineer is expected to install a certain number of sets in a given time period. However, in those public sector organizations which emphasize personal service, e.g. the social service departments of local authorities, the standard or level of service would appear to be a more appropriate measure. This is partly a qualitative matter and it is difficult to decide what standard should be expected from a department or organization of a given size.

If targets are to be meaningful to employees they must know their place in the organization and the limits to the authority. This may involve the preparation and distribution of job descriptions, organization charts etc.

10.2.4 Measuring performance

The measuring rod should obviously be the same as that used in setting targets, e.g. the quantity of goods.

10.2.5 Comparing actual with planned performance

The various techniques that can be used at this stage are discussed later in this chapter and also in Chapter 11. We confine our attention here to more general considerations.

It is important to decide the most appropriate time period over which the comparison is made. The longer the period, i.e. the less often measurements are taken, the less will be the cost involved. Furthermore, a more reliable measure will be obtained if what is measured has an erratic or uneven pattern of behaviour. For example in setting targets for the number of calls made by salesmen an allowance has to be made for the distance between potential customers. Assume that it is known that a salesman travels on average 20 miles to reach each customer. There would be no point in measuring his performance on a daily basis if on some days he worked areas where his customers were 10 miles apart. It might be necessary to consider his call rate over a month to average out these differences.

On the other hand the longer the period of measurement, i.e. the bigger the gap between taking measurements, the more likely it is that there will be a delay in identifying deviations from targets and in correcting those deviations. Moreover, the magnitude of the corrections will have to be greater in order to get back onto target.

Frequent (short-period) measurements are most likely to be undertaken when the measurement procedures are automatic (the increasing use of micro-computers in this context is discussed in Chapter 18). Frequent measurement is also required when the process involves a potential safety hazard. Inadequate monitoring in meat-packing factories in South America has resulted in loss of life. Less serious, but still unfortunate, is the death of fish and the pollution of rivers that has resulted from a failure to monitor the performance of effluent-treatment plant in this country.

We referred above to the cost incurred in measurement. The most obvious cost is that part of the wage and salary bill accounted for by the time spent in measuring performance. But the psychological cost is also important; a system involving frequent measurement can be very de-motivating ('the bosses in this place are always on your back').

10.2.6 Notifying any deviations

Any deviations of actual from planned performance must be notified to those responsible. This step should be taken as soon as the deviation is discovered so that corrective action can be taken as quickly as possible. Without a good communications system effective control is impossible.

As we showed in Chapters 4 and 5 one of the prime responsibilities of senior managers is to establish an adequate formal system of communications, with clearly defined channels of communication. Control information would normally be expected to flow through these channels. But it is also important to retain flexibility and to allow such information to be transmitted through informal channels if the established channels prove inadequate, e.g. if the unexpected absence from work of the officially designated recipient would cause corrective action to be delayed.

10.2.7. Identifying the reasons for the deviations

In some instances this stage precedes the previous one since it may become clear who is responsible for the deviation only after the reasons for the deviations have been identified.

Identification will probably be easiest when the reasons are internal to the organization. If output is less than planned it should be possible to discover from the company's records whether this was due to a labour dispute, a lack of components arising from poor production planning, the breakdown of machines etc. If, on the other hand, sales are less than planned it may be difficult to decide whether this is due to an inadequate performance by the sales force or to a fall in demand that has affected all suppliers.

10.2.8 Taking corrective action

The corrective action must be taken at the appropriate time. This will usually be as soon as possible after the reasons for the deviation have been identified. However, time should be allowed for adequate consultation with all individuals who will be affected by the corrective action.

Corrective action normally implies changing the current situation, e.g. if costs are too high steps must be taken to reduce them. But sometimes the horse has bolted by the time someone finds the stable door open. For instance, output might have been below target because of a strike at the supplier of a vital component. In these circumstances, the value of the control system is first that it enables the damage to profits caused by such an event to be estimated, and second that it demonstrates the need to prevent a recurrence, for example by dividing the orders for the component between two suppliers.

10.3 The areas of managerial control

We have given a number of illustrations of the operation of control systems relating to different areas of the organization's activities. We now discuss these and other areas in more detail.

10.3.1 Finance

Money is the key to the overall control of an organization. In the private sector sufficient profits must be earned to finance future expansion and to pay satisfactory dividends to shareholders. In the public sector, organizations have to operate within financial guidelines laid down by the government. Financial control is also concerned with cash flow; many organizations with promising long-term prospects have collapsed because they were unable to meet the short-term financial commitments (Laker Airways is a case in point).

10.3.2 Manpower

Since every person is unique, he or she is likely to react differently to a given set of circumstances. This obviously makes it more difficult to exercise control. But since manpower costs often account for 60% of total costs, the need to have close control of manpower is clear.

10.3.3 Physical resources

Plant, equipment, buildings and land involve heavy financial investment for many organizations. In addition, they represent long-term assets whose value can diminish substantially if maintenance is not undertaken when required.

10.3.4 Overall activity

Control must be exercised over finance, manpower and physical resources when the organization maintains a constant level of overall activity. When the level of activity changes, e.g. a new product is introduced or an existing product is dropped, control becomes, if anything, even more important. Otherwise a failure to meet targets due to inefficiency could be blamed on the change in activity.

10.3.5 Research and development

The introduction of new products and new processes often requires heavy expenditure on research and development. This is an area in which it is very difficult to exercise control, mainly because it is impossible to precisely define the target output (if the outcome of research is known in advance then there is no need to do the research). An argument that is often advanced when an R. and D. programme is not producing useful results is that to discontinue the programme would be to waste the money already spent. On the other hand to continue may mean throwing 'good money after bad'. There are numerous examples of inadequate control in the aerospace industry including the TSR2 (eventually abandoned) and Concorde (manufacture phased out).

10.3.6 Organizational

Total organizational control is the sum of all the individual control systems, and failure or managerial neglect in any of these systems can have serious and perhaps even fatal implications for the whole organization, as many managers have found to their cost. This total control ultimately is the responsibility of senior management. But all control systems, even the most computerized ones, are implementend by managers at all levels and in this respect all managers share the responsibility for organizational control. A tired supervisor, a slipshod maintenance operation, can undermine the most carefully designed control system.

10.4 Control techniques

In exercising control in the areas mentioned above, managers use a combination of techniques. The final mix will depend on the type of organization, whether it is in the public or private sector, and the influence of external forces, e.g. government economic policies. These techniques are used to differentiate stages of the control process. For example, critical path and network analysis are used in translating objectives into plans while budgetary control systems are used in measuring performance and in comparing actual with planned performance. All control techniques will include some or all of the following:

corporate planning
budgetary control systems
value analysis
operations research and other statistical techniques
programme evaluation review techniques
organization and methods and work study
project evaluation
management by objectives
market and product research
critical path and network analysis
statistical control systems of stock and production requirements
management audits
management appraisal systems.

The most important consideration is that managers should feel confident that they are receiving the information on the organization's activities and environment that enables them to exercise effective control.

10.5 Control and accountability

Managers in the private sector are accountable to their Board and their shareholders. In the public sector accountability and ultimate control is much more diffused, involving full-time professional managers, elected or appointed lay officials and possibly the general public in their capacity as taxpayers, ratepayers and electors.

Consequently, the control process is much more involved in the public than the private sector. Account may have to be taken of the views of individual chief officers, the management team, the chairman and elected members of a committee, outside pressure groups and the ratepayers, before a major control decision is taken in local government. In such a situation managers have to be sensitive to the attitudes of a wide range of people, and have to constantly check that their communications network is adequate.

10.6 Additional aspects of control

Our main aim in this chapter has been to show the importance of the control function and to examine the main features of the formal control processes that operate within organizations. These formal processes represent only one way in which the activities of individuals, groups and organizations are controlled. In this section we look briefly at forms of control which may or may not constitute part of a formal control process.

The form of control which we first meet, as children, is the *audible* control ('No!' 'Don't touch!'). This form is continued throughout life, the human voice being supplemented by other sounds, the klaxon or bell that tells us to start and stop work, the alarm that warns of a breach of security or safety.

We also experience a wide range of *visual* controls, in the form of written instructions, particular readings on a dial or a visual display unit, a particular colour or intensity of light etc.

Physical controls are also encountered early, whether in the form of a slap or being left in a play-pen. In later years the play-pen is succeeded by fences, barriers etc.

An example of *control by exception* is when a rise in the temperature of the water in a car's radiator causes a cooling fan to automatically switch on. Another example is when subordinates are required to report to their superiors only when things do not go according to plan.

Pre-control indicates that one tries to prevent something happening. For example in order to prevent a high failure rate on the first year H.N.D. Business Studies course, one might require all entrants to possess an O.N.D. To prevent a large number of road accidents drivers must pass a driving test.

Ad hoc control exists where no formal control process has been set up. When something untoward happens, managers make immediate decisions without reference to established procedures. The costs of a formal system are avoided but this saving is often outweighed by other costs arising from uncertainty, inconsistent decisions etc.

Control through motivation is quite different from other forms and indeed is control only in the sense that it affects behaviour. The motivation may be provided by a charismatic individual or may arise from membership of an organization; some economic historians believe that Britain's development as an industrial nation owed a great deal to the 'Protestant work ethic'.

10.7 Summary and conclusions

Control involves having a plan known and accepted within an organization, having information systems that measure deviations from this plan and notify those responsible, and the taking of corrective action. Control is exercised in relation to the financial, human and physical resources of the organization and may involve a combination of various techniques. The responsibility for control is spread widely and its operation affects every member of the organization. Consequently, managers have to pay as much (and possibly more) attention to the human element in control as in other managerial functions.

Revision questions and exercises

1   Answer *briefly:*
A   What is the essence of all control systems?
B   At what level of the managerial hierarchy is control mainly exercised?
C   What are the main costs involved in measurement?
D   What is the relationship between an organization's communication system and its control system?
E   Outline the steps involved in taking corrective action.
F   What is meant by total organizational control?
G   Give two examples of visual control.
H   How can one control through motivation?
2   Why is the control function of management so important?
3   Outline the main stages in the control process.
4   Outline the main areas of managerial control and discuss which you think is the most important.
5   'Control comes down to people in the end'. Discuss the validity of this statement, with examples drawn from your own experience.
6   Give five examples of different (types of) control systems and comment on the differences between them.

7   As a group choose a major event (e.g. relocating the office, moving house, the cup final) and discuss the various aspects involved in controlling it, paying particular attention to the main areas of uncertainty.

Further Reading

ANTONY, R. N. *Planning and Control Systems* (Harvard: Boston, 1965).

BEER, S. *Decision and Control* (Wiley: New York, 1966).

DRUCKER, P. *Management* (Pan: London, 1979).

DUCKWORTH, W. E. *A Guide to Operational Research* (Methuen: London, 1963).

GRASS, M. (Ed.) *Control of Working Capital* (Gower: London, 1974).

HULL, J. F. *The Control of Manufacturing* (Gower: London, 1973).

SMITH, I. G. *The Measurement of Productivity* (Gower: London, 1973).

TANNENBAUM, A. S. *Control in Organizations* (McGraw-Hill: New York, 1968).

THOMAS, A. B. *Stock Control in Manufacturing Industries* (Gower: London, 1970).

TOOLEY, D. F. *Production Control Systems and Records* (Gower: London, 1973).

WHITMORE, D. A. *Measurement and Control of Indirect Work* (Heinemann: London, 1971).

Part Three
Management in Action

In Part 1 we looked at the meaning and scope of the management function. Part 2 discussed the basic functions — communicating, planning, decision making, organizing, leading and directing, and controlling — that every manager has to carry out. In Part 3 we conclude by looking at the managerial function in action within organizations.

Chapter 11 analyses the role of the finance function in enabling organizations to operate effectively, and in allowing managers to exercise control and evaluate performance. Chapter 12 looks at the marketing function. This involves discovering what the customer wants, analysing changes in fashion and demand, and monitoring the effectiveness of the organization's products and services in the market place. Chapter 13 examines the main work areas covered by the production function including design, location and layout, and planning and control. Chapter 14 discusses the importance of the purchasing function. Chapter 15 analyses the main determinants of an effective personnel function. Chapter 16 considers the need for a variety of techniques that aid managerial and organizational efficiency and are covered by the term 'management services'. Chapter 17 surveys a workplace that is increasing in importance, i.e. the office. The information function of the office is analysed, the services it provides considered in detail, and some practical aspects of office management are discussed. In Chapter 18 we look to the future; we discuss changes in information technology that are likely to transform the way managers and organizations operate. We consider likely changes in the industrial and commercial environment, and we conclude by discussing the changing attitudes to work and leisure that are already affecting managers and organizations.

11

The Finance Function

11.1 Introduction

'It all comes down to money in the end', is a comment that is often heard. The finance function is a vital part of every organization's operation and survival. In this chapter after familiarizing the reader with the important elements of the finance function, as a basis for further study, we examine a number of the more important accounting techniques.

11.2 The sources of finance

Internal funds — retained earnings — account for over two-thirds of the total funds of industrial and commercial companies. These companies, and other private sector organizations, can also draw upon a wide range of external financial sources. The most important of these sources are as follows.

11.2.1 Clearing banks

Seven banks are members of the London Clearing House, (where the majority of cheques are cleared), Barclays, Lloyds, Midland, National Westminster (the 'big four'), and the smaller Williams and Glyns, the Co-operative Bank and Coutts. These banks, together with the corresponding Scottish banks, provide a widespread network of local and regional offices to meet the needs of organizations and individuals.

The banks provide money in the form of either an overdraft or a loan. With an overdraft an organization is allowed to overdraw its account (i.e. to borrow money) up to a specified limit. An overdraft is usually the cheapest form of finance since interest is charged only on the amount overdrawn. (The rate of interest equals the base rate plus a specified margin, usually 2 to 4%). This is especially advantageous when the organization's balance fluctuates from day to day, e.g. as wages are paid or purchasers pay their accounts. However, the overdraft is a short-term form of borrowing and leaves open the possibility that the bank may 'call-in' the overdraft (i.e. refuse to renew the facility) which can lead to severe liquidity problems. To avoid this danger, organizations sometimes prefer to take out loans for a fixed period, and to pay interest on the full amount of the loan outstanding.

The banks have been critized because of their reluctance to provide long term finance to companies and they have modified their policies in recent years in the light of this criticism. Although many loans are for short periods, say two to four years, term lending (up to twenty years) has become increasingly important. An article in the Midland Bank Review in 1981, showed that term lending now accounts for about a quarter of that bank's total lending to the manufacturing sector. (If officially sponsored schemes for exports and other arrangements which are in effect, if not in name, term loans, e.g. leasing, are included, term loans account for about 40 per cent of the Midland Bank Group's lending to industry).

The banks normally lend only against 'collateral' such as equipment or stocks of material. It is obviously easier for an established than a new business to provide suitable collateral. The budding entrepreneur may be obliged to use his personal possessions, including his house, as collateral and some people may be unwilling to take the risk involved in such a step. The Government has recently tried to alleviate this problem. Under the Loan Guarantee Scheme, introduced in 1981 for three years, the government will guarantee 80 per cent of the cost of loans made by banks, or other financial institutions, to new businesses. This guarantee encourages the banks to impose less stringent conditions on potential borrowers.

Despite the change in attitude of the clearing banks, they still play a less active role in the financing and guidance of businesses than their counterparts in many other countries. With a few exceptions British banks do not have direct shareholdings in industrial companies; nor do they play a part in their management, as in Germany and Japan. The closer relationships between the financial and industrial sectors in these other countries is said by some commentators to be one reason why those economies have grown more quickly than the U.K.

11.2.2 Merchant banks

Merchant banks do not have extensive branch networks and consequently provide funds to a more limited clientele than the clearing banks. They tend to be especially inaccessible to small firms, who often have to rely on local sources of finance. However some merchant banks are associated with institutions established to meet the needs of small firms, e.g. those in high technology industries.

In addition to providing finance from their own resources, merchant banks provide a variety of valuable services for the established firm. They may act as issuing houses when companies first go public or issue additional shares, or as underwriters, guaranteeing to take up any shares not bought by the public. They also provide help to arrange mergers and offer services in the foreign exchange and other specialized markets.

11.2.3 Hire purchase finance organizations

H.P. companies, as they are popularly known, compete with the banks in offering firms a means of finance for a variety of activities. Often if 'the friendly neighbourhood bank manager' is reluctant to lend money, a finance company will. Just as private individuals use H.P. finance for the purchase of a car or a household item, so firms use H.P. finance for vehicle purchase, equipment etc. To minimize the lender's risk, H.P. finance is normally offered only if the item to be purchased has a life expectancy longer than the period of the loan, and can command a reasonable second-hand value.

The benefit of this form of finance is that the firm becomes the owner of the item, but is able to offset the interest on the finance against tax. The disadvantage of hire purchase finance is that the rate of interest charged is often higher than the rate for bank loans. Nevertheless, H.P. organizations are more flexible in their loan requirements. Moreover many of the companies are subsidiaries of the major clearing banks, implying high standards in their procedures and advice.

11.2.4 Leasing

This method of financing has achieved prominence relatively recently. The main growth area has been in company car and commercial vehicle leasing, although the system also operates for office equipment and machines used in production. Tax benefits are a major advantage of leasing. The item leased remains the property of the leasing company, which therefore enjoys certain tax benefits; these are passed on to the customer in lower rentals, normally of three to five years duration.

The customer also benefits by avoiding the cash outlay that would be involved in purchasing the items, the cash released becoming available for other uses. Against this must be set the fact that the customer does not become the owner of the items; however this may not be important, e.g. where new, improved models appear at frequent intervals. Leasing also avoids the problems sometimes associated with the need to provide collateral. Finally it allows budgeting procedures to be simplified.

11.2.5 Rental

Whilst we have just discussed the benefits of leasing in assisting firms in their search for funds, we should perhaps mention that there are a variety of rental methods available to firms. This system retains ownership to the rental company, but has the advantage of spreading out payments over a period of time and releasing finance that would otherwise have been 'tied up' for other purposes. However renting does not often have the various tax advantages of leasing.

11.2.6 Insurance companies

Insurance companies are particularly active in the property market. They provide finance for property developers. They may also purchase the freehold of a firm's site and lease or rent it back to the firm for a period of time. (Multiple retailers have often obtained cash for expansion in this way).

The major impact of insurance companies on the financial scene in general is via their shareholdings in industrial and commercial companies. Generally speaking, the insurance companies try to limit their holding in a firm to 5 per cent of the total shares in that firm. But the Wilson Committee discovered that there were already numerous cases where this figure was exceeded.

11.2.7 Pension funds

Second only to the insurance companies as a source of investment in shares are the pension funds. Many of the largest funds are in the public sector, e.g. the National Coal Board, the Post Office, British Rail. It is perhaps somewhat ironic that employees in the public sector have, via their pension contributions, a personal interest in the survival and prosperity of the private sector.

11.2.8 The responsibilities of institutional investors

The shareholdings of institutional investors — insurance companies pension funds, investment and unit trusts etc. — now exceed those of private investors and their responsibilities have been extensively debated. One contentious issue is the type of company in which they invest. The Wilson Committee found that institutions had a balanced portfolio extending throughout the private sector. Only the smallest firms, or new-comers who had yet to establish their reputation, tended to be excluded.

The Committee's only criticism of these institutions was that they did not involve themselves in 'risky' investments, a situation which the institutions justify in terms of the need to protect the long-term interests (e.g. pension rights) of their members.

The institutions have tended to avoid the responsibility for sharing in the firm's management, that has traditionally gone along with ownership. Although they undoubtedly wield considerable influence 'behind the scenes', it appears that their intervention is confined to major issues, such as the price to be paid or accepted in a takeover, or the size of 'a golden handshake' given to a former director. The opposition to the payment to Mr. Jack Gill, initially proposed by A.C.C., was led by the Post Office pension fund. As the importance of the institutional shareholders grows, they may be forced to play a more active role in the management of the companies in which they invest. We noted above that individual insurance companies own more than 5 percent of the shares in some companies. It would be difficult to sell a shareholding of this size without making a loss; consequently if the firm is performing badly the major investors may be obliged to intervene.

11.2.9 Government-sponsored bodies

The Development Agencies in Wales, Scotland and Northern Ireland offer firms various forms of financial assistance, from rent-free properties to special loan facilities. Similar assistance is also provided in England by the Department of Industry.

Finance for Industry, whose shareholders are the clearing banks (85 per cent) and the Bank of England (15 per cent), has access to funds of £1,000 million intended mainly for medium-term lending. Its subsidiary, The Industrial and Commercial Finance Corporation (ICFC) provides long-term loans and equity capital from £5,000, and another subsidiary Technical Development Capital (TDC) provides finance to facilitate the commercial exploitation of technical innovations.

The Agricultural Mortgage Corporation caters specifically for the financial needs of farmers — agriculture is still one of our biggest and most efficient industries — and rural firms can look to the Council for Small Industries in Rural Areas (COSIRA), although the latter normally concentrates on craft industries employing under twenty people.

11.2.10 Sources of finance — conclusions

If any organization is well established and has good prospects there will be no difficulty in raising finance from the various sources discussed above. The main task is to decide what is the optimum financing package in terms of the mix of temporary and permanent finance, the type of security to be issued on the stock exchange and the price at which it will be offered etc. Such an organization is likely to receive many offers of assistance and advice. With money, as with many other things, 'nothing succeeds like success'.

11.3 Financial requirements

Having examined the sources from which private sector organizations might obtain finance, we now consider briefly the purposes for which this finance might be required. Many of these items would also apply to public sector organizations.

Depending on their size, the goods produced, the services offered and the sector they are in, organizations require finance for some combination of the following:

Rents and rates of premises
Purchase of materials, machinery, equipment etc.
Advertising, sales and other marketing costs
Wages and salaries
Insurances
Owner's remuneration, dividend payments
Hire purchase, leasing, rental, interest and other payments
Service charges: gas, electricity, water and telephone
Repair and maintenance costs.

The above list (which is by no means comprehensive) shows how complex can be the financial requirements of even a small firm. Those responsible for the financial function must ensure not only that the organization has access to adequate funds to meet all these needs, but also that the finance is available when required, i.e. that the cash flow is satisfactory. In addition, as noted above, the relative costs of alternative sources of finance must be kept under constant review (an aspect that received increasing attention when the 'monetarist' policies of the Conservative government led to, or were accompanied by, higher interest rates).

11.4 The public sector

Most of our comments up to this stage have concerned the private sector of the economy. Although some of these points can also be applied to public sector organizations, there are important differences between the two sectors, especially with respect to the sources of finance. The central government has always been able to raise the finance deemed necessary, although not always on the terms it would have liked. Other public sector organizations are more constrained, but benefit by having the backing, in one form or another, of central government.

The Government controls, directly or indirectly, major sources of finance for central government departments, the water industry, the National Health Service and the nationalized industries. For instance in the Health Service, prescription charges are directly set by central government. The latest round of increases is intended to assist in the financing of the restructuring of the Health Service (see Chapter 3) whose spending will reach nearly £11,650 million in 1982/83. National Insurance contributions are regularly increased to finance the cost of pensions and there are numerous other examples.

The government is trying to control the accounts of the nationalized industries by limiting each industry's borrowing limits. These cash limits mean that British Rail has to justify proposed investment in electrification on a line by line basis. The cash limit presently set for British Airways has led to employees being laid off and assets sold. For the year 1982/83 British Telecom's limit is £340 million, £40 million less than in the previous year. British Telecom is hoping to supplement this borrowing from the government by issuing a £150 million bond to the general public to finance its planned investment.

The only alternative source of additional funds for nationalized industries is via high prices for their products. But since this affects the rate of inflation there is sometimes strong pressure from central government, as well as various consumer groups, to minimize price increases.

The financing of local authorities has been discussed in Chapter 3. Despite inquiries into their financing, the most recent being the Layfield Report and a green paper issued in 1982 by the government, little has changed. The financing of local government is really tied with the issue of central versus local democracy, and both will have to be settled together.

11.5 Budgetary control

In the previous section we discussed the revenue aspects of the financial function. In this section we look at the finance function as a means of controlling an organization's operations. (One specific control technique, standard costing, is discussed in Section 11.10.) To assist the reader in his understanding of the importance of the financial control function, Figure 11.1 shows a typical organization chart for the finance department of a local authority in the London area.

A budget is a financial and quantitative statement of the policy to be followed in a given time period to achieve the objectives of the organization. A master budget is closely linked with the organization's yearly plans, and in addition budgets are prepared for major areas of the organization's activities:

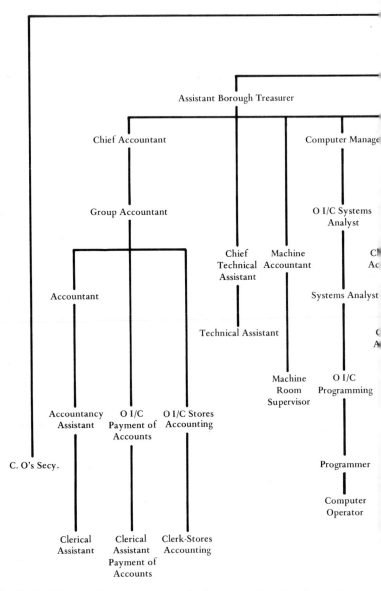

Figure 11.1   Typical finance department/organization chart (London borough).

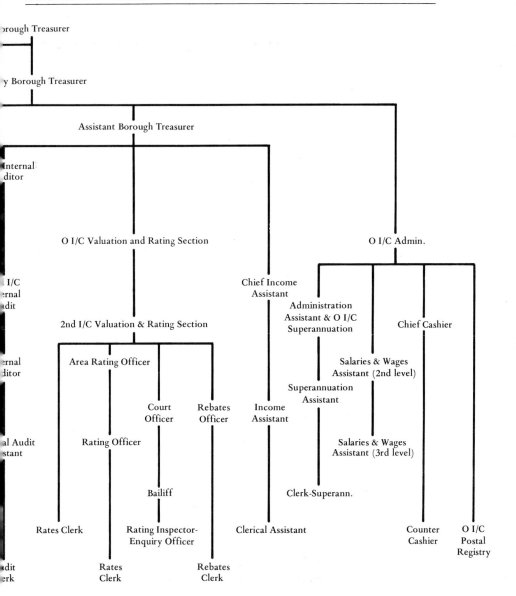

sales, marketing, production, research and development, wages and salaries etc. Each section and department has its own budget as part of the overall budget, and the managers concerned are responsible for meeting their objectives within the confines of their agreed budgets, i.e. they have to achieve results within certain financial constraints.

In some organizations there is the feeling that 'the accountants have taken over', that too much emphasis is placed on meeting a budget requirement, or cutting costs, rather than on ensuring that the organization is supplying the product that the market requires. Students will recall the maxim that 'the end of production is consumption'; some accountants feel otherwise and would replace the word 'consumption' by 'meeting financial targets' — this is obviously a mistaken viewpoint.

Whatever the pros and cons of this argument, no organization can allow its expenditure to exceed its income over any considerable period of time. Budgets are a way of avoiding this and of exercising management control throughout the organization. (The control function was discussed at length in Chapter 10).

11.6 Financial accounting

Whereas budgeting is concerned mainly with the internal operations of the organization, financial accounting is concerned with its external relationships. It provides an overall statement of the financial situation of an organization, and meets the legal requirements of companies to publish accounts and provide specified information. This information forms the basis of the actions of such bodies as the Inland Revenue, the Customs and Excise Departments, financial institutions and other investors existing and potential. (The balance sheet and the profit and loss account, two key financial statements, are discussed in Section 11.9).

11.7 The people

Financial accounting calls for specialized skills and experience in preparing accounts. In addition the staff concerned will be expected to order the company's financial affairs so as to obtain the maximum benefits (or minimum disbenefits) in relation to tax payments, V.A.T. costs, etc. Because of the skills required, financial accounting is often the preserve of people trained as chartered accountants, whereas budgetary control is best suited to people trained as cost and management accountants. The two professional bodies involved are now of equal status and both demand a rigorous training in the relevant aspects of the financial function. However, the end product is different and individuals tend to follow different career patterns. Cost and management accountants are orientated to careers with a particular firm or industry. Chartered accountants have wider horizons since, as well as working within organizations, they can operate in private practice as advisors to organizations and individuals, in the City, and in financial institutions.

The nearest equivalent profession in the public sector is the Chartered Institute of Public Finance and Accountancy which has members in the health and water services and throughout local government. These members undergo a similar rigorous training, but one slanted towards the particular needs of the public sector.

In conclusion, comment should be made about the auditing function. Some auditors work within an organization, to check that its financial procedures are being adhered to. Others are employed by outside specialist firms, who are required by law to audit the accounts of an organization annually. Yet others operate in government, e.g. the District Auditor who independently checks local authorities. Auditors are the financial profession's check on itself. In certain situations, however, their impartiality may be open to closer scrutiny, e.g. where a firm of outside auditors receives a large fee for auditing the accounts of an organization, and develops a close relationship with it in its day-to-day financial operation. Can an audit firm be expected to criticize the financial affairs of a company with which it has been working closely and advising?

11.8 Financial information

Having familiarized the reader with the operation of the financial function we now show how financial information can be used to increase an organization's efficiency. We consider information used in and derived from:

1 analysis of profit and loss accounts and balance sheets;
2 standard costing;
3 investment appraisal.

11.9 Analysis of profit and loss accounts and balance sheets

In analysing profit and loss accounts and balance sheets, comparisons are often made, especially by outside bodies such as investment advisors, between the performance of the firm in question and other firms in similar lines of business. Comparisons are also made between the performance of the firm in this and in previous years. We confine our attention to this latter comparison.

11.9.1 The profit and loss account

Table 11.1 shows profit and loss accounts for two years. As compared to 1981 sales revenue in 1982 rose by £1 million, or 10 per cent. But the

Table 11.1   The Profit and Loss Account

	1981		1982		Change 1981–2	
	£000s	%	£000s	%	£000s	%
Sales	10,000	100.0	11,000	100.0	+ 1,000	+ 10
less Cost of sales	7,800	78.0	8,800	80.0	+ 1,000	+ 13
Gross profit	2,200	22.0	2,200	20.0	—	
less Administration	750	7.5	770	7.0	+ 20	+ 3
Selling and Distribution	280	2.8	350	3.2	+ 70	+ 25
Finance	350	3.5	440	4.0	+ 90	+ 26
Net profit	820	8.2	640	5.8	− 180	− 22
plus Undistributed profit of previous years	1,750		2,170		+ 420	
	2,570		2,810		+ 240	
less Dividend	400		400		—	
Undistributed profit at the end of year	2,170		2,410		+ 240	

cost of sales also rose by £1 million (13 per cent), leaving gross profit unchanged at £2.2 million. This is unsatisfactory since, in a period of rising prices, it means a fall in gross profit in real terms. The firm would be advised to review its purchasing procedures in order to minimize the increase in the cost of raw materials and components. It should also try to increase the efficiency of its production processes, e.g. by reducing manning levels. Finally, it should consider the possibility of increasing its selling prices.

The position looks even less satisfactory when we consider the net profit. This has fallen by £180,000 or 22 per cent. As a proportion of sales, a ratio monitored carefully by outside bodies, net profit has fallen from 8.2 to 5.8 per cent. This fall has come about because of rises of around a quarter in selling and distribution costs and finance charges. Although one would expect some increase in these items as sales increases, such large increases would not appear to be justified. (Note the much more modest increase in administration costs). Areas for possible improvement include a more efficient scheduling of salemen's activities, tighter control of expenses, and a change to cheaper sources of finance.

In 1981 dividend payments accounted for less than half of net profit, the remainder being retained in the business. In 1982, despite the fall in profits, the directors decided to maintain the dividend at the same level, perhaps in order to support the share price. This dividend accounted for almost two thirds of the net profit, and the undistributed profit was correspondingly lower.

11.9.2 The balance sheet

Table 11.2 shows balance sheets for two years. By comparing the balance sheet at the end of each year we can measure spending during the year.

Table 11.2   The Balance Sheet

	31.12.81		31.12.82		Change	
	£000s	£000s	£000s	£000s	£000s	£000s
Fixed assets						
Premises, at cost		2,500		2,600		+ 100
Furniture, fittings						
& fixtures, at cost	2,100		2,300		+ 200	
less Depreciation	300	1,800	350	1,950	+ 50	+ 150
		4,300		4,550		+ 250
Current assets						
Stock	800		850		+ 50	
Trade debtors	1,300		1,700		+ 400	
Cash	80	2,180	65	2,615	− 15	+ 435
		6,480		7,165		+ 685
Less Current liabilities						
Trade creditors		1,430		1,875		+ 445
Net assets		5,050		5,290		+ 240
Share capital		2,880		2,880		—
Profit		2,170		2,410		+ 240
		5,050		5,290		+ 240

Spending on fixed assets was £300,000 (£100,000 on premises and £200,000 on furniture etc., against which is set a slightly increased depreciation charge). This spending indicates that the firm is expecting some increase in its scale of activity. As these new assets come into use, future profitability may be greater than that shown in the current profit and loss account.

Turning to current assets we see that both stock and trade debtors increased, while a small fall occured in cash. An increase in sales is frequently accompanied by an increase in stock and debtors. The higher the sales the higher the stock one expects to carry, and if all or part of the sales are on credit, trade debtors also tend to be higher. Furthermore, the drop in cash is not unexpected since an increase in sales often requires higher expenditure on other assets. (We have already noted the spending on additional fixed assets). Moreover the drop in cash, at £15,000 is modest as an absolute figure. But this represents a fall of almost one fifth and the firm will have to monitor its cash position very closely. (The drop in cash might even indicate that the firm should consider raising additional finance. But, as we saw above, the finance charge has increased, suggesting that this would not be a propitious time for increased borrowing).

11.9.3 Operating and financial ratios

The assessment of an organization's performance can be assisted by monitoring certain key ratios, such as those shown in Table 11.3.

Table 11.3 Operating and Financial Ratios

	1981	1982
Stock turnover rate (cost of sales/stock)	9.8	10.4
Debtor turnover rate (sales/debtors)	7.7	6.5
Creditor turnover rate (purchases/creditors)	5.5	4.2
Current ratio (current assets/current liabilities)	1.52	1.4
Liquid ratio (debtors + cash/current liabilities)	0.97	0.94
Net profit rate (net profit/½ opening capital +		
opening profit + closing capital + closing profit)	16.9 %	12.4 %

The stock turnover rate is the ratio of the cost of sales to stock. The cost of sales represents the value, based on purchase price, of the goods sold. Stock is valued at cost or market value if lower. The ratio increased from 9.8 in 1981 to 10.4 in 1982. An increase in the stock turnover rate would generally be welcomed as a sign of increased efficiency. But the firm should make sure that there are no undesirable consequences. Stock levels can become so low that the firm's delivery dates lengthen, or it may be unable to take advantage of an unexpectedly high level of demand.

The debtor turnover rate is the ratio of annual sales to total debtors at the end of the year. The fall in the ratio could be due to either an increase in the proportion of sales made on credit or to customers paying less quickly. Either outcome could be the result of a deliberate policy on the seller's part. But a slower payment rate could also indicate the firm's procedures in billing customers should be reviewed. It could also indicate that more sales were being made to customers who are a bad credit risk.

The creditor turnover rate is the ratio of purchase (cost of sales plus stock changes) to creditors. (The ratio for 1981 takes into account an increase of £50,000 in stock, calculated by comparing the balance sheets for 1981 and 1980). The fall in the ratio is due to a much steeper rise in creditors than in purchases. In effect this means that creditors have helped to finance the expansion of the firm's business. This has the advantage of reducing, or moderating, the increase in financing charges. On the other hand the firm may be forgoing discounts granted for early payment. Moreover a rise in creditors can indicate a deteriorating liquidity situation.

The importance of liquidity leads to the calculation of two other ratios. The current ratio is the ratio of current assets to current liabilities. The fall in this ratio indicates a slightly tighter liquid position. This is confirmed by the fall in the liquid (or liquidity) ratio, which is the ratio of 'quick' assets (debtors and cash) to current liabilities. Whereas it may not be possible to realize stock quickly without making a considerable price sacrifice, debtors can usually be turned into cash fairly quickly. (If the firm's usual cash collection procedures prove inadequate, it may use factoring; the factor immediately pays the moneys owed, less a discount, and subsequently obtains payment from the debtors). The liquid ratio is the best indicator of the ease (or difficulty) with which the firm could pay off its creditors quickly if called to do so.

The final ratio in Table 11.3 is the net profit rate (net profit as a percentage of share capital plus undistributed profit or as a percentage of net assets). The net profit rate gives an idea of the rate of return earned on the company's assets. It is an imperfect measure since there may be considerable divergence between the balance sheet value of assets and the market value of resources. Nevertheless the steep fall in the profit rate between 1981 and 1982 is a fairly clear indication that the firm has used its assets less profitably.

Shareholders are also very interested in dividend payments. The fact the total payment has remained unchanged despite the expansion of the business would disappoint shareholders. (However the company might have been tempted to cut the dividend in view of the lower net profit). The nominal rate of dividend (dividend as a percentage of share capital) is also unchanged at approximately 14 per cent. (In order to calculate the effective rate of dividend we would have to compare the dividend with the market valuation of the shares).

11.10 Standard costing

Standard costing involves the establishment of predetermined costs — usually in terms of cost per unit of output — and comparing these standard costs with the costs actually incurred. Table 11.4 presents a

Table 11.4   Standard Costs

	(£ per unit)	
	£	p
Direct materials (0.2 kg at £2.00 per kg)		40
Direct labour (0.2 hr at £2.50 per hr)		50
General overhead costs		20
Selling and distributon costs		70
Standard cost per unit	1	80

very simplified schedule of standard costs. The costs of direct materials
and labour are obtained by multiplying the amount used per unit of output
by the price of the input. General overhead costs are sometimes expressed
as a percentage of direct costs. Alternatively, the estimated overhead
figure is allocated among the various products made by the firm, and the
cost per unit is obtained by dividing the cost allocated to that product by
its estimated output during the period in question. Selling and distribution
costs may be established in the same way.

11.10.1 The calculation of variances

Variances may be calculated at various intervals, e.g. annually, monthly
or weekly. The more frequently they are calculated the more quickly will
the firm identify — and thus be able to correct — an unfavourable
deviation from the targets. On the other hand it is possible to calculate the
variance over too short a period to allow clear conclusions to be drawn
about the factor causing the variance. This is especially true for general
overhead costs and for selling and distribution costs, where the basis of
allocation is arbitrary.

We can demonstrate the principle involved in the calculation of
variances by considering one item, direct materials cost. In the period in
question, the firm manufactured 1,000 units, giving a standard material
cost of £400. The actual material cost was £450, an unfavourable variance
of £50. The analysis of this variance is shown in Table 11.5.

Two hundred kg of materials were purchased at a price of £1.90 per kg.
Since the expected price was £2.00, this yielded a favourable variance of
£20. On the other hand the quantity of materials used, 235 kg, exceeded
the expected use, 200 kg, yielding an unfavourable variance of £70. The
firm would wish to identify and correct the reasons for this unfavourable
variance. It might have arisen because the materials were of sub-standard
quality leading to a high reject rate, or because of faults in the
manufacturing process leading to a high scrap rate.

Table 11.5   The Analysis of Variances in Costs

Standard cost	$= 1000 \times £0.40 = £400$
Actual cost	$= 1000 \times £0.45 = £450$
Standard cost minus actual cost	$= $ variance $= £50$ unfavourable
Price variance	$= $ actual quantity $\times$ (standard price $-$ actual price)
	$= 200 \times (£2.00 - £1.90) = £20$ favourable
Quantity variance	$= $ standard price (standard quantity $-$ actual quantity)
	$= £2.00 (200 - 235) = £70$ unfavourable

11.11 Investment appraisal

A very important aspect of the finance function is making estimates of the return on investment — especially in plant and equipment — that the organization might make. Decisions as to whether or not to undertake major investments are usually taken at Board level, with the finance department providing the necessary information.

In some instances detailed financial information is not required, since the decision is determined by broader strategic considerations. When oil and petrol prices rose steeply all the major car manufacturers felt that the development of more fuel-efficient models was essential if they were to retain their market shares. In the public sector 'the major part of the investment programme in the Post Office and British Gas is determined by prior strategic decisions to maintain a certain standard for telecommunications services or to purchase the output of North Sea gas fields. Investment cannot in these cases be disaggregated for appraisal purposes because it relates to a total system — the telephone network or gas distribution grid — and consequently most of the investment programme becomes classified as inescapable or essential'. (N.E.D.O., 1976).

Even for such essential expenditure, investment appraisal may have a role, since there are often different methods of constructing, say, a network of gas pipelines, with different cash flow patterns. But there is most scope for investment appraisal when answers have to be given to such questions as: Should the firm expand the output of product A or of B? Should it purchase expensive, but labour-saving machinery? Should it renovate its existing premises in order to delay the purchase of new premises? The computation involved in answering such questions can be very elaborate and beyond the scope of this book. However it is easy to demonstrate the principles underlying the various methods of investment appraisal by means of very simple examples.

11.11.1 The discounted cash flow method

Assume that the firm is able to invest £100,000 is a project that is expected to yield £110,000 in one year's time. (The project might comprise the purchase and re-sale of a certain quantity of metal). Using symbols we represent the project as follows:

$$CO_0 = £100,000; \ NCI_1 = £110,000$$

where CO_0 is the initial cash outflow (it is conventional to designate the initial year as year nought) and NCI_1 is the net cash inflow in year one; (the cash inflow is measured net of all costs; in this example no costs are incurred in year 1).

The formula for calculating the D.C.F. or internal rate of return (r) is

$$CO = \Sigma NCI/(1 + r)^n,$$

where n is the year in which the cash inflow is received (one in this instance).

To obtain the rate of return (r) we substitute the cash flows into the equation and solve: £100,000 $= 110,000/1 + r$. It can easily be seen that $r = 0.1$ or 10 per cent. This means that the firm could borrow £100,000 at 10 per cent interest, invest it in the project, and out of the proceeds repay the capital (£100,000) and the interest (£10,000). It follows that the firm should undertake the project only if it can obtain finance at a cost of 10 per cent or less.

11.11.2 Net present value analysis

The D.C.F. method can be used to determine which projects would be profitable and which would be unprofitable. But if the company wishes to estimate the absolute change in profits it must use net present value analysis. The basic formula is $NPV = \Sigma NCI/(1 + i)^n - CO$

where NPV is net present value, NCI, CO and n have the same meanings as before and i is the cost of finance or capital.

This method of investment appraisal can be illustrated by considering a company which has to decide whether to replace one of its machines by an improved model which has just appeared on the market. The improved model costs £100,000 but would substantially reduce the cost of production. As shown below the cost savings would increase over time as the cost of labour, which the machine is designed to replace, increases. (To simplify the analysis we assume that the machine would have a useful life of only four years).

The total expected savings exceed the cost of the machine. However when these savings are discounted at the company's cost of capital (8%) they amount to less than the cost of capital. (The discounted values are easily obtained from tables or computer packages.)

Net present value = £89,493 – £100,000

= – £10,507

Table 11.6 Net Present Value Analysis

Year 1	Expected Savings (£)	Savings Discounted at 8% (£)
1	20,000	18,519
2	25,000	21,433
3	30,000	23,815
4	35,000	25,726
	110,000	89,493

11.11.3 The payback method

In some instances an organization may be less concerned with the overall return on a project than with the period required to repay the initial expenditure. This is most likely when the organization's liquidity is very tight or when more than the usual amount of uncertainty surrounds the project, e.g., because of rapid technological change or swings in fashion, as in the market for video games.

Assume that a manfacturer of video games is faced with a choice between investing in the facilities needed to make two different games. The initial investment is £200,000 in each case, and the estimated cash inflows are as shown in Table 11.7.

Table 11.7 The Payback Method

Year	Estimated Net Cash Inflows (£)	
	Game A	Game B
1	60,000	50,000
2	80,000	60,000
3	60,000	50,000
4	10,000	40,000
5	–	40,000
6	–	30,000

Game B is expected to retain its appeal for longer than game A. However A is expected to generate a higher cash inflow in the early years, and to repay its cost within three years as compared to four years for Game B. Using the payback method Game A would, therefore, be chosen.

11.11.4 The book rate of return method

This method is very easy to apply, which no doubt accounts for its popularity, especially with smaller firms. However it has serious deficiences, as can be illustrated by the following example.

A firm has sufficient capital to be able to invest in either of two projects. Each project has an initial cost of £100,000 and an expected life of five years, but with different patterns of profitability, as shown in Table 11.8.

Table 11.8 Book Rate of Return Method

| Year | Profit (after depreciation) £ | |
	Project A	Project B
1	50,000	10,000
2	20,000	10,000
3	10,000	20,000
4	10,000	40,000
5	10,000	20,000
	100,000	100,000

For each project the average annual return is £100,00 ÷ 5 = £20,000 and the rate of return, defined as the annual return as a percentage of the initial cost, is 20 per cent. The book rate of return method would suggest that the two projects are equally attractive. But when the time pattern of returns is taken into account, as in the other methods, it is clear that project A is the more attractive.

11.12 Summary and conclusions

In this chapter we have examined the importance of the finance function in organizations in the private and public sectors. We discussed the financial needs of organizations and the sources of finance available to them. The difference between financial and cost accounting was illustrated. Finally we showed how financial information can be used in helping to monitor the organization's performance. This information can be helpful both to central management and to the other functions in the organization, discussed in the following chapters.

Questions and exercises

1   Answer briefly:

A   What are the clearing banks?

B   What are the differences between an overdraft and a loan?

C   What collateral can be offered against a bank loan?

D   What are the main conditions to be fulfilled before an H.P. company is likely to grant a loan?

E   Give two reasons for the growth in popularity of leasing.

F   Name two pension funds in the public sector

G   Why do pension funds indulge mainly in 'safe' investments?

H   Name two government bodies that offer business finance.

I How does the government try to control the finances of the nationalized industries?

J What is the main aim of budgetary control?

2 'The problem with a new business is that it is almost impossible to raise adequate finance'. Discuss this statement with reference to the financial sources open to businessmen.

3 A relative has the option of buying a small print firm, but before committing himself he asks you to draw up a schedule of the areas for which he will require finance (in both buying and operating the business). Prepare a schedule, together with any other financial advice you may think relevant.

4 'One of the problems of British industry is that the accountants have taken over. All they are concerned about is meeting financial targets rather than producing the right product'. Discuss.

5 Role play a board meeting at which line managers, i.e. production, development, sales and marketing, want more funds to develop a product, and the finance department say that the product is already over budget. (Suitable examples include a new model car, a domestic appliance such as a vacuum cleaner, and a social service such as the provision of homes for the elderly or nursery facilities.)

Further Reading

BROOD, H. W. and CARMICHAEL, K. S. *A Guide to Management Accounting* (H.F.L. Publishers Ltd: London, 1965).

BULL, R. J. *Accounting in Business* (Butterworths: London, 1980).

FRANKS. J. *Corporate Financial Management* (Gower: London, 1974).

HOULTON, M. L. *An Introduction to Cost and Management Accounting* (Heinemann: London, 1980).

N.E.D.O. *The Nationalized Industries* (H.M.S.O.: London, 1976).

PARKER, R. H. *Understanding Company Financial Statements* (Pelican: London, 1981).

SIZER, J. *An Insight into Management Accounting* (Pelican: London, 1979).

12

The Marketing Function

12.1 Introduction

Marketing is a key managerial function. Finding out what the customer wants, monitoring changes in the market place, and anticipating future trends are essential factors in an organization's survival. In this chapter we examine the various elements of the marketing function and look at the way marketing has developed in recent years.

We concentrate on marketing in the commercial or market sector, and in particular on the marketing of consumer goods. There is less need for marketing in organizations which do not supply goods for sale. But even in these organizations marketing concepts, and especially the need to discover what consumers want, have become increasingly accepted.

12.2 The development of the marketing function

Marketing is a relatively young function. Until the industrial revolution most markets were local in origin, small in size, and served by individual craftsmen and producers. Factors such as the weather, wars and the condition of transport routes tended to pre-determine the availability of goods and services for large parts of the population.

With the agrarian and industrial revolutions, it became possible to produce goods on a larger-scale than previously. But in order to obtain all the advantages of large-scale production it is necessary, of course, to be able to sell large quantities of a given product. This was made easier by developments in mass transportation (especially canals and railways) which created many regional and national markets. But it was also necessary to persuade consumers to purchase one particular type of product rather than another. Marketing techniques (such as advertising, branding and sales promotion) that we now take so much for granted, were regarded as revolutionary when they were first introduced on a large scale towards the turn of the century.

The pace of change has continued to be extremely rapid, by historical standards, throughout this century. Such factors as the increased availability of materials e.g. steel and (more recently) plastics, the development of the internal combustion engine, the creation of a national grid for the distribution of electricity, the introduction of computers and micro-processors, have resulted in perpetual change in the pattern of production and consumption. A constant stream of new products has led to the creation of new, and the decline of old, markets. Many new products involve substantial expenditure on research and development. Helping to recoup this expenditure before competitors introduce rival products is one of the tasks of the marketing function.

12.3 The marketing function

The focus of the marketing function is the potential customers for the organization's products. In order to plan effectively the organization needs information on the likely sales of its products, the pattern of sales over time, and the geographical pattern of sales. It also needs to know why things are as they are, what factors cause consumers to buy one firm's products in preference to others.

It is difficult to obtain reliable answers to these questions because purchasers differ in terms of income, attitudes and preferences. In order to simplify the issue it is useful to divide the population, the potential customers, into groups. The classifications most frequently used by the producers of consumer products are (a) decision-making units (DMUs), (b) socio-economic categories. We consider each classification in turn.

12.3.1 Decision-making units

A typical classification would be:

1 Young singles.
2 Young marrieds with no children.
3 Young marrieds, youngest child under six.
4 Young marrieds, youngest child over six.
5 Older marrieds with children under eighteen.
6 Older marrieds with no children under eighteen.
7 Older singles.
8 Other (widows, orphans, etc.).

Classifying people in this manner can help the marketing of a product in many ways. For example a young married couple with no children, probably both working and therefore having a good income, will, when setting up their home, have a considerable amount to spend on consumer durables (fridge, washing machine, furniture etc.) Suppliers of these products, in forecasting future sales, will try to estimate the numbers of such families and to predict changes in their circumstances, e.g. how their disposable income might be affected by future changes in taxation. Suppliers will design products to cater for the tastes of this group, e.g. products with clean, uncluttered lines and bright colours. They will also try to appeal to this group in their advertising, e.g. by stressing the convenience in use that is so important to the working wife.

The marketing approach would differ if one was aiming at the older single DMU. These people are more likely to have all or most of the consumer durables they require and to be fairly settled in their lifestyle. But because they are at the peak of their income earning capability they are able to indulge in luxury spending, on holidays to exotic places, electrical gadgets, expensive fashion clothes, and on dining out.

12.3.2 Socio-economic groups

The underlying rationale of this classification is similar to that for the DMU, namely that different groups have different expenditure patterns, (and hence respond to different marketing programmes). The main groupings are shown in Table 12.1.

Table 12.1   Socio-Economic Groupings

Social Group	Social Status	Occupation	% of Population
A	Upper Middle Class	Senior Managers, Professionals, Doctors, Professors	3.0
B	Middle Class	Middle Managers, Lecturers	10.9
C_1	Lower Middle Class	Supervisors, Clerical Staff, Receptionists	21.7
C_2	Skilled Working Class	Skilled Manual Workers	32.0
D	Working Class	Manual Workers	23.0
E	The Rest	Pensioners, Unemployed, Students	9.4

Example based on system used in Institute of Practitioners in Advertising

It is important to take account not only of the numbers in each group, but also of the expenditure patterns. For example group C2 forms a large proportion of the total but its expenditure pattern is fairly low cost. It is unlikely, therefore, to contain many potential customers for Rolls Royce cars. Advertising for expensive cars would be better aimed at group A which, although small in number, has the highest disposable incomes and wealth. (The top 3 per cent of the population own 50 per cent of the wealth).

12.3.3 Psychological factors

Although classifying people into groups can provide useful guidelines for marketing activities, such activities must also take account of the psychological factors that influence and motivate individual consumers. As an illustration of the range of motivations, consider spending on food. On a purely physiological level we need food to survive, and there is little need for marketing in this context. However most people's incomes (in developed countries) allow spending on food to satisfy additional motives. Hence we find marketing promoting the idea of healthy, pure and natural foods, the benefits of instant and frozen foods, and the advantage of dining out as opposed to eating at home.

A desire for security and safety is widespread. At the general level, heavy advertising of brand names is justified by the need to instill a sense of confidence in the consumers of those products. In some instances the appeal is much more specific, e.g. Volvo cars incorporate a large number of safety features, a fact that is emphasized in the company's advertising.

In marketing clothes (and other fashion items) an appeal is made to conflicting motivations. At the top end of the market emphasis is placed on the distinctiveness and exclusiveness of the dress or hat. In garments aimed at the mass market, on the other hand, advertising recognizes the need for acceptance, the need to belong to a group. The group may be associated with a particular part of the pop scene or with a particular life-style (e.g. the Martini set).

Marketing takes account of people's needs to fulfil their various roles in life. An employer may be persuaded to install hand-drying machines, soap dispensers etc., because he feels that his employees will benefit; a housewife may use a new detergent because her husband and children will enjoy having cleaner clothes. In other instances appeal is made to the individual's narrow self-interest; he is encouraged to spend his hard-earned income on a sports car, a suit of clothes, or a fishing rod.

Psychologists have undertaken a great deal of research into cognition, i.e. our interpretation of the stimuli to which we are exposed, and the results of this research have influenced marketing, and in particular advertising. A theme in a long-running advertising campaign was that '7-stone weaklings' could become big and strong by using a certain exerciser. Women would then fall for them and other men would no longer 'kick sand in their face' as they lay on the beach.

12.4 The marketing elements

The marketing function comprises a number of key elements: market research, product planning, pricing, packaging, advertising and sales promotion, and distribution. We discuss each in turn, beginning with market research.

12.4.1 Market research

Market research seeks to provide an answer to the question: what marketing policy should be adopted in order to achieve the organization's objectives? In order to answer this question it is necessary to obtain information concerning the needs, motives and attitudes of consumers (discussed in the previous section), since these will determine how consumers react to alternative policies. Information must also be gathered on the marketing policies of any competitive firms. Finally it is necessary to monitor any changes or trends that might affect the demand for the firms' products including changes in consumers' incomes, taxation, exchange rates, tariff barriers etc.

In the space available it is impossible to do more than give a few examples of the types of information gathered and the methods used in market research. (The discussion, in the following sections, of the remaining elements of marketing policy will provide an indication of other areas covered by market research).

12.4.1.1 The future pattern of demand

An assessment of demand in various markets and a prediction of the future pattern of demand can guide a company in the allocation of its resources. Other things being equal, a high or expanding demand provides a more favourable environment than a low or declining demand, and a firm will try to identify markets with favourable demand characteristics. Information on demand can guide decisions concerning which products to introduce, which to retain and which to discontinue, and which geographical markets (including overseas markets) to supply.

12.4.1.2 New products

If a firm is contemplating the introduction of an industrial product, say a machine, it may estimate the amount of money that the purchaser would save by installing the machine. This cost-saving could then be emphasized in its sales promotion.

If the new product is intended for the consumer market there are various ways in which consumers' reactions can be tested. A sample of consumers could be presented with a description of the product, or with a mock-up, and asked to comment on its convenience, styling, price etc. Different samples of consumers can be presented with slightly different mock-ups and their reactions taken as a guide in the final design.

If it is felt important to test consumer reactions in a more realistic situation, the product may be test marketed, i.e. sold on a trial basis in one area. (If the product is to be advertised on television, one of the independent television regions may be chosen).

12.4.1.3 Price sensitivity

It is often important to be able to predict, at least roughly, how consumers will react to a change in price. It is sometimes possible to conduct an experiment in which actual prices are changed, or in which different prices are charged in different outlets. Although this method is realistic, it is difficult to control. For example a shop that is not taking part in the experiment may suddenly change the price it charges for the product, or an advertising campaign may be waged for a competitive product.

An alternative method is to ask consumers how much of the product they would buy at various prices. This gets over the problems noted above, but has the disadvantage that the consumers do not have to 'put their money where their mouth is'.

A third method is to fit out a large caravan etc. so that it resembles part of a store, and to ask consumers to simulate their normal shopping behaviour. The prices of the products can be systematically varied before different groups of consumers enter the 'shop'.

12.4.1.4 Monitoring sales

The effectiveness of the firm's sale force can be assessed by monitoring changes in sales over time and differences between one sales territory and another. Such information can also be used in assessing the effects of such things as changes in salesmen's routes and pattern of calls, incentives to salesmen, and reporting systems. For example, I.C.I. recently experimented by giving greater discretion to a group of sales representatives, allowing them to decide when to visit customers and whether to pass information to their superiors, allowing them to make immediate cash settlements of up to £100 in cases of customer complaint, and giving them a discretionary range of about 10 per cent on prices. Their sales rose by 18.6 per cent over the same period in the previous year, compared with a 5 per cent decline in those of a control group using established, supervised methods.

A good market research unit will combine a range of quite diverse skills. The staff will be able to utilize techniques incorporating statistical and psychological concepts, to design and analyse questionnaires, to conduct personal interviews, both extensive and intensive (in depth), and to maintain familiarity with relevant sources of data. To these skills are added the intuition and 'feel' for the market developed through experience.

12.4.2 Product planning

For an established organization, product planning or policy involves answering two questions. First, to which of its existing products should the organization devote (a) more (b) less and (c) the same amount of resources as at present? Second, what type (if any) of new products should be introduced?

These two questions should be examined together, and the organization should consider its 'portfolio' of products as a whole when drawing up plans for the future. For example if demand for all of its existing products appears to have levelled off it should begin to search for possible new products, so that these will be ready for introduction when the demand for existing products declines. If it appears unlikely that new products will be available within the required time scale, attention should be given to the possibility of extending the product range by modifying or developing existing products, e.g. a new version of a cake mix might be created by adding a new ingredient, an estate or a GT variant of a family saloon car might be developed.

12.4.2.1 The introduction of new products

Many of the factors influencing decisions relating to new products (the second question noted above) also influence decisions on existing products (the first question). But some additional considerations have to be taken into account, mainly because of the possible impact of a new product on the organization's existing activities. The main factors to be considered can be grouped under three broad headings.

Gap in the market

New products are, in general, successful only if they fill a gap in the market. This does not necessarily mean that the product is entirely new to the market. But it does imply that the introduction of the product will increase consumers' satisfaction, because any existing producers are unable to supply the product in the quantity, quality or at the price desired.

It is also important to ensure that the gap in the market is wide enough to render the new product viable, i.e. to be produced on a scale that allows an acceptable profit. In fact very few new products yield a profit until some time — typically two or three years — after their introduction. During this initial period sales increase as consumers become more familar with the product, (the gap in the market widens). The firm also benefits by a reduction in unit costs as experience is gained in production.

The firm must also be aware, however, of the possibility that the gap might narrow if it enters a market already supplied by other producers. These producers may react to this entry by lowering their price or by increasing their advertising and sales promotion, thus reducing the relative attractiveness of the new product.

Product life

Ideally a product should have a long life so that it can repay the initial research, development and set-up costs, and remain in production for some years thereafter, as happened with the Morris Minor and the Volkswagon 'Beetle'. Finding products with such a long life is difficult when rapid technological change quickly reduces the significance of a new product's distinctiveness. (Firms often seek to protect their position from imitation by taking out patents on new products, but this is not of much use if technological progress allows competitors to develop better products).

Firms are often able to prolong the life of a product by various means, and these should be considered before the decision whether or not to introduce the product is taken. When the home market becomes saturated or subject to very severe competition, it may be possible to begin exporting. Model variants may be introduced. Expenditure on advertising and sales promotion may be increased. Finally it may be possible to extend sales by reducing price and so appealing to new market segment. (The pricing of new products is considered in detail below).

Compatibility with existing products

A new product may be highly compatible with, or complementary to, existing products in two ways. First, it may utilize spare capacity in the production and/or distribution systems, e.g. spares, factory space, machine time, space in delivery vehicles, time in salesmen's schedules. If the new product shoulders some of the cost of this capacity, the costs allocated to existing products will be reduced accordingly.

Second, the new product may enhance the sales of existing products. Purchasers often prefer to deal with a limited number of suppliers in order to reduce administrative costs, and in these circumstances it is clearly advantageous to be able to offer the purchaser a wider range of products.

For example the financial services offered by the large banking groups include facilities for the deposit of money, the provision of finance in various forms — overdraft, term loan, hire purchase, factoring, etc. — foreign currency transactions, investment advice, arranging new issues, export documentation services and so forth.

Even if new products do not yield any of the above benefits, they may still be compatible with existing products in that they draw upon the organization's expertise and experience. This may be in production or marketing or in both, as when the producers of frozen fish fingers and peas extended into more exotic dishes such as frozen pizzas.

At the other end of the spectrum are those situations where the new products would be incompatible with existing products. For instance the new product might require a more highly skilled and highly paid workforce. The recruitment of such workers could lead to claims for higher wages on the part of the existing workforce. To avoid this problem it might be necessary to produce the new product in a separate location, but this could add substantially to costs.

A second source of incompatibility is when the new product would conflict with the 'image' of existing products. When the Parker Pen Co. introduced ball-point pens it kept well away from the low price, mass production end of the market since this might have damaged the high quality, high prestige image of its fountain pens. Some manufacturers of well established, branded food products have set up subsidiary companies to produce cheaper private-label products.

A final possible source of incompatibility is the loss of sales of existing products that might follow the introduction of a new product. When B.L. introduced the Metro, they were aware that it would attract buyers from the existing Mini range. Whether this will hasten the disappearance of the Mini will become clear in due course.

As we said above, an organization should consider its total portfolio of products. One of the factors favouring the introduction of highly compatible products is that these products make least demands on management time, thus reducing the danger that existing products will suffer from a lack of attention by management. If it is decided that less compatible products shall be introduced, they should be strictly limited in number.

12.4.3 Pricing

A broad distinction can be made between decisions relating to the basic price of a product and subsidiary pricing decisions.

The basic price indicates the place of a given brand or type of product within the price structure pertaining to all brands or products. In setting this price the producer will take account of four factors: his costs, the elements of his marketing mix (other than price), the marketing mix of his competitors, and the attitudes of consumers.

If a producer believes that his product has a more favourable image or reputation than competitive products, e.g. because of superior product quality or heavier advertising, he will tend to add a higher profit margin. On the other hand if he believes that on balance his product does not offer an advantage over competitive products, he is unlikely to set a price above average.

If a producer wishes to increase his share of the market he may set prices below those set by his main rivals. However an aggressive pricing policy often gives rise to retaliation; other producers reduce their price to protect their market share. Another danger of price reductions is that they may be seen by consumers as indicating a deterioration in the quality of the product, with the result that sales do not increase.

12.4.3.1 The pricing of new products

If a producer introduces a new product in a market already supplied by existing producers, the prices of these competitive products are likely to act as a benchmark. But if the product is entirely new, i.e. a pioneer product, the producer has much more discretion in setting price.

He can choose between two broad strategies. First he can set a high initial price to extract the maximum revenue from the few consumers who value the product most highly. Subsequently, this price is reduced, usually in a number of steps, in order to extend sales into other market segments. Alternatively, he can set a low price designed to gain maximum penetration of the market and to deter potential competitors. At this low price profits may initially be unsatisfactory; indeed loses may be incurred. But as sales increase, unit costs fall and profitability improves.

12.4.3.2 Subsidiary pricing decisions

Decisions on basic price are extremely important and are taken at a high level in the organization, e.g. by the marketing director or by the Board. But there are many other pricing decisions which, although less important individually, occupy a great deal of management time in total. Especially important are decisions relating to price differentials and discounts.

12.4.3.3 Price differentials and discounts

Price differentials may relate to different geographical markets, e.g. British firms tend to earn lower profits on export than on domestic sales. Differentials may relate to the time of purchase, e.g. rail fares and telephone calls are cheaper at off-peak times.

Discounts are offered for a variety of reasons. Most firms have quite elaborate quantity discount schedules, intended to encourage purchasers to buy larger quantities. Cash discounts (for immediate or early payments) are also common. Manufacturers give discounts off the retail prices to distributors (wholesalers and retailers) designed to cover the distributors' costs and yield a profit.

Price differentials and discounts can sometimes be justified on the ground that they reflect lower costs on the part of the producer. For example if quantity discounts result in larger order quantities, this reduces the unit cost of production and order processing. In other instances the main justification is that differences exist in the responsiveness of different customers to price changes (technically there are differences in the price elasticity of demand).

12.4.3.4 Rules of thumb

Prices are sometimes set, not as part of a carefully considered policy, but in accordance with rules of thumb. For example most retailers and many manufacturers apply a standard mark-up to cost in order to arrive at price. This simplifies decision making, but is to be recommended only provided that prices are constantly monitored to ensure that they are competitive. In many markets in recent times an increase in competition has required manufacturers to reduce mark-ups below those prevailing earlier.

12.4.3.5 Psychological aspects of pricing

We have already referred to the fact that a low price may be seen by the consumer as indicating inferior quality. The other side of this coin is that a high price can convey a high quality or high prestige image. Hence we have advertisements for 'the most expensive pen in the world'.

Provided that the producer is assured that a low price will not deter consumers it might choose a price just below a round figure, e.g. setting a price for a car of £3,995 would enable it to advertise 'the car that costs less than £4,000'.

12.4.3.6 Customary pricing

There are many examples of prices that people have become used to, e.g. 10p or 20p for a bar of chocolate. A price of 11p or 21p would probably 'feel' strange and might lead to a dramatic fall in sales.

When the principle is extended to a range of products it is known as price lining. For example, men's shirts — in a range of qualities — may be sold at £6.99, £7.99 and £8.99. (This example indicates that there is a link between customary and psychological pricing).

12.4.3.7 Pricing in the public sector

As noted in Chapter 3, it was originally envisaged that the nationalized industries would set prices designed to cover their costs, and would be free from detailed government intervention. In practice, governments have intervened frequently, usually to persuade the industry to modify proposed price increases, occasionally, as with the gas industry at present, to cause prices to increase more rapidly than industry wished.

Most other public sector organizations supply their products at zero price (many educational facilities) or at a price well below cost (many medical services). If such 'merit goods' were sold at the prices needed to cover their costs, it would discourage their consumption, especially by low income families. On the other hand it becomes very difficult to assess the demand for such products in the absence of a price. Moreover rationing by price is replaced by other forms of rationing, e.g. by one's place in the waiting list for treatment in a National Health Service hospital.

12.4.3.8 Consumer information

The spread of agencies providing information to the consumer about the relative merits of alternative brands, ensures that pricing policies will continue to occupy a central role in marketing policy. This will also be ensured by the fact that price is the only element in the marketing mix that gives rise to revenue; all the other elements give rise to costs.

12.4.4 Packaging

The importance of packaging obviously varies from product to product. In most industrial goods packaging, in the form of crates or containers, is designed merely to protect the product and to make it easy to transport. In some consumer goods, on the other hand, packaging is also intended to persuade consumers to buy the product or brand, and packaging costs may exceed other marketing costs.

12.4.4.1 Packaging and purchasing decisions

There are several ways in which packaging can influence consumers' purchasing decisions. A packet, tin or bottle with an eye-catching colour or design can persuade consumers to pick up and examine the product. An increasing proportion of products are sold on a self-service basis, often in very large stores stocking several thousand items. In such situations the need to attract the consumer's attention can be of paramount inportance, especially where new products are concerned.

The consumer, having examined the product, will be encouraged to buy if the package helps to meet her needs. The needs may be practical, e.g. a certain shape or size of package will fit easily into a shopping basket or kitchen cupboard, a plastic bottle may appear to be less substantial than a glass one, but will be lighter to carry.

Other needs may be psychological, as noted earlier. Some colours are warmer and more reasurring than others; chocolate bars often have brown wrappers. Other colours give a clean or clinical impression e.g. washing-up liquids and scourers are often found in white and green containers.

Ideally, packaging will meet both practical and psychological needs. Note the success of 'After Eight', a chocolate mint sold at a premium price. The design of the box reinforces the advertising message that, by offering the mint along with coffee, a hostess of good taste is seen to be concerned with the comfort of her guests. Furthermore by wrapping each mint is its own packet one reduces the chances that anyone will be embarrassed by sticky fingers.

Finally, packages often give information about the products and how they should be used, e.g. washing or cooking instructions, sample recipes.

12.4.4.2 Packaging and the welfare of consumers

In the previous section we examined the various ways in which a producer might use packaging to persuade consumers to buy his products in preference to other products. In general we can assume that these practices benefit both the producer and the consumers. In this section we discuss other aspects of packaging, and we shall see that the implications for consumers' welfare are not always favourable.

The provision of information

Although packaging can provide consumers with useful information, as noted above, it can also mislead, in particular by suggesting that the consumer is getting more for her money than is so. Packets of detergents or breakfast cereals may have unnecessary wasted space inside; tins of meat may contain a low proportion of meat and a high proportion of jelly, fat and gravy, in contrast to the picture on the front of the can; jars of face and hand cream may have false bottoms and double skins (at the time of writing it seems that this form of packaging may be declared illegal).

An increasing number of grocery products are bar-coded, enabling them to be 'scanned' as they pass through the cash-out, the scanners being linked to a central computer. The information permits better stock control and enables the retailer to reduce his costs. If these cost reductions are passed on in the form lower prices, consumers benefit.

Information is not confined to consumer products. It is increasingly common to find, on industrial containers and road and rail tankers, notices relating to dangerous substances, fire treatment codes etc. In many instances international coding systems have been agreed to help customs, fire and emergency services, and the general public, in the event of an emergency.

Re-use versus disposibility

When 'no deposit' bottles and throw-away plastic containers first came onto the market they were greeted with enthusiasm by the general public. But as refuse disposal problems grew, as beaches and the countryside became littered with bottles, beer cans and plastic containers that were not degradable, the public reaction was less favourable, and indeed quite hostile on occasion. For example the Friends of the Earth deposited a large quantity of bottles outside the head office of a well-known manufacturer of soft drinks.

Manufacturers have responded to this criticism in several ways. They have increased their use of bio-degradable plastics, which are gradually broken down by bacteria etc. A number of producers have re-introduced refundable deposits on bottles which are then re-used. The bottle manufacturers have increased their use of cullet (glass already used) including supplies from the 'bottle banks' set up by local authorities. In addition to reducing environmental pollution, these practices help to make better use of non-renewable resources, such as the energy used in the manufacture of glass.

Safety

Increasing attention has been paid in recent years to child safety, in both product design and packaging. In packaging this has manifested itself in such things as special tops on drug bottles, child-proof locking systems, and alternatives to plastic bags that could cause suffocation.

A different aspect of safety is involved in the use of aerosols. The convenience of aerosols has led to their use for an increasing number of products: hair spray, shoe-polish, paint etc. But several environmentalist bodies have protested about possible damage to the ozone level in the atmosphere, and the consequent health hazards. Although the evidence on this point is by no means clear, it is possible that some countries may introduce legislation banning the use of aerosols, and the future of this form of packaging is uncertain.

12.4.5 Advertising

There are many types of advertising, ranging from long-running television advertising on a national scale of consumer products, e.g. beer, washing up liquids, holidays, through advertisements of purely local interest in evening newspapers and local radio e.g. cinema programmes and sporting events, to public interest advertising compaigns e.g. 'Save It' (energy saving) and 'Clunk-click' (safety belts). We shall be mainly but not exclusively concerned with the first type.

12.4.5.1 The aims of advertising

The advertising of commerical products has two basic aims: to inform potential customers about the nature and availability of a product, and to persuade them to buy the product. These two aims go hand-in-hand in the sense that a potential customer must be aware of a product before he can decide to buy it. But individual advertisements carry varying mixes of informational and persuasive content. An announcement of the time and venue of a forthcoming whist-drive is mainly informational; the statement that 'Guinness is good for you' is mainly persuasive.

The most obvious sign of successful advertising is an increase in sales, via an increase in either the number of customers or the amount bought by existing customers. But this does not mean that the advertising must be deemed to have failed if sales do not increase; without the advertising sales might have fallen. Moreover, advertising may allow price to be raised without a loss of sales volume.

As we show when we discuss distribution below, large organizations have achieved a substantial increase in their share of the retail trade. In order to persuade these multiple retailers to stock their products, manufacturers are often required to demonstrate a level of advertising sufficient to create the consumer demand that would justify giving shelf-space to the product.

Some advertising has a much longer time horizon, being designed to create a favourable image of the organization as a whole. The organization may be portrayed as supplying high quality products, researching at the frontiers of knowledge for the benefit of mankind, and preserving the nation's culture and heritage by supporting the arts. Organizational advertising has a wide target audience and can be effective in several spheres. It can make the salesman's task easier, it can help recruitment of workers, and in some instances it may influence political attitudes, e.g. concerning nationalization.

12.4.5.2 The parties involved

There are three main parties involved in advertising: the advertiser, the advertising agent and the media owner. We dealt with the aims of the advertiser in the previous section. The interests of the media owner are self-evident — to gain as much advertising income as possible for his paper, magazine, T.V. or radio channel.

This leaves us with the advertising agent, the man in between. Advertising agencies supply a number of services; they conduct research into the effectiveness of various forms of advertising, advise on choice of media, create and implement advertising campaigns. We can summarize their role by saying that the successful agency ensures that the advertiser's

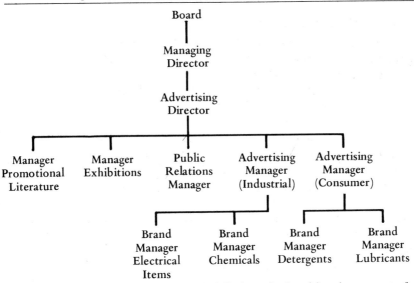

Figure 12.1 Organization chart of typical 'in house' advertising department of a large company.

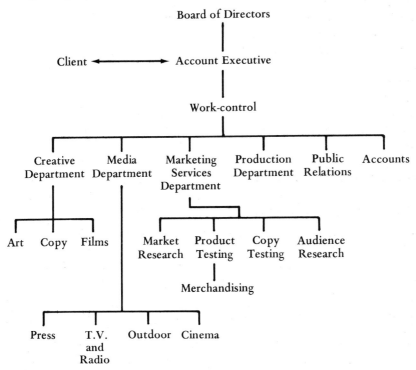

Figure 12.2 Organization chart of a typical advertising agency.

money is spent to the best effect.

Large advertisers have to choose between setting up their own advertising and promotion department and utilizing the services of an outside agency. The choice is a personal one and is mainly decided on grounds of costs and convenience. Figures 12.1 and 12.2 compare an 'in house' department with that of an outside agency.

12.4.5.3 The media

In choosing between the various competing media, advertisers take several factors into account: the cost, geographical coverage, audience type, physical characteristics, and ability to reach special sections of the market.

The press

The Sunday press with its colour supplements has the advantage of a long reading (i.e. non-working) day for most people. The cost of advertising in colour supplements is high in relation to press advertising in general. Moreover an advertiser is able to give his message only on a weekly basis. Like the Sunday press, much of the daily press has national coverage. Its readership has fairly well-defined profiles, e.g. *The Guardian* is read by many academics, the *Daily Mail* has a high proportion of female readers and *The Financial Times* a high proportion of readers in management and the professions. One paper is more suited to the advertising of certain types of product, another paper to other types. Different locations within the paper attract different advertising rates. The spaces opposite page 3 of the *Sun* became a best selling slot when the *Sun* began to compete in the Page 3 'glamour stakes'.

Local and regional newspapers, published on a daily or weekly basis, are obviously more suitable for advertising aimed at a limited geographical audience, or when there are marked differences in consumer preferences. They can also be used as a trial run before a decision as to whether a product should be launched on a national basis. Local newspapers are usually taken into the home and so read by more than one member of the family.

Magazines

There are three main types: general, specialized and retail trade magazines. General magazines often have larger circulations but specialized magazines offer a pre-selected readership, e.g. the type that are read by people who are interested in video games or model making. Magazines are often read at leisure, whereas newspapers are often skimmed through quickly.

Annuals
This category includes the yearly or twice yearly catalogues of mail order houses, which reach large numbers of readers. The inclusion of a product in one of the better catalogues can give a substantial boost to sales.

Television
Ninety per cent of homes receive commercial television, which is now the best way of reaching a national audience. However the cost of advertising reflects the size of the audience, rates being especially high at peak viewing time. The costs of producing television commericals can also be very high. An advertiser who is content to reach a more limited audience at lower cost can confine his advertising to a single television area, e.g., Thames or Granada.

Radio
Commerical radio is comparatively new to the advertising scene. Until recently there was only Radio Luxembourg and the pirate stations (Radio Caroline being the most famous). Now every big urban area has its own channel and even the small businessman or shopkeeper can make an immediate impact on customers in the locality.

Cinema
The number of admissions is falling, but the cinema has a 'captive' audience and can be used to advertise cigarettes (banned on television). 'Young adults' constitute the primary target for advertisers utilizing the cinema; the very young, the middle aged and the old prefer to stay at home and watch televison. Home video could hasten the decline of the cinema, but create additional opportunities through advertising on rented video films.

Direct mail
This method is expensive (postal costs) unless circulars are delivered privately on a local basis. Local distribution often precedes a door-to-door approach for house improvements, double glazing etc.

Outdoor
Posters can be very effective but they have high production and distribution costs and are prone to vandalism. Advertising on buses combines the advantages of posters with mobility. Sponsored buses, completely devoted to one product or company, and painted in the appropriate 'livery', are becoming increasingly common. Signs, such as those in Piccadilly Circus, are eye catching but often do not remain in people's minds: it is the effect rather than the message that comes across.

Advertising signs now appear at many sporting events. The rate charged is increased substantially when the event is covered by television.

12.4.5.4 Arguments for and against advertising

In recent years the effectiveness and ethics of advertising have probably been the subject of more debate than any other management function. The proponents of advertising argue that a well-designed and implemented advertising campaign has a number of advantages.

1 It encourages competition, makes the consumer more aware of each product's capabilities and price, and so enables him or her to make a more informed choice.
2 It assists in planning production; by reducing fluctuations in demand it leads to greater production efficiency.
3 Product identification with a particular manufacturer helps to ensure that quality and service standards will be maintained.
4 By familiarizing consumers with new products and ideas it helps to improve our standard of living.
5 It allows a reduction in expenditure on other forms of sales promotion, e.g. personal selling.

The opponents of advertising would argue that:

1 Advertising costs money and therefore must lead to a higher price for the finished product.
2 It is a waste of resources that could be used for better uses, e.g. education.
3 It is no guide or guarantee of consumer satisfaction or value after they have bought the product, and can be positively misleading. (Complaints of misleading advertisements are heard by the Advertising Standards Association).
4 Heavy advertising by existing producers can prevent the entry of potential competitors into a market.
5 Advertising leads to people wanting things that they cannot afford. A failure to achieve this 'level of expectation' can lead to a sense of failure or depression.

12.4.6 Other forms of sales promotion

12.4.6.1 Personal selling

We are all familiar with personal, face-to-face, selling, since it is used by all retailers, except in self-service stores. It is also widely used by the producers of industrial goods, who tend to spend relatively little on advertising.

A sales force can be organized on a geographical, product or customer basis. A geographical basis is usually chosen when the producer sells throughout a wide area (e.g. nationally). It minimizes travelling time and costs, and allows regional differences in tastes and expenditure patterns to be taken into account.

A product basis is most appropriate when salesmen need to have technical expertise, e.g. in order to be able to explain, and not merely describe, differences in performance between their company's machines and those of competitors.

A sales force is usually organized on a customer basis when a substantial part of the producer's sales are accounted for by a few large customers. Negotiations with these customers are conducted by 'key account executives', the rest of the salesforce being organized on some other basis.

If a manufacturer is selling to different types of customer, e.g. wholesalers, retailers and other manufacturers, he may organize his salesforce in line with those distribution channels.

12.4.6.2 Other methods

Marketing executive are constantly striving to find a new method of sales promotion in order to get ahead of the competition. In addition to the methods discussed above, many others have been used, with varying degrees of success. These include free samples, 'money-off' offers, free gift offers, competitions, and sponsorship of events of various kinds.

12.4.7 Distribution

Distribution is the link between producer and consumer. A large number of people are occupied in maintaining this link. The number of employees in the distributive trades — wholesaling, dealing and retailing — is around 2¾ million, one eighth of the total in all industries. There are also thousands of workers outside this sector involved in the transportation of goods.

Transport costs form a large proportion of total costs and hence of the final price of goods. This proportion has been rising, largely due to increases in fuel costs, and more attention is now given to physical distribution management: the location of warehouses and departments, the choice of routes, the scheduling of vehicles etc.

12.4.7.1 The functions of distributors

The basic functions of distributors are to:

1 Transport goods from the production unit — factory, farm etc.
2 'Break bulk' i.e., reduce the size of package, e.g. a retailer who receives

cases containing twenty packets of detergent will put individual packets on his shelves.

3 Display the smaller packages in a manner convenient to the consumer or user; this usually means displaying the actual goods in a shop, but we also include here alternative methods such as display in mail order catalogues.

Distributors also undertake other functions such as advertising and the provision of credit.

We now examine the channels of distribution for five types of product: energy items, other raw materials, agricultural products, industrial goods and consumer goods. We shall see that distribution is undertaken by producers as well as by specialist distributors, and we consider the reasons for this.

12.4.7.2 Energy items

Distribution is usually wholly or partially undertaken by the producers, who are often government agencies of one type or another. For example, in the U.K., the National Coal Board is responsible for distributing coal to the depots of local merchants, while nationalized industries are responsible for the supply of gas and electricity to factory, office and home. At the end of the last war most crude oil was extracted by the companies which subsequently refined it and then distributed the refined products. But the governments of the individual countries in which the crude oil is extracted have, over the years, gradually extended their control over initial distribution and price and this control is now exerted on a multi-national basis via OPEC.

The involvement of producers in distribution can be largely explained by the advantages of combining large-scale production with large-scale distribution. At the later stages of distribution, when there may be few economies of scale, independent distributors have a more important role, e.g. coal merchants, petrol filling stations. (But note that the oil companies have increased their ownership of filling stations in order to guarantee an outlet for their petrol.)

12.4.7.3 Other raw materials

Producers are also involved in the initial stages of distribution of many raw materials. These producers are often government-controlled, and attempts have been made to operate control on a multi-national basis. But with a few exceptions, e.g. tin, these attempts have been unsuccessful.

12.4.7.4 Agricultural products

Most agricultural products require fast collection and specialized storage.

Agricultural marketing boards, e.g. the Milk Marketing Board, control distribution at least up to the wholesale stage. Under the Common Agricultural Policy of the E.E.C., control over distribution is combined with a system of guaranteed prices. In some instances high prices have resulted in supply surpluses, e.g. the butter mountain and wine lake. The persistence of these high prices is largely due to the powerful farm lobbies, especially in France.

12.4.7.5 Industrial goods

The manufacturer often supplies machines and large pieces of equipment direct to the user (usually another manufacturer), especially where the item is a 'one-off' designed to that user's specifications.

Specialist agents and stockists are employed in the distribution of smaller, standardized goods, and for components (spare parts). Most of these stockists operate on a regional or local, rather than a national, basis, and their location reflects the location of the industries they serve, e.g. stockists of equipment and components used in the vehicles industry and engineering are heavily concentrated in the West Midlands.

12.4.7.6 Consumer goods

Very few manufacturers produce the range of goods that would justify setting up a retailing organization. Some manufacturers have taken over established retailers, but these retailers usually stock the products of a large number of manufacturers, and are run as semi-independent operations.

But many manufacturers undertake the wholesaling of their products, especially food products and other fast-moving consumer goods. The manufacturer is thereby able to ensure that retailers are familiar with his product. The manufacturer is also in a better position to judge whether a deviation of sales from target is due to inadequate wholesaling or to a failing elsewhere, e.g. poor product quality.

If a manufacturer sells into virtually all retail outlets he may decide to supply direct only to the largest retailers, and to supply other retailers via independent wholesalers. It has become increasingly common for manufacturers to undertake merchandising (filling shelves and replenishing stocks) on behalf of the retailer. Manufacturers who do this consider the additional cost to be justified by being able to ensure that their products are given adequate space on the shelves most likely to catch consumers' attention (e.g. at eye-level).

12.4.7.7 The role of the retailer

As noted above, retailers break bulk and display products. They also advertise; the majority of the largest advertisers are now retailers, but manufacturers often contribute to the cost of advertising featuring their products. They offer specialist advice and information (especially important for complex products such as electrical equipment), provide credit of various forms (budget accounts, credit cards, 'the slate' etc.), and in some instances they deliver goods to the consumer's home.

The more functions performed by the retailer the higher his unit costs will be (unless these functions generate a corresponding increase in sales volume). Increased wage rates have caused many retailers to look for means of reducing their labour costs, and the self-service store is the most obvious manifestation of this. Self-service is most common in grocery retailing, but it is now spreading quickly into other trades, including chemists, and even into department stores which have emphasized personal service.

As noted above, the growth of self-service has important implications for packaging. Manufacturers have also to decide whether to sell through self-service stores which offer consumers lower prices or through shops offering better service, albeit at a higher price.

12.4.7.8 The types of retail outlet

Table 12.2 shows the changes that have occurred in the share of retail trade. It can be seen that multiples have increased their share and now account for over two thirds of the total.

Table 12.2   Share of Retail Trade, by Form of Organization

	1971	1979	1980
Single outlet retailers	41.7	31.7	31.0
Small multiples	12.6	14.1	14.4
Large multiples	45.7	54.2	54.6
Total	100.0	100.0	100.0

Source: *Business Monitor*

The multiples

The main reasons for the increased share of the multiples are (a) their prices are lower than those of small specialist shops; (b) having bigger shops they stock a wider range of goods; consumers are thus able to obtain a high proportion of their total requirements from one store.

Table 12.2 shows that the highest rate of growth had been achieved by the large multiples, with ten or more shops (often of above average size). The share of large multiples is especially high in groceries where Asda, Tesco, etc., operate chains of supermarkets stocking several thousand lines. They have also moved into non-foods in a big way, either in their own name, or by acquisition, e.g. Asda owns Wades furnishers and Allied Carpets. Multiples prominent in other trades include Boots, Comet, Dixons and M.F.I.

Single outlets retailers
The numbers of outlets operated by single outlets retailers fell from 338,000 in 1971 to 198,000 in 1980. In trying to withstand competition from the multiples small shopkeepers emphasize personal service, including long opening hours. They can also obtain some of the benefits of large-scale retailing — including bulk buying and advice on shopfitting, stock control etc. — while retaining their independence, by joining a *voluntary group*. (Although most members of voluntary groups have only one shop, a few have several shops.)

Voluntary groups retailers are better able to withstand competition from the multiples and the groups — Spar, Mace, V.G, Wavy Line etc. — increased their share of grocery turnover in the 1970s. However they have recently lost market share as conditions became even more competitive. Although the voluntary groups are best developed in the grocery business, they are also found in other trades including chemists (Numark and Unichem), hardware (Osmat) and paint and wallpaper (Trend Decor).

Mail order
The share of total retail trade accounted for by mail order increased from 2.5 per cent in 1961 to 3.9 per cent in 1971 and 4.7 per cent in 1982. The size of mail order catalogues has grown and the consumer can now choose from among a wide range of goods in the comfort of her home. Credit facilities compare favourably with those offered by other retailers, and almost all purchases are made on credit. The orders are taken and money is collected by agents, and the main factor limiting the future growth of the mail order houses may be the number of agents able to bring in sufficient business to yield a profit to the company (there are currently an estimated 5 million agents). The increasing cost of postage is another problem facing mail order houses, a number of which have established their own delivery systems.

Another factor favoring mail order trading is the restrictions on opening hours faced by shops. These restrictions have become particularly significant as the number of working wives has increased (although some retailers have responded by introducing one or two late closing nights). Another response to these restrictions has been an increase in the number of vending machines.

Vending

When vending machines were first introduced, criticisms were made of the quality of the goods sold, and especially of food products. Quality problems have been overcome by new preparation and storage systems, and a wide range of food products, from chocolate bars to complete meals, are now sold through vending machines. Other products supplied in this way include cigarettes, paper-back books and money (the banks' cash points).

Franchising

If a company with a new product wishes to penetrate the market as quickly as possible, but has only limited finanical and management resources, it may grant a franchise, permitting an individual or company to supply the product in a given area. The franchisor usually advertises the product on a national basis and supplies training and advice on choice of store location, stock control etc.

There are various methods of charging for a franchise, but the most usual is an initial flat fee plus a percentage of profits or turnover. The franchisee also has to provide and equip the premises (shop, garage etc.) and is required to adopt policies laid down by the franchisor with respect to purchasing, price, presentation and decor.

The biggest growth area in franchising has been the fast food businesses, Wimpy and Kentucky Fried Chicken probably being the best known names. But the idea has been adopted in many other areas including car maintenance (Ziebart rust-proofing, Hometune car-tuning) document-reproduction (Prontaprint) estate agents (Realty) and drain-cleaning (Dyna-rod).

12.4.7.9 Future trends in retailing

The recent changes that have occurred in retailing have originated within the industry itself. Future changes are more likely to reflect external factors, particularly various aspects of the information revolution.

In the not too distant future consumers with a televison set and telephone will be able to call up for details of the price and availability of various products in local shops and to phone in their orders. The items will be taken from the retailer's warehouse or store-room and packed ready for collection or delivery. Consumers will pay for their orders by giving details of their bank account, from which money will be automatically transferred to the retailer's account.

This form of shopping is obviously less suitable for some products than others. Consumers will still wish to inspect some products before purchase (although mail order companies have constantly widened their product range, as noted above) and to have personal service. But there is no doubt that some dramatic changes will occur. The trend towards increasing concentration in retailing will continue, since only the larger organizations will be able to afford the necessary hardware. There is likely to be a further blurring of the distinction between wholesalers and retailers (many wholesale cash-and-carry depots are in effect open to members of the general public).

Manufacturers will have to modify their distribution policy in line with these changes in the channels of distribution. Changes may also be required in packaging; for example they may develop one form of packaging suited to 'made-up' orders, while retaining another with more eye-appeal for display purposes. (Incidentally it has also been suggested that manufacturers will have to re-think their advertising policies if the spread of video-recorders enables consumers to 'record-out' the commerical breaks).

12.5 Summary and conclusions

Marketing focuses on the needs of the consumer, and marketing policy is designed to meet these needs and to yield a profit to the producer. The major elements of policy, discussed in detail, are market research, product planning, pricing, packaging, advertising and sales promotion, and distribution. In our discussion of distribution we showed why producers choose particular channels of distribution; we also examined the polices of various types of distributors, the multiple, small shopkeeper, mail order house etc.

Since commercial organizations must sell their products in order to survive, good marketing is clearly essential to commerical success. Marketing policy is formulated and implemented by specialists. However, successful marketing also depends upon the effects of other departments. It is not much use creating a demand if one cannot supply products of the right quality, at the right price, and at the right time. This is largely the responsibility of the production department, whose functions are discussed in the next chapter.

Revision questions and exercises

1   Answer briefly:
A   What is meant by a DMU?
B   What are the main elements of the marketing function?
C   Why is breadth of market so important to a product's success?
D   What are the main aims of packaging?
E   Name three future trends in packaging.

F   What factors does the producer take into account in setting prices?
G   What are the main functions performed by retail outlets?
H   What is franchising?
I   What are the main advantages of door-to-door selling?
J   Why do firms advertise?

2   Select about 20 advertisments in every day use and note any good or bad features. Try to identify any common advertising themes in particular product areas.

3   'Sex in advertising exploits women but sells newspapers and products'. Discuss, giving examples.

4   'In a world where many people are starving and on the poverty line, advertising is a luxury that should be eliminated as socially unacceptable'. Discuss.

5   You have a 2-year-old Mini 1000 to sell. Draft an advertisement and outline the approach you would adopt when potential purchasers come to look at the car.

6   Pick a new fashion in clothes, hairstyle, or make-up and discuss ways of marketing it.

7   Suggest a marketing campaign to sell more paper clips.

8   How would you market: Margaret Thatcher, David Steel, Michael Foot and Roy Jenkins (or their successors).

9   You are appointed chairman of the British Tourist Authority and are anxious to increase the number of foreign visitors coming to this country. Explain the various marketing alternatives available to you and say what steps you would take to achieve your objectives.

10   *Student numbers*
      You are employed by a large provincial marketing agency that has gained a reputation for dealing with unusual assignments. The local polytechnic approaches you and asks your advice on the following. They are worried about the falling birth rate and their ability to continue to attract students to their courses in sufficient numbers. The polytechnic runs a number of courses of national standing including HND and HNC courses, a business studies degree, engineering and chemistry degrees, an accountancy degree, professional courses, and a variety of management courses. The polytechnic, which is based at Preston, has a large catchment area although, by tradition, most of its students come from a close radius to Preston. Many of the buildings are modern and include a new library and students union, although living accommodation is still a problem. Discuss the steps you would take to ensure that the polytechnic recruits sufficient students in the future.

11   *The salesman*
      You have just taken up an appointment as Sales Director of a national organization making gas fires and gas logs. The organization employs some 40 salesmen, all based at the head office in Runcorn, covering the whole of the United Kingdom.
      Having settled in your job after a couple of days it becomes apparent that your predecessor has left major problems. First, there is a large turnover of

salesmen, approaching 40%. On investigation this appears to be due to low earnings, lack of objectives and the fact that some of the salesmen are having to spend long periods away from home during the week, visiting customers a long way from the head office.

The salesmen also complain that the production people cannot meet delivery dates that they promise their customers. When you raise this matter with the production director he says that the salesmen give unrealistic delivery dates and that there is no guidance given to him on which models to produce. This leads to shortages in some lines and surplus stocks in others. Storage is also a problem; your vehicle fleet is becoming old and increasingly costly to maintain, and a recent drivers' strike has produced a three week backlog of deliveries.

At the same time your major customer, the British Gas Corporation, starts complaining of the fact that spares are insufficient and that your model range is becoming outdated compared with other manufacturers. They also complain of poor service from your sales force, especially in the areas of technical information and after-sales service. The salesmen keep changing before a satisfactory relationship can be built up and standards vary from one part of the country to another. The Gas Corporation is organized into four main geographic areas.

You call a weekend meeting of the whole of the sales force but only about 50% turn up. Those who do are very dispirited and feel that they do not get sufficient guidance from head office, that they are selling an inferior product, that they have no promotion prospects and that the fringe benefits offered them are inferior to other companies. They quote examples of having to deliver gas fires to customers during the recent strike using their company Minis.

The Managing Director sees the latest sales figures and being very worried asks you to produce a report stating the steps needed to rectify the situation and regain the company's position as a market leader in its field.

Discuss the steps you would take and the contents of the report.

Further Reading

BIDDLECOMBE, P. *Financial Advertising and Public Relations* (Business Books: London, 1971).

CANNON, T. *Basic Marketing* (Holt, Rinehart and Winston: New York, 1980).

CHISNALL, P. *Marketing — A Behavioural Analysis* (McGraw-Hill: New York, 1975).

DE LOZIER, and J. M. WAYNE *The Marketing Communications Process* (McGraw-Hill: New York, 1976).

ENGEL, J. and BLACKWELL, R. *Consumer Behaviour* (Holt Saunders: New York, 1982).

FOSTER, D. W. *Planning for Products and Markets* (Longmans: London, 1972).

FRAIN, J. *Introduction to Marketing* (Macdonald Evans: London, 1981).
KOTLER, P. *Marketing Management* (Prentice Hall: New York, 1980).
MAJAVO, S. *Marketing in Perspective* (George Allen and Unwin: London, 1982).
STANTON, W. J. *Fundamentals of Marketing* (McGraw-Hill: New York, 1981).

13

The Production Function

13.1 Introduction

In this chapter we examine the main work areas covered by the production function: product design and development; plant location, layout and equipment; production planning and control.

Some of the issues that we discuss apply to all sectors of the economy. But in general the production function is seen as being particularly important in manufacturing. Consequently, our discussion focuses on that sector. The decline of British manufacturing receives constant attention in the media, and it is appropriate to begin with a brief examination of this topic.

13.2 The decline in manufacturing

The U.K. has travelled the usual route of economic development; a movement of workers out of agriculture into an expanding manufacturing sector is followed by decline in the *relative* importance of manufacturing and an increase in the relative importance of the services (education, health, entertainment etc.).

The decline in the importance of manufacturing can be measured in various ways. If we examine employment we find that the number of employees in employment in manufacturing fell by 13 per cent between 1966—75 and by a further 11 per cent between 1975 and 1980 (an even faster rate of decline). By 1980, manufacturing accounted for only 30 per cent of total employees in employment, as compared to 40 per cent in services (or well over 50 per cent if the distributive trades are included). Increasing productivity has meant that output rose between 1966 and

1975. But a 5 per cent fall in output occurred between 1975 and 1980.

As noted above it is quite usual for countries to reach a point in their development at which manufacturing begins to decline in relative importance. But this decline has been greater in the U.K. than in other countries. Figure 13.1 shows that productivity growth in manufacturing in the U.K. has not kept pace with our competitors, particularly in the years 1971—79. The U.K.'s share of the value of exports of manufactured goods fell from 26 per cent in 1950 to 9.5 per cent in 1980. (Our share was down to 8.5 per cent in 1976, and whilst the subsequent upturn is encouraging, we have, of course, recovered only a small part of the ground previously lost. Moreover the decline in our share of the *volume* of trade has not been reversed.)

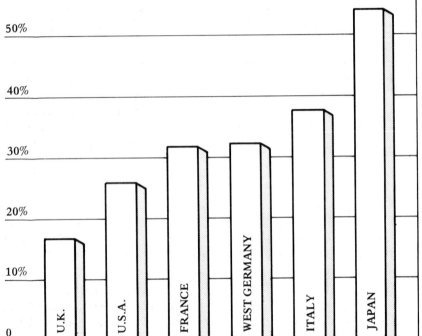

Figure 13.1   Productivity growth in manufacturing, 1971—9. Source: *Barclays Review*, August 1981.

Experience has varied from one branch of manufacturing to another. If we look at broad industry groups we find that in the decade 1970 to 1980 the U.K. chemicals and electrical engineering industries increased output albeit to a modest extent. On the other hand, substantial declines occurred in mechanical engineering, vehicles and textiles.

Particularly disturbing is the loss of sales in markets in which Britain was previously very prominent. A virtual monopoly of textile equipment has disappeared; even British textile manufacturers frequently choose Swiss or German rather than British machinery. We import the majority of our cars, and B.L. Ltd., the only remaining major British-owned manufacturer, has seen its share of the British market dip from 60 to 17 per cent. Imports now account for a large share of the market for domestic appliances — 96 per cent of dishwashers, 45 per cent of washing machines, 30 per cent of spindriers — and for nearly 90 per cent of office equipment etc. I.C.L., our sole surviving large computer manufacturer, has been forced to close several factories and substantially reduce its labour force, despite the rapid expansion of the world market.

What has gone wrong? Why has the U.K. manufacturing sector done less well than its competitors when the world economy has expanded, and been more vulnerable in times of recession? Diagnoses of 'the British disease' have emphasized the following areas:

1 The level of investment in new plant and equipment has been lower in the U.K. than in most other industrialized countries. (The gap was in fact much wider in the 1960s than subsequently.) As we noted in the previous chapter, some commentators have argued that the banks have taken too short-term a view of their involvement in industry. Other commentators have suggested that industrial companies also have too short a time horizon, preferring to distribute dividends to shareholders rather than plough back profits. (It is further suggested that this attitude is fostered by the emphasis placed on current dividends by finanical commentators in the media and by the City in general). An alternative explanation of the low level of investment is its low yield. There is no point in installing machinery if it cannot be fully utilized, either because of union pressure or an inadequate demand for the final product.

2 Many parts of British industry have been characterized by restrictive working practices and overmanning. We have already mentioned that union pressure sometimes prevents the efficient utilization of new plant and equipment. The organization and attitudes of British unions have also resulted in a work force that is less flexible than those of Germany, Japan, U.S.A. etc. Demarcation disputes (which union's members have the right to do what job) tend to be more common in this country. The unions also tend to insist that more rigid conditions should be applied to training (including the length of apprenticeships) and re-training. Finally, strikes can disrupt industry and hence cause a loss of efficiency. In fact, overall, the U.K.'s strike record is not very different from the average for all industrialized countries. But a relatively high proportion of strikes in the U.K. are unofficial (without

union backing). Since unofficial strikes are difficult to anticipate, they tend to be especially disruptive.

3 It is sometimes said that there is no such a thing as poor unions or a poor work-force, only poor management. Although this is an oversimplification, it contains an element of truth. Good managers will foster a co-operative attitude on the part of unions and workers. Even if workers and their representatives are determined to be militant, good managers will minimize the number of issues that can be exploited.

Managers are, of course, concerned with many issues other than those involving the unions, and it appears that in some sectors of manufacturing British managers have proved less skilful than their counterparts in other countries. British firms have a good record in producing new ideas and even in pioneering new products, but frequently fail to translate these into commerical successes. The E.M.I. scanner changed, in only a couple of years, from a highly profitable world leader to a commerical burden of such a magnitude as to result in E.M.I.'s being taken over by Thorn. British Leyland closed the most modern car assembly plant in Europe, built to manufacture Rover cars, only shortly after its opening and without it ever approaching full production.

Sir Freddie Laker built a thriving airline, but was then tempted to expand at a time when competition was becoming much more intense. The expansion, which was mainly financed by borrowed money, came to an abrupt end in 1982. The company was unable to meet its financial commitments and a receiver was appointed.

Isolated examples such as these may not in themselves be of much significance. But they are evidence of a more widespread failure on the part of British firms to meet customers' requirements. A recent report by the National Economic Development Office identified a number of reasons for loss of sales to overseas competitors, including inferior design, poor product quality, and a failure to meet promised delivery dates.

4 In earlier chapters we have stressed the point that managers can learn to improve their performance. But performance is also affected by native ability, and there is no doubt that in the U.K. career opportunities, including prospective salaries, have been less attractive in production, engineering and manufacturing in general than in the City and the professions. In Germany and Japan the best graduates want to go into production, since that is where the money and status are, and this undoubtedly helps to explain the success of German and Japanese manufacturing companies. In the U.K., on the other hand, the 'best minds' tend to become lawyers, accountants or academics.

Incidentally these attitudes tend also to be found among politicians. Conservative governments are generally felt to be favourably disposed towards industry. But the members of Mrs. Thatcher's cabinet with full-time experience of business, usually obtained this experience not in manufacturing but in the City, in farming or as lawyers.

These, then, are four fundamental, deep-seated reasons for the relatively poor performance of British manufacturing industry. In some years these factors may be overshadowed by others, including government policy. For example, the tough economic policy of Mrs. Thatcher's government, with high interest rates and a strong pound, contributed to the rapid rundown of industry and the record number of bankruptcies in the early 1980s. (On the outher hand it also led to a substantial improvement in labour productivity). But a decline also occurred under the preceding Labour government, suggesting that government influence is limited and that we have to look more widely for a solution to our problems.

As suggested above this may require an increase in investment in manufacturing, better training, a change in working practices, more attention to marketing, and so forth. It would be helpful if governments could adopt policies which led to a steady increase in demand, and they could assist the interests of British exporters by persuading other governments to reduce barriers, and in particular non-tariff barriers, to trade.

13.3 The production process

Each production process may be regarded as unique. Whether we are talking about the potter moulding clay on his wheel into the shape of a jug, the refining of crude oil into a variety of finished products, or the robot assembly line that produces Maestro cars, each and every process has its own problems, its advantages, its unique style and atmosphere. Among the variables are the machines, the materials, the consumables and last, but by no means least, the people involved in the process: shopfloor workers, foremen and supervisors, line managers in charge of departments, designers and planners, right up the organizational hierarchy to the production director.

Four main types of production can be distinguished. (In practice two or more types may be found in combination).

1 *Mass production* is the manufacture of articles in large numbers with few variables as to types or range, e.g. the modern car assembly plant.
2 *Process production* also takes place on a large scale. But whereas in mass production a large number of individual items is produced, the

output of process production is usually large volumes of liquids or powders. Moreover process production normally requires large amounts of specially designed plant, operated by a relatively small work-force. The modern, purpose built chemical plants and oil refineries are examples of process production units.

3 *Batch production* is common in the engineering industry. A number of similar items are produced in batches within a certain time scale. This method is often wasteful in time and resources as it requires stocks of materials and semi-furnished parts to be stored close to the production unit, and involves the items being transported several times over. It is therefore usually confined to situations where the demand for the item is insufficient to allow mass production methods to operate efficiently.

4 *Jobbing* involves the production of different products in unit quantities and covers such items as engineering components designed to meet the specifications of individual customers, individual pieces of glassware etc.

The production process may be regarded as the ultimate management test since it requires people, information, machines, materials, buildings, transportation and storage systems to be brought together in a given sequence against a required timescale.

A change in one of these variables has an impact on all the others. For example an interruption in the supply of materials due to industrial action may cause the whole production process to slow down or stop. This may affect employees' take home pay as bonus earnings are reduced. Machines will not be operating at capacity, which will affect their maintenance schedules. The level of finished stocks will be reduced, while stocks of other consumables used in production and not affected by the industrial action will increase, unless management reduces quantities ordered. The amount of finished product available for sale will be reduced, and the sales and marketing people will become involved in explanations to customers as delivery dates are altered. Finally the process comes full circle as the production planners alter their schedules and issue new instructions to all the sections involved. Moreover these revised schedules will have to be changed again when the industrial action ends and the supply of materials returns to normal.

A similar set of interactions would result from a change in any of the variables in the process, and production managers are constantly carrying out 'fine tuning' exercises as the resources under their control vary. Patience, as well as technical skills, is required by managers in this area.

Whatever the type of unit he controls a production manager is concerned with a number of decision areas. These are discussed in detail below, but first it is useful to examine the distinction between long- and short-term decisions.

Long-term decisions are generally made by senior management at Board level on the advice provided by specialist managers, and the production director in particular. They are major decisions that determine the shape, size and future activities of the organization as a whole, as well as of the production division or department. Issues decided at this level include:

1 The type of product to be manufactured and its major design features.
2 The type of production process to be used.
3 The detailed design of all the elements in the production process, including the layout of the unit itself.
4 The location of the production unit.

Short-term decisions cover many of the areas of 'fine tuning' mentioned in the previous section, and stem from the flow of information to the production division. The areas involved are:

1 Stock levels
2 Production capacity
3 Maintenance
4 Quality control
5 Financial control
6 Utilization of labour

We now examine the major decision areas relating to production, beginning with product design and development.

13.4 Product design and development

13.4.1 Design costs

New products often require new machine tools and materials, and these re-tooling and re-equipment costs must always be in the forefront of management's mind when the final design is being decided. Design changes to existing products can also involve expensive modifications to the production process.

New or modified designs arise from a variety of reasons. A brand new product may be introduced to fill a gap in the market; this may involve an extension of the frontiers of science and technology, as with the first television set and the first computer. In such situations it is often difficult to estimate correctly the overall design, development and production costs, as changes will undoubtedly have to be made to the original design as tests and experience dictate. Being first in the field is fine if you get the sums right first time, But experienced managers know that this is rarely the case in practice. Over-runs on budgets are common in high technology projects, from atomic power stations to multi-role combat aircraft, from Concorde to the Advanced Passenger Train.

In other industries, design changes arise from the need to follow the dictates of fashion. The length of hemlines and the width of trouser legs change from year to year. Changes in the popularity of particular colours occur in clothes, and also in wallpaper, furnishings etc.

Products can also become outdated for reasons other than fashion. If one manufacturer introduces a product with superior performance characteristics, competitive products may have to be modified if they are to survive. For example increasing imports of fuel-efficient cars into the U.S.A. made many of the American 'gas-guzzlers' obsolete. Sometimes there is a need to support the existing range with a product that appeals to a particular section of the market, e.g. the B.L. Mini 1275 G.T. was aimed at the younger, sportier section of the Mini market.

New products are sometimes introduced to utilize spare capacity and to keep people in employment. While these are worthy motives it is important to ensure that there is an adequate demand for the new products.

Finally a new design may arise because the designer and owner wants to achieve fame and fortune, for example the QE2.

13.4.2 The stages in the design process

13.4.2.1 Ideas stage

The originator comes up with a good idea and turns this into a rough design or specification. This often involves discussion with the sales and marketing divisions to obtain as much information as possible about likely consumer reactions, the nature of competitive products, if any, etc. (In some instances, the stimulus for a new product comes from the identification by marketing and sales staff of an unsatisfied consumer need).

13.4.2.2 Decision stage

Designers, technicians and other specialist staff work on a detailed specification for the product, incorporating such factors as technical requirements, performance statistics and styling. An estimate will also be made at this stage of cost, selling price and output. If, in the light of this information the proposal appears to be feasible, the work will continue; if not the idea and the design are dropped.

At this stage a working model is often constructed. Use may also be made of computer design simulation. This allows a comparison between alternatives to be made at a fraction of the cost that would be required to construct several working models. Computers can also be used to simulate the effects on the different parts of the organization: production, purchasing, sales etc.

13.4.2.3 Transference stage

The information collated above is translated into detailed requirements for the production division. Often, a 'design and development team' is set up composed of people with a variety of specialist skills, utilizing a 'matrix type of organization' (see Chapter 8). The aim of this group is to ensure that the final design can be easily produced; once the production unit is 'tooled up' any changes in design will involve disproportionately heavy production costs.

13.4.2.4 Pre-production

A 'pilot' or 'test' run is arranged to try out, on a trial basis, the production system and ancillary management functions, and to enable the employees to gain practical experience under actual production conditions. Tools, machines, drawings, work specifications, cost estimates and training requirements are all tested out. At this stage it is not unusual to find easier, more economic means of producing parts of the product. Although computer simulations can be very useful, there is no substitute for practice in a real work situation, and close monitoring and attention by management at this stage will help to maximize efficiency when full production begins.

13.4.3 Value analysis

As part of the quest for greater efficiency in the production process, a technique known as 'value analysis' was originated in the U.S.A. by L.D. Miles of the General Electric Company in the late 1940s. The aim of this technique is to ascertain, by mean of a series of tests and questions, the true value of every part or product used in the production process, and thus to assist management in making resource decisions.

Value analysis questions the whole purpose and function of a part or product, and thus has a broader scope than cost reduction systems which, while aiming to minimize costs, take for granted the functional elements of the part or product.

Value analysis works best when a small multi-disciplinary team can look at all the aspects involved, each member bringing his particular skill and experience to bear on the problem or item in question. The project team would proceed as follows:

1 A product or part (preferably of major importance) is selected.
2 Financial costs are estimated.
3 The number of components used is listed.
4 All possible uses for the product or part are considered and the number likely to be sold is estimated.
5 The major objective of the part or product is agreed and all the means of achieving this objective are examined. For example is a lubricant additive going to be used solely in the gearbox of a car or can it be used in motor mowers, boat and motorcycle engines? What changes would be required to meet these major aims?
6 The major objectives being agreed, detailed financial costs are estimated for each of the options and a final choice is made on the most suitable mix of components in terms of cost, function, design etc.
7 The final stage involves deciding what other functions or uses for the final product have to be incorporated into this choice of components so that all possible uses are catered for. This may mean that further thought and design work is involved before the new product or part is accepted in the market place.

13.4.4 Quality and reliability in the design process

All managers have to set quality standards. These targets are strongly influenced by the sector of the market the organization is aiming at, and the price charged, e.g. a Rolls Royce car has a high price and caters for the top end of the car buyer's market, and must therefore maintain the highest quality.

The quality standard achieved depends, of course, on the capabilities of the organization. High quality requires good control standards, and monitoring throughout the production process. Feedback from the sales force and marketing department on customer reaction also helps to maintain high quality standards.

Reliability is linked, but not directly proportional, to the standard of quality. Reliability depends on many factors such as the number of moving parts, usage, the materials and servicing arrangements. Reliability will be enhanced by the following factors:

1 The use of well-proved and tested designs. The closer one approaches the 'frontiers of knowledge' or the current design limits the more likely it is that reliability will suffer.
2 Simplicity of design. The more complex a product, the more faults are likely to occur, and the more difficult they may be to correct. Consider the scope for faults in the modern car with its electric windows, turbocharger, electronic ignition, special lighting systems, heated seats, warning display systems, etc. and the difficulties that can face

the owner who wishes to service his own car. Even garage mechanics are now having to specialize as no one person can encompass the necessary knowledge. We now have auto-electricians, fuel specialists, car tuners, in-car entertainment shops etc.

3 The use of reliable components in all parts of the product with high tolerance factors should minimize maintenance and breakdowns. Each component must be tested not only in its own right, but also in conjunction with the other components to be incorporated in the unit or product.

4 The incorporation of 'fail safe' systems or products having 'set lifespans' will assist the user in planning maintenance schedules and avoiding unwarranted stoppages and breakdowns.

5 Production in accordance with the designer's specifications is the greatest guarantee of reliability. Slipshod workmanship, incorrect tolerances, a wrong materials mix will all affect reliability, sometimes with very serious cost implications. For example in 1979 and 1980 the Lancia car company was faced with a massive corrosion problem in some of their models, due in the main to a faulty batch of steel produced several years earlier. In other instances the problem is discovered after an even longer period of time, e.g. corrosion in nuclear power station cooling pipes. In both cases the result was a dissatisfied customer, the spending of vast sums of money to put the problem right, and bad publicity and considerable loss of prestige for the manufacturer of the end product. Even the Japanese, whose reliability record is excellent on the whole, are not exempt from these problems; the Honda car company had to recall some of their models in the North American market for safety checks in 1981.

13.5 Plant location, layout and equipment

13.5.1 Plant location

There are many advantages in locating a new production line in close proximity to exisiting lines, in adjoining factories or even within the same factory. But in some instances there may not be sufficient space to permit this. In addition, even if there is sufficient space, the manufacturer may decide to locate elsewhere for a variety of reasons (outlined below). Manufacturers are usually faced with a wide range of alternative locations, and in choosing between these alternatives the following factors will be taken into account:

1 *Proximity to other units within the organization.*
   In this respect government intervention has often been to the detriment of British organizations' overall efficiency, by preventing them from

locating at their preferred site. In the car industry, for instance, particular governments, often for purely political reasons, have forced vehicle manufacturers to locate in areas they would not themselves have chosen, putting, for example, engine assembly plants in Wales, and axle and gearbox plants in Scotland, while the major assembly units remained in the Midlands. The additional transport costs involved, and the co-ordination problems that arise when groups of managers are hundreds of miles apart, have put British manufacturers at a disadvantage when competing with Japanese manufacturers, most of whose activities are concentrated in one huge site.

2 *Labour availability.*

With the present high levels of unemployment this factor is no longer so important. Nevertheless firms must ensure that there is sufficient labour to meet their needs. This is especially important when the unit is heavily dependent on one type of labour e.g. skilled engineers or women with the dexterity required for complex assembly operations. Manufacturers often look for workers with the requisite skills and experience. But sometimes they prefer to train 'green' labour, since new recruits are less likely to bring with them unwanted habits, including restrictive working practices. (The desire to evade such practices is one reason why manufacturers who could expand on their existing site may prefer to move).

3 *Housing availability.*

This particularly applies to temporary housing for their workers. The New Towns are often able to offer a company instant housing for its employees, often in modern surroundings. This gives them a considerable advantage over local authorities which have long waiting lists for council houses from existing inhabitants, and which are, therefore, reluctant to provide housing for newcomers.

4 *Amenities.*

People are now demanding better surroundings and amenities including leisure centres and recreational facilities of all kinds. Public expenditure on these amenities began to increase in the 1960s, with most provision being made in the New Towns and in the suburbs of established towns rather than in old, overcrowded inner city areas. (Having encouraged a movement of firms and population away from city centres during the last twenty years, governments are now trying to reverse the trend in order to prevent further decay of the economic and social fabric of these areas).

5 *Transport.*

Another advantage that New Towns are fond of publicizing is the fact that housing is available close to factories and offices, so that workers can avoid the long, uncomfortable and expensive journeys to work which are frequently the price of suburban life.) Factories built in New Towns or rural areas can also offer better car-parking facilities, a factor of increasing importance with the rise in the level of car ownership.

The organization also has to take into account the ease and cost of transporting raw materials, components and finished products. The development of the motorway system has widened the choice of locations and many industrial developments have been established close to motorway intersection points. Similarly the development of airports and container-ports has influenced the location of industrial units.

6 *The availability of materials.*

The development of the motorway system, discussed above, has made it easier to transport materials over long distances. But there are still advantages to be gained from locating near to the source of materials, especially when these are heavy or bulky. Brick-making factories are located close to clay deposits, coal-fired power stations close to coal mines.

7 *Access to markets.*

Although modern transport systems have made it easier to transport finished goods over long distances, there are advantages in being close to markets. The concentration of population in the South East helps to explain the development of light industry in that region in the post-war period. For manufacturers of industrial goods, and especially of components, nearness to industry is desirable since quick delivery can be an important competitive weapon.

8 *Space.*

The lack of adequate space at the existing site is the main reason why manufacturers choose to expand in new locations. The space requirement can sometimes be very big indeed; when the Nissan car company examined possible sites for a British plant they only considered sites of several hundred acres. In other instances the manufacturer may have special site requirements, e.g. flat land or land which will take the foundations required for high buildings.

9 *Climate.*

Climatic conditions were once an important influence on the location of industry, e.g. the cotton industry needed the damp climate of Lancashire. Climate has become of less direct importance as methods of controlling humidity and temperature within factories have been perfected. This has enabled firms to choose locations with a pleasant climate. Note the massive growth of industry in the 'sun belt' and West Coast of America, to the detriment of the traditional East Coast

States. Another aspect of climate is the existence (or absence) of large quantities of water. Some industries use water on a large scale, either in the production process, or in the treatment and disposal of effluent.

10 *Safety*.

Hardly a day goes by without the press commenting on the dangers from some chemical plant or nuclear power station. The 'Flixborough disaster' of a few years ago awakened the general public to the danger of chemical plants being built close to housing. The danger still exists in many areas, but the trend is to separate the two so that any accidents can be contained without the general public being affected.

11 *Finance*.

This is obviously a vital issue, and most of the factors considered above are brought together in a cost benefit analysis of alternative sites. But account must also be taken of the substantial government assistance available in the Assisted Areas (Special Development Areas, Development Areas and Intermediate Areas).

12 *Politics*.

Jim Callaghan gained notoriety or gratitude, depending on your viewpoint, when he persuaded Ford to build their new European engine plant in Wales near his constituency. The arrival of a large multinational in an area means jobs, increased prosperity (or less misery), and this means votes.

13.5.2 Plant layout

In designing the layout of an office building or production unit, a manager has to make decisions concerning:

1 The positioning of departments within the overall site.
2 The detailed design of each department so that the appropriate sections are adjacent to one another.
3 Individual workplace or machine design.

Incorrect decisions in any of these areas can give rise subsequently to a variety of increased costs, including the need to rent additional space, inadequate communications, double-handling and other transportation costs.

Systems of plant layout may be based on:

1 Process or function; examples include the catalytic crackers used in the refining of crude oil into kerosene, petrol, wax etc. (a process unit), and the designing of one plant, the press shop, to make car bodies, and another, the spray shop, to paint them, (functional units).
2 A fixed position; this type of layout is used in the construction of large products, e.g. shipbuilding, oil rig construction.

3 The product; in this, the most common type, the layout is determined by the requirements of the manufacture of the product, be it beer, whisky, biscuits or bread. This layout often requires long production runs of nearly identical products, usually with a high degree of automation to minimize human fatigue and error.

The detailed preparation of a design for a factory layout involves making use of all the information that is available at the time and trying to estimate likely future changes. The marketing department should estimate the likely future demand for the product, and the final design should ensure that there is sufficient room for expansion to cater for future needs.

Having completed this investigation the following procedure could be used as a brief guide to layout planning:

1 Using a plan of the building and site, ensure that the relevant services are available in the right places.
2 Examine the operational sequences, so that operations and sections are located in a correct relationship to one another.
3 Ensure that the 'major' or 'key' operations are correctly situated, since this is a major determinant of the overall efficiency of the production process.
4 Position the remaining operations and ancillary services, e.g. stores, dispatch, canteens, washrooms, and all transportation and communication routes.
5 Plan the individual work areas in detail and ensure that all ancillary equipment is correctly located.
6 Test out the plan, either utilizing a model or by carrying out pre-production runs.
7 Fully familiarize employees and management with the layout and make any final adjustments as working experience dictates.

All layout plans may be regarded as a compromise between conflicting pressures: time, space, costs of storage, ease of access. While every unit or plant is unique, as noted at the beginning of this chapter, and while what is a good layout for one plant may be a bad layout for another, there are certain criteria by which any layout may be judged:

1 It must do the job it was designed to do, efficiently and effectively, paying due regard to the human factor in the production process.
2 Flexibility is vital. Changes in product design will inevitably take place over a period of time and the production process must be capable of adapting to them.
3 The whole process should be well co-ordinated to make maximum use of all the resources involved, eliminate unnecessary storage and minimize waiting time between operations.

4 Visibility and accessibility are important for machine maintenance, safety, and management control and supervision; if you cannot see what is going on, you cannot manage and control it.

5 Handling, particularly human handling, should be minimized as it wastes time and money (wages and equipment costs).

6 Health and safety requirements must be met and the overall working atmosphere should be a pleasant one. People will only give of their best and take pride in what they produce if management create the right environment.

7 The plant must be secure, well fenced and guarded, with a minimum number of supervised entrances and exits. In some production processes e.g. drugs, chemicals, security is obviously vital and special precautions have to be taken.

In Britain there is a shortage of engineers qualified in the production management area. Planning is often carried out by well meaning amateurs or left to architects, who are more concerned with matters of style, than practical work realities. The situation is changing and some of our modern factories are every bit as efficient as those of our overseas rivals. But there are still many manufacturing units housed in old buildings with inefficient layouts. Not surprisingly, their production costs do not compare well with those of the robot-dominated, computer-controlled production systems of our rivals in Japan, Germany and America.

13.5.3 Equipment

Any purchaser of industrial equipment will, of course, make sure that the equipment does the job for which it is required. He will also be concerned with the cost of the equipment, and with the return on his expenditure. (Most equipment is bought for replacement purposes, and if the cost is too high it may be possible to continue using the existing equipment).

In considering these issues the purchaser will take account of a range of factors, including the price of purchasing and operating the machine, its reliability, ease of maintenance, its safety standards and the delivery period. A view should also be taken of possible design changes which might outdate the present equipment and thus affect its economic life.

This is always an area of potential conflict between the needs of the accountant, in terms of finance, and the requirements of the production manager concerned with the job in hand. When sales are booming and capacity is stretched the production manager is more likely to triumph; conversely in times of recession and low profits the hand of the accountant is strengthened.

13.6 Production planning and control

13.6.1 The system

Planning and control of the production process has been revolutionized in recent years with the advent of computerized systems. While traditional manual/paperwork systems do still exist, the necessary documentation and information is being increasingly prepared by computers.

The process starts with the arrival of an order from the sales department and ends when the finished items arrive in the stores for onward transportation to the customer. Each organization has its own production planning system (although computer-based systems are often of a standardized format), but most systems incorporate the stages shown in Figure 13.2 (overleaf).

It can be deduced from Figure 13.2 that the ability of the system to meet agreed delivery dates, requires the successful co-ordination of a number of variable factors. To ensure that progress is maintained care has to be taken to avoid any of the following occurences:

1 Delays in materials or parts from the stores.
2 Machine breakdowns or unplanned stoppages for maintenance.
3 Problems with outside organizations, e.g. sub-contractors.
4 Strikes, stoppages, or other industrial action by employees.
5 Inadequate quality of parts or materials.

Production controllers and managers have to constantly check progress, and make adjustments to their overall timescales should any of the above occur. To facilitate control a number of sources of information and techniques can be utilized, including:

Flow charts
Network planning techniques
Production schedules
Machine loading charts
Labour cost/performance details (from work study)
Inspection and maintenance systems
Financial budgets
Parts and materials lists.

Computerized systems enable information to be closely monitored and updated, and prepare the necessary documentation for action to be taken.

Whichever combination of the above information systems management eventually chooses, all production managers are faced with the need to control five main functions in the production process: scheduling, loading, dispatch, progress and materials.

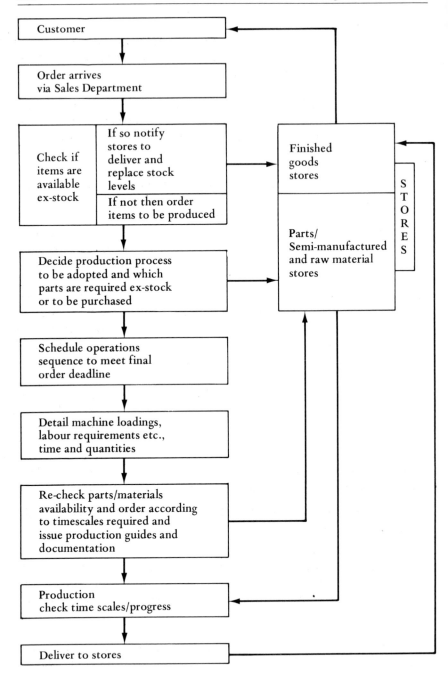

Figure 13.2   Production planning and control system.

1 *Scheduling*
This involves an overall plan that has as its aim the completion of a particular job. It takes account of existing work priorities, labour and materials availability and the required delivery date.

2 *Loading*
This involves a more detailed schedule, relating to a particular machine, operator, or operation, the objective being to maximize output and minimize costs. The most variable factor in this situation is the performance of the operator. His or her interest, attention and output may vary considerably over a period of time, whatever the incentives offered. (This is not true of robots, which is one of their advantages.)

3 *Dispatch*
This covers all the activities involved in moving parts, materials and finished goods in and out of the stores. It also includes the preparation of the necessary paperwork and documentation, e.g. drawings, instructions, time scales.

4 *Progress*
This refers to what is, perhaps, the most unenviable task of all. A progress chaser has to try to persuade people to make good for other people's mistakes and ensure the whole system runs to schedule. Progress chasers require patience in abundance, a cheerful disposition, tenacity and a good memory. Unfortunately the pay does not often match these requirements.

5 *Materials Control*
The objective is to make sure that the right materials, parts etc., are available in the right place to a given timescale. In any factory there is a constant movement of materials, parts, finished and semi-finished goods into and out of the stores and along the production lines. Materials control is a major function that has to be undertaken against tight time schedules, and has to cater for strikes, shortages etc. The aim at all times is to keep the production lines moving to meet the agreed order dates.

There are two further important links in the overall control of the production process:

1 *Estimators*
These employees provide estimates of labour costs, direct manufacturing costs, materials, plant and equipment charges. These estimates constitute control information to line management, and may also be used as a guide in the setting of prices.

2 *Finance staff*
We dealt with financial control in Chapter 11, and it is sufficient to note here that operating budgets, incorporating financial information, are used as a means of comparison and control. It is in the production process

perhaps more than in any other area of the organization's activities that financial staff work close to reality, seeing their figures being turned into identifiable physical items such as stocks of materials or finished goods.

13.6.2 Quality control

Maintaining agreed standards of quality is much easier today when increased mechanization has reduced the impact of the 'human factor' with all its variances. Nevertheless most production functions involve human action, and even machines can vary in their operational effectiveness. Consequently quality control will remain an important management function.

Quality control requires inspection, and this should extend to all aspects of the production function, not just the finished product. The inspection department of manufacturing organizations has as its aim the maintenance of established standards and the provision of data to management so that design or material content changes can take place if required.

Inspection takes place at a number of locations in a production unit to ensure that any 'loss of standard' can be isolated to a particular function or individual at the earliest opportunity. Some of the areas covered are:

Goods inwards inspection
Inspection on the production line of work in progress
Process control in chemical industries
Part and tool room inspection
Finished goods inspection.

Some organizations inspect every product e.g. each car that comes off an assembly line. Others adopt a statistical sampling method, inspecting a certain percentage of items. In process industries a sample is often taken at different stages of the process, e.g. in the brewing industry, and tests are run on this sample to determine the quality of the total batch or production run.

Whichever system is in operation, management must ensure that their tolerances and quality levels are acceptable to customers and in line with those used by their competitors. Customers now demand quality as well as price competitiveness and if British manufacturers cannot achieve these, there are often imported products that can.

13.7 Summary and conclusions

In this chapter we showed the importance of the production function, and manufacturing industry in general, to the health of the economy as a whole. We discussed the types of production processes and the decisions managers have to make. We analysed the elements of the production process, from the design and development of new products (including value analysis techniques) through the options available when choosing the location of a manufacturing unit and the requirements of layout and equipment, to production planning and control and the need to maintain quality standards.

The management of the production function is a highly skilled job involving knowledge of technology, engineering, design and the ability to control people, coupled with the need to balance all sorts of conflicting interests and factors against a timescale i.e. the final delivery date. Unfortunately, these skills have not been sufficiently recognised in terms of status and salary in this country, and our manufacturing competitiveness has suffered accordingly. It is to be hoped that we will take advantage of the opportunties offered by micro-chip technology to close the gap in competitiveness; however, there are few signs of this so far.

Revision questions and exercises

1   Answer briefly:
A   Give two reasons for the poor performance of British manufacturing industry.
B   List four main types of production process.
C   Give examples of long-term production decisions.
D   What is the first stage in the design process?
E   What is value analysis?
F   What factors can assist the reliability of a product?
G   Why is production planning so important?
H   What is meant by materials control?
I   Give two examples of management techniques that can assist in controlling the production process.
J   What do estimators do?
2   What factors should be taken into account in designing a new product?
3   What steps can an organization take to improve the quality of the products or the services it offers?
4   *S.P.G. Engineering Co. Ltd., Case Study*
      Your company, a large multi-purpose engineering group, is considering setting up a brand new factory in South Wales to take advantage of Government grants and to be close to the new micro-chip centre near Newport, Gwent, to which it will be supplying parts.

      All major decisions are the subject of company-wide consultation, and shop stewards and representatives have the opportunity to present their views. A special consultative committee is set up to consider the move, comprised of representatives of management and unions, and on the agenda of the first meeting there is an item: 'Layout of plant'. When discussions start it is obvious that everyone has his own view on what should be considered under this item. To make progress the Managing Director suggests that you, as project manager for the move, prepare a report for the next meeting, detailing the various matters to be considered in designing the layout of the new plant.

1 Write the report.

2 Role play the various participants at the next meeting at which the report is considered.

5   *New Car Design Case Study*

You are chief designer for a car manufacturer with a dated medium-sized car range. You are requested to draw up a draft design for a medium-size family car, to be produced in three years time to compete in the Maestro grouping. You have a free hand apart from being required to observe the following guidelines:

1 Economy is a key factor.

2 The car must appeal to female drivers as well as males.

3 The company wants to avoid too many variations on the basic design.

4 A life span of ten years is required for the model range.

5 Servicing costs should be minimized.

Draw up a design specification of the new car.

6   *Factory Location Case Study*

You are the production controller of a medium-sized company employing 80 males and 150 females. You produce jeans and leisure wear and your factory is situated in the centre of Preston, in old premises. For some time now your present production facilities have been a cause for concern. Space for storage is at a premium, you need to expand your product lines but have not got the space. In addition, staff and your transport department are having difficulty with access and parking. However, most of your employees are recruited locally and female employees, in particular, use public transport, most of them having small children at a nursery school close to the factory. You have a small canteen but many of the employees use pubs and restaurants in the town. Your firm obtains a large export order and it is evident that existing facilities will have to be considerably expanded to meet the new production targets. It would be possible to move to new premises on a Central Lancashire Development Corporation site, adjacent to the motorway at Bamber Bridge about 3 miles South of Preston. You have the choice of either a ready made factory unit, which will require only slight modification, or a factory to be built to your own specification. There are obvious advantages in moving, including financial ones, and you are asked to prepare a report listing all the advantages and disadvantages of the move.

1 Prepare the report.

2 The shop stewards, while appreciating the benefits the contract will bring to their members, express concern about the move and its effect on their members, e.g. the working mothers' ability to deliver and collect their children from play school, travel, shopping needs etc.

Role play the various participants at a meeting requested by the shop stewards with management to discuss the move.

Further Reading

BAILEY, P. and FARMER, D. *Managing Materials in Industry* (Gower: London, 1974).

BETTS, P. *Supervisory Management* (Macdonald Evans: London, 1980).

BUFFA, E. S. *Modern Production Management* (Wiley: London, 1965).

BURBRIDGE, J. *Production Planning* (Heinemann: London, 1980).

EVANS, D. *Supervisory Management* (Holt, Rinehart and Winston: London, 1981).

LOCKYER, K. G. *Factory Management* (Pitman: London, 1976).

TOOLEY, D. F. *Production Control Systems and Records* (Gower: London, 1974).

WILD, R. *Production and Operations Management* (Holt, Rinehart and Winston: New York, 1979).

WILD, R. *Management and Production Readings* (Penguin: Harmondsworth, 1980).

14

The Purchasing Function

14.1 Introduction

The purchasing function has increased in importance in recent years, as managers have come to realize how much money can be saved by having a professionally managed buying operation. In this chapter we examine alternative ways of organizing the purchasing function and the major responsibilities of the purchasing department. We conclude by considering various aspects of stores control, an area of responsibility which can either be considered as falling within the purchasing function or as a separate, but closely allied, function.

14.2 Organization of the purchasing function

Purchasing may be organized on a centralized or a de-centralized basis. We consider the advantages and disadvantages of each basis in turn.

14.2.1 Centralization

Most large organizations operate a centralized purchasing department, often allied to a central stores. This practice is particularly common in public sector organizations where the arrangement is even extended to purchasing consortia covering, for example, several local authorities in an area.

Proponents of centralization point to the following advantages:

1 Centralized purchasing gives the benefits of bulk buying. It enables the organization to negotiate maximum discounts by placing one or two large orders per year rather than a number of small ones. (The

discounts reflect the benefits of bulk purchasing to suppliers, e.g. longer production runs and easier production planning). These benefits are maximized when all orders are placed with a single supplier. In 1982, B.L. Ltd. announced that many components were thereafter to be purchased from one rather than two or more suppliers.

2 Bulk purchasing from one source helps staff in the supplier's production or sales department to identify their precise requirements. It also enables communication systems to be simplified.

3 Centralization aids consistency in purchasing policy and makes standardization easier. There is always the risk where a number of people are involved in placing orders that goods of differing qualities or standards will be purchased. (Even when 'one-off' items are purchased, a centralized system can be beneficial; the large orders for standardized products can enable better terms for the one-off items to be negotiated).

4 Expertise and specialization in different areas of purchasing are facilitated. Buyers can, for example, give all their time and attention to one or two products. In a de-centralized system the buyer is concerned with a wider range of products, with a danger of becoming 'jack of all trades and master of none'.

5 Information, management control and computerized invoicing systems work more smoothly when purchasing is centralized. The chances of losses or mistakes in ordering are minimized.

6 Finally, a centralized system often has the advantage of being located with a central stores. This makes inspection and quality control easier; stock control is simplified and management of the total operations can be more easily co-ordinated.

14.2.2 De-centralization

The 'small is beautiful' supporters would argue that a centralized system is unwieldy and impersonal, and that there are advantages in having smaller de-centralized units, or individuals working in each operational department or section of an organization.

1 Smaller units can be more flexible. They can purchase according to current requirements rather than to the dictates of some standardization procedure. For example if stocks of some material were about to run out and halt production, it might be better to purchase from a local supplier than to risk a delay in delivery by purchasing from an 'authorized' supplier located further away.

2 Close liaison can be maintained with suppliers, particularly local suppliers, and a more personal, as opposed to departmental,

relationship built up with salesmen.
3 De-centralization puts purchasing responsibility 'where the action is',
   i.e. alongside line management.

The balance of advantage between these two approaches depends upon
the size of the organization, its type and range of products etc. However,
one of the present authors has had considerable experience of both types
of systems and in his opinion the benefits of centralization, in particular
the opportunity for bulk purchasing, specialization and better
management control, far outweigh any disadvantages. Moreover, it seems
likely that these benefits will become even greater in the future; further
economies of scale in production arising from technological change will
enable bigger discounts to be obtained for bulk purchases.

14.3 The responsibilities of the purchasing department

1 The purchasing department's primary responsibility is to form and
   maintain good relationships with suitable suppliers. This means taking
   a positive approach: going to exhibitions, reading the trade press,
   obtaining suppliers' names from other purchasers and so forth. There
   is much more to purchasing than sitting in an office and waiting for
   salesmen to call. As part of this responsibility, it is necessary to ensure
   that the vendor organization has a sound financial base (i.e. it is not
   going to go bankrupt in the middle of delivering a vital order) and that
   quality standards are maintained.
2 Suitable suppliers having been identified, the purchasing officer must
   use his negotiating skills and knowledge of the market to obtain the
   most competitive price possible. However, he must, of course, take
   account of other factors, including quality and speed of delivery.
   There is often a 'trade-off' among these various factors and a
   purchasing officer's expertise is put to the test in trade-off situations.
   He has to decide whether, for example, is it worth paying 5 per cent
   more to a supplier who offers earlier delivery; or whether he should
   risk buying from a new company which is selling at a price below that
   of the existing suppliers whose products have always been of a
   satisfactory standard.
       When a purchaser accounts for a high proportion of a supplier's
   output, he must beware of extracting so good a bargain that the
   supplier's financial viability is threatened. A bankrupt supplier is of no
   benefit to a purchasing department.
3 It is the responsibility of the purchasing department to ensure that the
   right goods are delivered in the right place at the right time. This

involves developing a good relationship with one's suppliers and being aware of their problems. Marks and Spencer's purchasing staff are particularly good at doing this, being helped by the fact that many of their suppliers are former Marks and Spencer managers, who are aware of the company's systems and requirements.

4 If things do go wrong, it is the duty of the purchasing department to notify all concerned, production, sales, research etc., and to try to obtain alternative supplies. This is where the purchasing function has a particularly close link with the manufacturing function.

5 The purchasing department has two main financial functions to perform. First, it has a responsibility to verify invoices and ensure that stock levels are properly costed. Second, it can help other departments estimate costs and prices by advising them of the likely prices of 'bought in' goods and materials. In providing this advice it may need to predict prices several months ahead.

6 The purchasing department will receive a considerable amount of information from salesmen, exhibitions, the trade press, T.V., radio, catalogues, suppliers etc. Much of this information will help it to discharge the responsibilities listed above. But it should also pass information on to other interested parties within the organization. So for instance it would be helpful for the design department to know that a company has introduced a new component that could be incorporated in machines currently being designed.

Purchasing departments that try to play things 'close to their chest' soon lose the confidence of their colleagues, and the whole success of the purchasing function can be jeopardized by suspicion and mistrust. Just as the purchasing department must recognize its responsibilities to other departments, so these other departments must beware of usurping the purchasing department's authority. If a co-ordinated purchasing policy is to be maintained, personnel in other departments must resist the temptation to 'go behind its back' in dealing with suppliers. While it is acceptable for line managers to discuss their requirements with salesmen, they should not allow themselves to be persuaded to sign orders when the responsibility for doing so has been given to the purchasing department.

The purchasing function has developed considerably in recent years. Managers are now aware of the immense savings that can be made in the purchase of materials, components and services, and also of the costs that can arise when supplies are disrupted. With the advent of a professional qualification and training schemes, purchasing staff are now professionals in every sense of the word, and can command appropriate salaries and status in organizations, large and small, in the public and private sectors.

14.4 Stores control

Stores control involves the management of all the items in a store, from the moment they arrive up to the time they leave. One of the major tasks is checking the quality of the items that come into the stores. Prior to this acceptance stage it is possible to return faulty goods to a manufacturer for rectification, or to query problems with the carrrier.

Staff in the 'Goods Inward' section acknowledge receipt of goods and carry out the documentation required to incorporate the goods in the stock control system. The good are unpacked and checked for quality and quantity against the standards on the original order form. Faulty items are noted and returned, as are packing systems that are re-chargeable to a supplier or carrier. The necessary documentation is then forwarded to the accounts section to ensure that the financial arrangements are progressed. The stores staff also notify other interested departments, e.g. production, of the item's arrival.

14.4.1. Computerized Systems

Stores management in large organizations has been revolutionized by the use of computerized systems. These process all the necessary documentation, maintain checks on stock levels, and notify management to re-order as required. They can even control the location of the stock and of the equipment for extracting and issuing it. The stores counter and shelves has given way to floor to ceiling pallets, stacked to great heights in special artificial environments, handled with modern equipment using the latest micro-chip technology. With such systems man handling is a thing of the past; modern conveyor systems, computer floor tracking systems and a variety of other devices extract and deliver the items to the workplace almost without the touch of a human hand.

But however sophisticated the stores system may be, managers are required to make the same decisions as in the past. The major decisions relate to the following areas.

14.4.2 The location of stocks

The location of stocks will be influenced by the physical design of the stores, by the need for adequate storage space and for good circulation space, and by the desire to use modern handling equipment and documentation systems. Stocks are located partly in stores, and partly in user departments throughout the organization — in offices, at particular stages in the production process etc. It is therefore important to have adequate coding and classification.

14.4.3 Stock levels

There is often a tendency to carry too large a stock of certain items 'just in case'. In many instances 80-90% of turnover is derived from products accounting for 15-20% of stocks; therefore turnover and stocks should be fairly closely related. Once the desired level of stocks has been determined, systems can be established to 'trigger' ordering procedures once the minimum stock level has been reached.

Nowadays there are often a variety of sources of instant supply for standardized items. For example, garages used to have to maintain stores for all items on the cars they sold and serviced. Nowadays they call on the services of specialized 'factors', small organizations that operate in car electrics, clutch parts, etc. It is cheaper to use these outside suppliers than maintain vast stores of their own.

Standardization of parts between different manufacturers, and such systems as the British Standards Institute seal of approval on the quality of goods, have helped considerably in this respect.

14.4.4 Handling procedures

Handling procedures should be reviewed periodically so as to minimize dual handling, e.g. putting an item on to a storage shelf and then getting it out again shortly afterwards for issue. Dual handling involves additional paperwork as well as physical effort. If the stores system is properly managed as part of an overall materials procurement system, there is no reason why some items should not be delivered direct to the workplace, (providing the control procedures are adequate). A periodic review of procedures also ensures that opportunities for introducing new and improved handling methods are not neglected.

14.4.5 Human resources

The 'people costs' of stores operations are often high, even in the most mechanized stores operation. Unfortunately, some managers see the stores as a backwater, a dumping ground for the old, sick, disabled and troublemakers in their organization. But the approach to stores management is gradually changing as modern accounting systems cause senior managers to re-assess the cost of their stores operations. Well-qualified, well-trained and enthusiastic staff can be a tremendous help to any organization in achieving efficiency within the stores department, and in ensuring that the manufacturing or service section operates smoothly and without interruptions.

14.5 Summary and conclusions

In this chapter we have surveyed the purchasing and stores functions, operations which in many organizations have only recently been given the attention and status that they deserve. We considered the relative advantages of centralized and de-centralized purchasing functions, and concluded that in most instances the balance of advantage lies with centralization. We examined stores control and identified the major decisions facing managers.

We explained why an organization's efficiency depends upon effective management in both purchasing and stores control. We also showed that efficiency requires that there should be close links between these two functions.

Revision questions and exercises

1   Answer *briefly:*
A   Why is the purchasing function so important?
B   What benefits can computers bring to the purchasing function?
C   Give two examples of financial functions that are the responsibility of a purchasing department.
D   Define the meaning of stores control.
E   Why do purchasing departments need to know a supplier's vendor rating?
2   Discuss the advantages and disadvantages of centralization and de-centralization of the purchasing function.
3   You take over as Chief Administrative Officer in the Chief Executive's department of a large Metropolitan District Council. The Chief Executive feels that the authority is wasting a great deal of money in its purchasing operations (which are based in the Chief Executive's department as a central service to all departments). He proposes transferring the section to your control, and as a first step asks you to prepare a report for him on the responsibilities of the purchasing department, as you see them.
    Write the report.
4   You are asked to prepare a report for a large multi-national on energy purchasing. What factors would you advise them to take account of?
5   What are the advantages of purchasing from a single supplier, as operated by firms such as British Leyland and Marks and Spencer?

Further Reading

BAILEY, P. H. J. *Purchasing and Supply Management* (Chapman and Hall: London, 1971).
BATTERSBY, A. *A Guide to Stock Control* (Pitman: London, 1970).
BURTON, J. *Effective Warehousing* (Macdonald Evans: London, 1979).
COMPTON, H. *Storehouse Management* (Macdonald Evans: London, 1980).

HEINRITZ, S. and FARRELL, P. *Purchasing* (Prentice-Hall: Hemel Hempstead, 1981).

LOCK, D. *Factory Administration Handbook* (Gower: London, 1979).

WARMAN, J. *Warehouse Management* (Heinemann: London, 1980).

WILD, R. *Production and Operations Management* (Holt, Rinehart and Winston: New York, 1979).

15

The Personnel Function

15.1 Introduction

In 1963, its golden jubilee year, the Institute of Personnel Management described personnel management as being:

'A responsibility of all those who manage people, as well as being a description of the work of those who are employed as specialists. It is that part of management which is concerned with people at work and with their relationships within an enterprise. It applies not only to industry and commerce but to all fields of employment.'

Since this statement was made, the role of the personnel specialist has increased dramatically, particularly in the public sector. Recent legislation and the current economic and political climate have ensured that the personnel function now plays a major role in the overall managerial environment of organizations.

To assist the reader's comprehension of this complex function, we divide the personnel function into the following main work areas: Employment, Training, Payment Systems, Welfare and Safety, and Industrial Relations. Each of these areas is discussed in turn.

15.2 The employment function

This is one of the most important areas of the personnel function. All organizations have to decide who to employ, how many people to employ, and when to employ them (i.e. the right number of people, in the right place, at the right time).

The employment function covers the areas of: manpower planning, recruitment and selection, assessment, promotion and termination of employment.

15.2.1 Manpower planning

If manpower planning is to be effective, the organization must have clear objectives and operating plans that can be broken down on a departmental and an individual basis. This implies a need for information on both internal and external labour markets. The relationship between these two markets is illustrated in Figure 15.1 below.

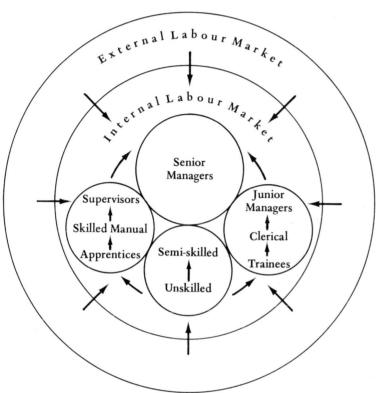

Figure 15.1   Internal and external labour markets.

The internal market comprises a flow of employees, via transfer and promotion from one type of job to another. In Figure 15.1 we have identified four main job categories, and we have shown that, for example, senior managers are drawn from the ranks of supervisors and junior managers, and that the pool of skilled manual workers is replenished both from semi-skilled workers and apprentices. Practice varies, of course, from one organization to another. For instance, in some organizations the route from semi-skilled to skilled manual workers is blocked because of differences in the aptitudes required for the two jobs, or because of trade union restrictions on entry.

The external labour market provides new entrants to all levels of the organization. Practice will vary depending on the organization concerned. Some organizations may only appoint senior managers from within. Others will make use of the external labour market on frequent occasions to bring in a 'fresh outlook' at senior management level.

If the range and volume of the organization's output is stable, the internal labour market flows will tend to be steady. As senior personnel leave the organization, by retirement or death, these vacancies will usually be filled by internal promotion (unless external recruitment is the practice), which in turn will give rise for recruitment at the more junior levels. On the other hand, if the organization is expanding very rapidly, vacancies at the various levels may not be capable of being filled by internal promotion alone, and external recruitment as well as internal promotion, for all job categories, may become the norm. Even in times of economic depression, forward-looking organizations may still recruit apprentices and trainees externally to protect their future needs for skilled and qualified employees.

15.2.1.1 Factors influencing future labour requirements

The organization's demand for labour depends upon the products supplied by the organization and the technology utilized in their production and distribution. These factors are themselves subject to a wide range of influences. Since these influences are discussed elsewhere (see Chapter 12 on the Marketing Function), it is necessary here to list only a few by way of illustration: ideas for new products arising from market research or the research and development department; new and existing products supplied by competitors; government policy; developments in micro-technology etc.

Having estimated its future manpower requirements, the next step is to decide what part of these requirements the organization is likely to be able to meet from its existing employees. This requires an assessment of the internal labour supply, not only in terms of total numbers, but also by skills, qualifications, physical capabilities, potential for training and acquiring new skills, etc.

The gap between demand and internal supply will need to be met by recruitment from the external labour market. The factors affecting the external supply include: demographic trends (age and sex structure), educational facilities, trade union attitudes (e.g. towards apprenticeships, the closed shop and demarcation limits), legislation (covering e.g. employment conditions) and, of course, the demand for labour from other employers.

Having taken all these factors into account, the organization may decide that some of the 'gap' that has been identified cannot be met by recruitment. Its options are then to try to improve the internal labour supply, e.g. by increased training, or, if this is not feasible, to modify its planned output of goods and services.

15.2.1.2 Summary

To summarize, effective manpower planning helps management to:

1 Estimate recruitment requirements well in advance.
2 Identify future needs for training, including management development.
3 Avoid unnecessary redundancies.
4 Estimate financial requirements in the manpower area.

These benefits of manpower planning accrue both to the organization and to individuals. On the other hand the costs fall mainly on organizations who should, therefore, constantly monitor the balance between costs and benefits.

15.2.2 Recruitment and selection

All organizations have to recruit and select people and unless this function is carried out properly an organization is storing up serious industrial relations problems for itself at a future date.

15.2.2.1 The recruitment procedure

In this section we consider the procedure that might be followed when a vacancy occurs.

1 The first step is to consider whether it is necessary to fill the vacancy at all. It might be possible to allocate the functions and responsibilities to other employees or to use more machinery. It may even be possible to reorganize so that the functions are no longer required. To assist them in their deliberations management must possess job descriptions, giving information about all the duties and relationships of the post. (See the appendix to this chapter for an example.)
2 If the decision is taken to fill the post, a personnel specification is drawn up, giving information about the type of person required, the skills, qualifications, physical characteristics, personality profile, age, etc.
3 From this specification an advertisement is prepared. This is then circulated internally (if the appointment is to be internal only), or internally and externally if the widest circulation is required. Because advertising space costs money, care should be taken in the choice of newspaper or journal chosen for the advertisement. Personnel staff will be aware, for instance, that if the job is a very junior one with a low

salary, then a local, rather than a national advert would be preferable. The readership of a newspaper or professional journal will also help to determine the placing of an advertisement. Should the post be a very senior one it may be worthwhile employing specialist selection consultants to prepare and place the advertisement on the organization's behalf.

The advertisement will include brief details of the post, the salary or wage rate and promotion prospects. The closing date and the method of application should be specified, the choice being between a self-composed application and a standard application form supplied by the organization.

A self-composed application can provide deeper insight into the character of the applicant and is most appropriate when the post is a very senior one. However, it has the disadvantage that the applicant may leave out some of the required information because he did not realize its importance.

The standard application form avoids this danger. It also has the advantage — which is particularly important when there are a large number of applicants — of enabling essential information e.g. age, qualifications, etc. to be extracted for shortlisting purposes.

It is also often useful to include some general information about the company's future plans and prospects in the advertisement. This may increase the attractiveness of the post to potential applicants and may also enhance the organization's general standing with the result that future advertisements attract more attention.

4 The applications having been received, a short list is drawn up. The size of the shortlist will obviously depend on the number and quality of the applications. But rather surprisingly it is often found that, no matter how many applications are received, no more that six to eight people have the required qualifications and experience. Other factors influencing the size of the shortlist are the time it will take to interview those shortlisted, and the finance involved in paying interview expenses.

5 The next step is to seek references for the shortlisted candidates where this is thought appropriate. References can give an independent assessment of a candidate but as no candidate is going to use as a referee someone who will give him a bad reference, the whole reference system should be treated with caution.

6 The next vital step is the interview itself. Interviews should be two-sided and provide an environment for a frank exchange of information and views between all the parties concerned.

The personnel department should have made prior arrangements within the organization to cover: reception of the candidates, interview room arrangements, provision of information about the candidates to those carrying out the interview, and miscellaneous issues such as catering, payment of expenses, etc.

An interview should be so structured as to cover the following four main areas:

1 Relate each candidate's education, qualifications, experiences and outside interests to the job requirements.
2 Identify ancillary factors such as each candidate's age, health, salary (relevant and required) and availability.
3 Ascertain, via skilful questioning, why each candidate is leaving his present job and any personal factors that may inhibit his future mobility in the organization he is now applying to.
4 The interview panel have then got to make a choice out of all the candidates. In making this choice, as well as paying attention to the factors mentioned above, interviewers take account of such things as: candidates' manners, attitudes, speech, outside interests, appearance and even political viewpoints in certain cases.

When a job offer is made, there is much to be said for the public sector system of making the offer to the successful candidate on the day of the interview. This enables any queries to be settled there and then. Moreover, if the candidate refuses the job offer then it can be made to another shortlisted candidate, avoiding additional interview and advertising expenditure.

As soon as is practicable the job offer should be confirmed in writing and arrangements can then be made for the contract of employment to be drawn up and for the successful candidate to join the organization.

15.2.3 Assessment, transfer, promotion, termination of employment

An important function of the employment section of the personnel department is the establishment and operation, in conjunction with line managers, of a system of objective assessment for all employees. Such a system helps to ensure that procedures relating to transfer, promotion and termination of employment are widely acceptable. An assessment system can also be used in reviewing salary scales and fringe benefits.

By definition, an assessment scheme is concerned with the performance of employees. If follows that this performance must be related to the functions attaching to the posts held by employees. These functions are frequently laid down in a formal job description (see the example in the Appendix to this chapter) which is related via the functions of departments to the structure and objectives of the organization.

$$\text{Objectives of the organization}$$
$$\downarrow$$
$$\text{Structure of the organization}$$
$$\downarrow$$
$$\text{Functions of departments}$$
$$\downarrow$$
$$\text{Individual job descriptions}$$

A typical assessment scheme would operate as follows:

1 Each employee's superior completes at regular intervals a written report on his subordinates.
2 This report is shown to the employee concerned, preferably with a member of the personnel department present.
3 The employee is encouraged to make a positive response to the report, e.g. commenting on difficulties encountered, reacting to criticism, etc.
4 The personnel department is then able to use the information and views obtained in decisions concerning:
   (a) Promotion or transfer designed to enhance the employee's contribution and career prospects.
   (b) Further training or work experience.
   (c) The termination of the employee's services if all other efforts to improve his performance fail.

A few years ago a system of assessment and planning known as 'Management by Objectives' or MBO became very fashionable. This system tried to link each employee's agreement to his own objectives, as discussed with his superior, to improved organizational and individual performance. The system was based on the principle that:

agreed objectives = better commitment = improved performance.

Recently, the costs of introducing a system of MBO, the time taken in agreeing objectives and reaching conclusions in a fast-changing economic and political climate, have led many organizations to re-assess the benefits to be gained from this type of assessment system.

15.2.4 The contract of employment

A contract of employment is a document that gives legal recognition to the relationship between the employee and the organization. The document lays down the terms and conditions of employment, covering such work areas as: salary, working hours, holidays, sickness, superannuation and pension schemes, leave, notice, trade union membership, etc.

The contract is the document that is used as a basis for agreement or arbitration when a dispute arises between employer and employee. It also describes the method to be used, should it become necessary to terminate an employee's employment, so that no doubt or dispute in these unfortunate circumstances can arise.

New legislation is constantly affecting the terms of contracts of employment and it is essential that personnel staff keep up to date in this particular area, otherwise their organizations may find themselves liable to substantial damages if the law is not followed correctly.

15.3 Training

The training function is concerned with (a) induction training, i.e. the training of newcomers to the organization, and (b) general and specialist training of existing employees.

15.3.1 Induction training

The aims of an induction programme should be to:

1 Introduce the employee to the organization and enable him to make an effective contribution as quickly as possible.
2 Create a favourable and committed attitude towards the organization.
3 Prevent high labour turnover rates in the early months of employment.
4 Bridge the gap between two organizations or between school or college and work.

The production of an employee handbook for distribution to all new employees can be seen as the first stage in the induction programme. Such handbooks normally explain the aims and objectives of the organization, its structure, the lines of communication to be used if problems arise, welfare benefits, trade union rights, etc.

The training section of the personnel department frequently has responsibility for the handbook and also for subsequent elements in the induction programme. It decides the length and time of the programme, the place ('in house', or an external venue), the speakers, etc.

When they finish the programme new employees should have an overall impression of the organization, know some of the senior managers and have listened to their views, and be familiar with the requirements of their own jobs and how they fit into the overall organization.

15.3.2 Training of existing employees

Most organizations require their employees to undergo training at several points during their career. The training provided will depend upon an assessment of needs and objectives, undertaken by the training staff.

15.3.3 Needs and objectives in training

Training needs can be ascertained by a variety of methods. The most comprehensive involves an analysis of each employee's record card, and discussions with supervisors and managers. Using the job description, an assessment is made of whether the employee possesses all the relevant skills to perform satisfactorily, e.g. the job description in the Appendix requires skills in report writing. (Perhaps the postholder may require some specialized training in this area).

Alternatively, the assessment process of an MBO scheme, described above, or some other assessment method will often highlight areas of further training needs. In setting training objectives, particular care must be taken to ensure that the objectives are measurable in terms of changes in the employee's performance or attitude.

15.3.4 Training plans

These should be based on the 'needs' described above and should be concerned with the overall arrangements for training: the costs and benefits expected, the methods of selection to be used, and the type of training staff and facilities required.

15.3.5 Training methods

These are divided into 'on the job' and 'off the job' varieties.

1 *'On the Job'*, i.e. work-based training schemes, include:
   Job rotation — moving an employee to different jobs to improve knowledge and experience;
   Demonstrations — learning from an expert's demonstration;
   Coaching/supervision — where an employee does the job under close supervision and guidance by a skilled employee.
2 *'Off the Job'* systems include:
   Programmed learning — enables employees to work at their own speed.
   Lectures — useful for ex-students, who are familiar with this method, but of doubtful benefit to experienced managers.
   Discussion groups — useful to experienced employees who can learn from others' experiences.

Case studies — much featured at some universities, but care must be taken in selecting appropriate material.

Role playing and group exercises — can provide participants with skills in a controlled learning environment.

Discovery techniques — these allow participants to find out principles and relationships for themselves guided by a skilled tutor; useful for engineering or science-based training schemes.

15.3.6 Training evalution

This answers the question as to whether the training plan and methods chosen have met their needs and objectives. The most usual method is to obtain the reaction of employees on completion of their training and then to monitor their progress. If the training has been successful, the employee will be more effective in his work using the new skills obtained on the course, and his attitude to the job and to other colleagues will have improved.

15.3.7 Training course options

Most training sections in personnel departments nowadays have the option of choosing from a wide variety of courses offered by colleges, polytechnics, universities, consultants and government bodies. Courses offered cover:

1 Degree and diploma courses in, for example, engineering and business studies.
2 Post-graduate and post-experience courses including general management subjects.
3 Professional courses e.g. accountancy, law, personnel.
4 Short experience courses.

The range is now so varied that anyone, from a school leaver to the chairman of a multi-national conglomerate, can be catered for somewhere. Because of this variety and the time and cost involved, most organizations rely on their training staff, not only to assess the need for training, but also to make the necessary choice and arrangements from the multitude of facilities available. Training staff are now 'professionals' in every sense of the word.

15.4 Payment systems

15.4.1 Aims

Any organization that wishes to attract and retain employees of the right calibre has to pay particular attention to its wage and salary structure, referred to in this section as its payment system.

All payment systems have the following aims:

1 They must be definitive, equitable and consistent with the demands of the job and acceptable by the participants concerned.
2 The system must be capable of being easily controlled and administratively effective.
3 Flexibility must be built into the system to cater for future changes in overall circumstances.
4 The system must relate to 'the going rate' or 'national norms' if it is to stand the test of time.

15.4.2 Elements

Most payment systems are made up of one or a combination of the following:

1 A basic minimum rate or base rate
2 An incentive allowance
3 Special allowances
4 Fringe benefits.

The final composition will, of course, depend on the circumstances at the time and the relative bargaining strengths of employers and employees. The employees usually try to obtain, via their negotiators, the highest basic payment rate they can, partly for its own sake and partly because other additional payments are often based on a percentage increase on the basic rate.

15.4.3 Collective bargaining

Most payment systems in this country are arrived at by a process of free collective bargaining, i.e. open-ended negotiation between employers and employees, the latter often being represented by trade union officials. Negotiations can cover an individual employee, a group of employees, a work unit or office, a company, or even a national grouping e.g. public sector pay is determined nationally and applies throughout the country.

From time to time governments have tried to influence the free collective bargaining process as an attempt to control inflation. In several instances they have issued 'pay norms', which they have tried to apply to their own employees in the public sector. In other circumstances they have introduced statutory controls over pay, normally accompanied by some system of price control, e.g. in 1975 the Government introduced maximum wage/salary increases of £6.00 per week with no increases at all for those people whose wage/salary exceeded £7,500 per annum. The maximum increase was reduced to £4.00 per week the following year.

In the long term, attempts by Government to influence pay policy in this way have failed for a variety of reasons among these being the unwillingness of trade unions to accept more than a temporary limitation of their freedom to negotiate on behalf of their members. Controls on pay have also disturbed differentials (e.g. the £7,500 limit). Finally, incentive schemes and productivity deals (sometimes phoney) and workplace bargaining, often result in 'norms' or 'prescribed rates' of increase being evaded.

In recent years public sector employees, in an attempt to maintain their living standards, have agreed to systems of pay comparability. These have used either statutory bodies, e.g. The Civil Service Pay Review Board, or outside commissions, such as the Clegg Commission, to mediate in cases of dispute. At the time of writing the trend appears to be away from this comparability system; indeed the civil service strikes of the spring of 1981 were mainly caused by trade union anger at the Government's abandonment of the comparability system and the setting of a pay norm for their annual pay negotiations.

15.4.4 Payment techniques

Within the confines of whatever bargaining system is in operation, an organization can use a number of techniques to assist in setting the salaries of its employees. One of the most used in recent years is 'Job Evaluation'.

This method entails considering jobs, rather than individuals, and aims at relating the worth of one job to another so that they can be ranked in relative importance within an organization.

A variety of systems are available, but the procedure is much the same in many cases. The job, or a number of jobs (sometimes referred to as 'key' or 'benchmark' job) having been selected, a job evaluation panel is convened composed of representatives of management and employees. This panel then evaluates the job, using the job description and information supplied by the post or job holder, and taking account of the views of all the members of the panel. The job can be 'ranked' or placed in position relative to other jobs by one of two systems:

1 A non-analytical system which merely ranks the job in relation to others using a number of key contents, e.g. keyboard skills or:
2 Factor comparison or points rating, using analytical and quantitative techniques given to the various factors of the job itself.

In addition to using a system of job evaluation, many organizations make use of incentive schemes and productivity agreements to increase the pay of their employees and help boost productivity. These systems are examined in more detail in Chapter 16 on Management Services; suffice it to say at this stage that use of these systems of payment is widespread in both the public and private sectors, especially for manual or blue collar employees.

Despite the success of incentive schemes and productivity payments, particularly in the public sector, where they were introduced to overcome the problems of low basic wages in the 1960s, recent high unemployment figures have led to a reaction against such schemes.

High rates of inflation, together with attempts to control wages and salaries by statute, have led to a tremendous growth in fringe benefits, which supplement wages and salaries. These benefits include: company cars, interest free or subsidized loans, free telephones, health insurances, club membership, credit cards, subsidized canteens, luncheon vouchers and many others.

Occupational pension schemes can also be seen as a fringe benefit, especially where the employer assumes full responsibility for the payment of contributions. Alternatively pension schemes could be seen as part of the organization's payment system.

Fringe benefits are usually provided on a greater scale in the private rather than the public sector, and for senior white collar staff rather than for other employees. Most public sector employees, however, enjoy the benefit of index-linked pension schemes and following complaints by the private-sector employer organizations and other pressure groups, a commission was set up to examine the situation. The Scott Report recommended that index-linking of pensions should be extended to the private sector, an outcome the private sector pressure groups and the Government had not been expecting.

Fringe benefits are gradually being extended to all levels of employees, e.g. the recent decision of the electricians' union to offer private medical insurance to its members despite strong criticism from other unions. This trend towards 'equalization' of fringe benefits is likely to continue in the foreseeable future as trade unions press for all employees to be treated more equally in this area.

15.5 Welfare and safety

15.5.1 Welfare

Just as with fringe benefits, discussed above, so too the welfare facilities offered to employees have increased in recent years. (Indeed many of the fringe benefits such as private medical insurances obviously contribute to employees' welfare.)

Most personnel departments have a particular individual with specific responsibility for the welfare of employees. This may or may not be a full-time job depending on the size of the organization. As well as practical help and guidance to employees on a wide range of problems, both in the home and the workplace, the welfare facilities offered by organizations now cover:

1 Sickness schemes. The days of 'being off sick' without pay have now all but disappeared.
2 Canteens, with subsidized food, are now quite common in large organizations.
3 Sports and social facilities. These help break down barriers between employees; it is far better to 'let off steam' on the squash court than 'take it out of someone else' at an important office meeting.
4 Transport — subsidized rail or bus tickets, private mini-buses, coaches, cars, etc.
5 Accommodation — in addition to contributing towards removal expenses, organizations help with accommodation, e.g. by providing temporary accommodation for new employees. This facility aids the mobility of new and existing employees by removing some of the worry a change of location brings about.

15.5.2 Safety

Safety at work has long been controlled by legislation in this country, the main statutes being: the Factories Act 1961, the Offices, Shops and Railways Premises Act 1963, and the Health and Safety at Work Act 1974.

The last Act is by far the most comprehensive piece of legislation. Based on recommendations of the Robens Committee it operates as follows:

1 All employers must produce a written statement of their general policy with respect to health and safety and inform employees of it.
2 Management have the responsibility for designing and operating safe working practices. Failure to do so makes them liable at law.
3 Employees have a responsibility to take care that they work safely; this can often involve wearing certain types of protective clothing, using particular machines, doing a job a certain way. They must therefore follow the instructions laid down by their employers.
4 The Act lays down that there shall be designated safety representatives. These representatives often form a safety committee (although the Act does not insist that employers set up such a committee), which controls and inspects working practices and the workplace environment.
5 Training, with paid leave, for safety representatives is now common, as is safety training, in various aspects of their jobs, for all employees.
6 The Act operates through a Health and Safety Commission with a Health and Safety Executive running the day to day affairs. The Employment Medical Advisory Service and the Factory Inspectorate

are two arms of the Executive who can carry out inspections to ensure safe working practices are in operation. The Act also allows for inspectors to issue 'improvement notices' on any individuals or organizations who are in breach of Health and Safety regulations; in the last resort a 'prohibition notice,' which stops the operation where there is a risk of serious injury, can also be issued.

The Act was a milestone in health and safety policy. It covers all people at work and for the first time insists that employers and employees follow safe working practices. The Act brought the force of the law to a situation for which many progressive employers had reorganized for some time. It also brought about an increase in the responsibilities and the workload of personnel staff in all organizations who have to ensure their organization follows positive health and safety policies in line with the law.

15.6 Industrial relations

This term refers to the overall working environment within an organization, and in particular to the relationship between management and employees. It may appear strange to be dealing with this subject last of all in a chapter on the personnel function, but in practice good industrial relations depends on all the personnel policies already outlined and discussed. Industrial relations is a specialist area in its own right only when aspects of the law dictate certain relationships between employers and employees, and when the negotiation procedures to achieve agreement call for specialist managerial and other skills.

The major pieces of recent legislation relating to this area of the personnel function are as follows:

15.6.1 1974 Trade Union and Labour Relations Act

This Act repealed the 1971 Industrial Relations Act, provided greater protection against unfair dismissal, and confirmed 'the closed shop' system or union memberships' agreement.

15.6.2 1975 Employment Protection Act

A major provision of this Act was the establishment of the Advisory, Conciliation and Arbitration service, ACAS, which provide conciliation, arbitration and mediation services in disputes, and advisory and information services to industry. It examines and determines applications for recognition by independent trade unions. It promotes collective bargaining arrangements and has issued various codes of practice.

The Act also extended the maternity rights of female employees. Any pregnant woman having two years continuous service is entitled to a national insurance maternity allowance for a six weeks minimum period. She also has the right to be re-instated in her previous or similar job should she choose to return to work within twenty-nine weeks of the birth of her child.

Among the other provisions of the Act were guaranteed payments for short-term lay offs, enhanced time off arrangements, e.g. for officials engaged in union activities, the specification of procedures to be followed in cases of dismissals (including minimum periods of notice), and the obligation of employers to provide employees with itemised pay statements.

15.6.3 1975 Equal Pay Act and 1975 Sex Discrimination Act

The aim of these Acts was the removal of many of the then existing discriminations between sexes in the fields of employment. Under the Acts the Equal Opportunities Commission has the power to make enquiries and, if necessary, intervene in cases of discrimination between sexes.

15.6.4 1976 Race Relations Act

This Act forbids discrimination on grounds of race, colour, ethnic group or national origin. The Race Relations Board was replaced by the Commission for Racial Equality which has similar powers to the Equal Opportunities Commission.

The overall effect of the above legislation has been to constrain managements' freedom of action. Failure to act correctly is not only costly in money and industrial relations terms, it is also a blot on the image of an organization as a good employer and on the capabilities of its managers. Consequently, most organizations now employ industrial relations specialists in their personnel departments, who are able to offer expert advice on the interpretation of legislation.

Almost all the activities of the personnel department, whether or not they arise from the provisions of legislation, influence industrial relations. The system of collective bargaining, consultation procedures, participation arrangements and communication methods all affect the relationship between managers, trade unions and employees. As we implied during our discussions in Chapters 4 and 5, good communications are essential to good industrial relations. It follows that the personnel department should take an active role in the design and operation of systems of communication between all areas of an organization. A lack of information, badly conducted negotiations, poor consultation systems can all lead to a hardening of attitudes by one side or the other which may take a long time to overcome.

15.6.5 1980 Employment Act

This Act made provision for payment out of public funds towards expenditure in respect of ballots, for the use of employers' premises in connection with ballots, and for the issue by the secretary of state of codes of practice for the improvement of industrial relations. An employee's right to return to work after maternity leave is made dependent on written notification and is subject to certain time restraints. Moreover small firms, who were having particular difficulty operating the existing legislation in respect of maternity rights, were exempted from most of the provisions of this section of the Act.

15.6.6 The 1982 Employment Act

This Act followed extensive consultation procedures by the Government with over 100 organizations and numerous individuals. Its main provisions are to:

1 enable the Government to compensate certain people dismissed from closed shops under the Labour Government's legislation;
2 increase the protection for non-union employees working in a closed shop;
3 promote regular reviews of existing closed shops by secret ballots of the employees concerned;
4 outlaw union-only requirements in the awarding and making of contracts;
5 restrict lawful trade disputes to disputes between workers and their own employer;
6 make trade unions liable, in the same way as their individual officials, if they are responsible for unlawful industrial action.

15.7 Summary and conclusions

In this chapter we have tried to illustrate the importance of the personnel function in organizations today. We started off by showing that the personnel function was the responsibility of all managers who have to control and supervize people. We looked at the main work areas of the personnel function: employment, recruitment and selection, training, payment schemes, welfare and safety, and industrial relations. We showed how, in recent years, the growth of legislation has affected the whole operation of the personnel function and led to an increase in the importance to all organizations of professionally qualified personnel staff. The personnel function is now firmly established. Looking to the future one can only envisage a growth in these activities as organizations become more 'people-orientated,' and as employees demand more say in the conditions and decisions that shape their working lives.

Revision questions and exercises

1   Answer *briefly:*
A   Describe the main aims of a personnel manager.
B   What are the main areas covered by the personnel function?
C   What is meant by industrial relations?
D   Define manpower planning.
E   What is the main requirement of a good training scheme?
F   What are the main sources of recruitment?
G   Name two pieces of legislation that have affected the personnel department in recent years.
H   What are the main work areas covered by the employment section in a personnel department?
I   Give three examples of fringe benefits.
J   What is meant by collective bargaining?
2   'I do not believe there is such a thing as the specialist personnel function; all managers are operating the personnel function over staff for whom they are responsible'. Discuss.
3   On what basis should a firm institute a scheme for staff training and development, and how might the success of such a scheme be judged?
4   'Good industrial relations means paying employees an adequate salary' Do you agree with this statement?
5   Do you think women have opportunities in management equal to men? What areas are barred to women in practice and in what areas do women have advantages over men?
6   If you were a personnel officer and had four candidates equally qualified in terms of experience and qualifications, one of whom was a twenty-six year old women who had been married for three years, would you give this woman serious consideration against two male and one female applicant (divorced with grown up children)? Give the reasons for your decision.
7   You work for a firm of consultants that is invited by a new District Health Authority to advise them on the structure of their Personnel Department.
     The new Authority takes over the functions of the existing Area and District Health authorities and it is required to absorb existing administration and medical staff.
     The Authority intend to operate a complete personnel function and asks you in your report to pay particular attention to:
     (a) The structure and function of the Department.
     (b) Points to be considered when merging staff at present employed by District and Area Health Authorities.
     (c) Guidelines for effective recruitment of additional staff that may be required.
     Write your report.

8   You have recently taken up an appointment as Director of Personnel of a large County Council. The monthly staff statistics show that the turnover figure for clerical and secretarial staff is particularly high, being at an annual rate of nearly 45% over the last five months. Discussions with the other staff in the Personnel Department reveal that,
   1 Departments interview their own staff for appointments and also outsiders, but without any assistance from the Personnel Department.
   2 Adverts are sometimes dealt with by the Personnel Department and sometimes by other departments without any reference to Personnel.
   3 The staff who have been appointed to vacancies are often, to your mind, not really suited to the requirements of the job.
   You approach the Chief Executive and the Chairman of the Personnel Committee about the issue and they instruct you to rectify the problem and prepare your recommendations in a report as soon as possible.
   (i)   Outline the methods of standardizing the recruitment procedure so that all departments know the correct steps to take when recruiting staff.
   (ii)   Describe how the actual interviewing procedure can be improved and draw up a guide that departments can follow to ensure the right people are recruited.
   (iii) Indicate which factors you would take into consideration in justifying your proposals financially to your Chairman and Chief Executive.

Further Reading

ANSTEY, E., FLETCHER, C. and WALKER, J. *Staff Appraisal and Development* (George Allen and Unwin: London, 1976).

BENNETT, R. *Managing Personnel and Performance* (Business Books: London, 1981).

CLEGG, H. A. *The Systems of Industrial Relations in Great Britain* (Blackwell: Oxford, 1973).

CUMMING, M. *The Theory and Practice of Personnel Management* (Heinemann: London, 1977).

CUMMING, M. *Personnel Management in the National Health Service* (Heinemann: London, 1978).

DUNN, J. and STEPHENS, E. *Management of Personnel* (McGraw-Hill: New York, 1972).

INBUCON CONSULTANTS *Managing Human Resources* (Heinemann: London, 1976).

JONES, J. and MORRIS, M. *A-Z of Trade Unionism and Industrial Relations* (Heinemann: London, 1982).

KING-TAYLOR, L. *Not for Bread Alone* (Business Books: London, 1972).

PIGORS, P. and MYERS, C. *Personnel Administration* (McGraw-Hill: New York, 1977).

STAINER, G. *Manpower Planning* (Heinemann: London, 1971).

THOMASON, G. *A Textbook of Personnel Management* (IBM: London, 1981).

TORRINGTON, D. and CHAPMAN, J. *Personnel Management* (Prentice Hall: New York, 1979).

TORRINGTON, D. *Face to Face Management* (Prentice Hall: New York, 1982).

Appendix   Sample Job Description

COUNTY COUNCIL

JOB DESCRIPTION

Department	County Secretary's
Section	Productivity and Common Services
Title	Organization and Methods Office
Post No.	CS 34
Grade	Principal Officer Grade 1

1 *Job Purpose*

Under the supervision of the Principal Organization and Methods Officer (Post CS 25), to provide an internal consultancy service, designed to increase efficiency by means of improving work methods, systems, procedures, control and organization structures.

2 *Main Duties and Responsibilities*

(a) To plan, programme and control the project work of the section by:

  (i) Preparing assignment briefs in consultation with user departments

  (ii) Allocating appropriate O. and M. staff to assignments

  (iii) Determining appropriate O. and M. techniques

  (iv) Assessing benefits and preparing interim and final reports.

(b) To build up and maintain good working relationships with departments by:

  (i) Consultation

  (ii) Written reports on projects

  (iii) Amending and updating proposals after discussion with departmental staff.

(c) To ensure proposals are accepted and implemented by:

  (i) Presenting an implementation programme

  (ii) Carrying out follow-up reviews.

(d) To train and develop O. and M. staff in the section by:

  (i) Recognizing training needs in consultation with the Personnel Department

  (ii) Allocating work so as to provide experience

  (iii) Keeping up to date with new techniques and trends and informing staff of these

  (iv) Ensuring confidentiality is maintained by all staff where required.

3 *Postholder*

The postholder should be a graduate, full member of the Institute of Management Services and have at least five years O. and M. experience in the public sector covering some or all of the following work areas — O. and M., work study, systems design, statistics, job evaluation, operational research, industrial relations.

4 *Age factors*

Immaterial subject to qualifications and experience.

5 *Supervisory responsibility*

Responsible for eleven O. and M. officers.

6 *Supervision received*
   Responsible to Principal O. and M. Officer (Post CS 25) but would be
   expected to use initiative after the preparation of assignment briefs.
7 *Contacts*
   Maintain contacts at all levels within the organization and other outside
   professional and other appropriate bodies and persons.
8 *Special conditions*
   The postholder will work within the flexitime arrangements of the County
   Council but may at any time be required to work outside these hours. He/she
   may be required to visit other local authorities or outside organizations from
   time to time.

Dated April, 1983

16

Management Services

16.1 Introduction

Management services refers to a variety of techniques (the main ones being organization and methods and work study) that assist management in improving the efficiency of their organizations.

In this chapter we look at some of the techniques used, see how the management services function is organized, and assess its future development.

16.2 What is management services?

The term 'management services' is based on the title chosen by the professional body which represents staff working in this area. The Institute of Management Services was established in 1978, with Sir Monty Finniston as its first president. Its predecessor was the Institute of Practitioners in Work Study and Organization and Methods, itself created in 1974 by a merger between the Institute of Work Study Practitioners and the Organization and Methods Society. The change in title in 1978 was due to a feeling that the existing title did not reflect the wide range of techniques used by staff engaged in this work. Management services is, of course, a more comprehensive term. The wide range of activities undertaken by management services personnel was also noted in the Bains Report, 'Local Authority Management Structures' which preceded the 1974 local government re-organization. The Report quoted evidence received from the Society of Town Clerks:

> 'The term ''Management Services'' comprises all those services which help management to plan, control and improve the activities of the

organization in a general sense. The term is wider than the orthodox interpretation which is generally limited to efficiency and productivity services.'

Although management services personnel have extended their range of activities, they still use, in the main, techniques based upon two areas of specialization, O. and M. (organization and methods) and work study. A few years ago these techniques tended to be operated separately. O. and M. was concerned with efficiency in the office, whereas work study was concerned with problems on the shop floor and payment schemes for manual or blue collar workers. But even before the new Institute was formed this demarcation was breaking down and staff were becoming more interchangeable between these two work areas. However, for ease of presentation we discuss each of these two, and other techniques, separately.

16.2.1 Organization and Methods

The formal use of O. and M. can be traced back to 1919 when a small team was set up in the Treasury following the Bradbury Report on *The organization and staffing of government offices*. O. and M. has often been better developed in public than in private sector organizations. This is perhaps no surprise when one considers that much of the public sector operates on bureaucratic lines, in an office type of environment. Nevertheless it shows that innovations in management techniques are not confined to the private sector, contrary to the impression sometimes given by critics of the public sector.

In fact, O. and M. covers most of the management functions found in either the public or the private sector. It is mainly concerned with:

1 Defining the true problem that exists and the facts required.
2 Examining work methods, i.e. information systems, administrative systems, office equipment etc.
3 Analysing how employees spend their time and scrutinizing staffing levels.
4 Examining the introduction of the latest types of office equipment, i.e. communications equipment, reprographics, mail etc.
5 Undertaking research into specific areas.
6 Advising on organizational structures and re-organizations, including responsibility levels, gradings and salaries, command structures, departmentation etc.
7 Ensuring that the organization has effective communication systems.
8 Advising on office and factory layouts.
9 Introducing computerised systems (and operating the computer in certain organizations).

10 Examining work planning and programming systems.
(See the sample job description in the appendix to the previous chapter).

From the above list it will be evident that O. and M. staff are involved throughout the organization, from junior clerical levels up to Board or policy committee level. They use a variety of methods and techniques, statistical, analytical, observational and behavioural, as appropriate. But whatever the area of investigation and whatever the methods used, the following steps would normally be involved.

16.2.1.1 Selecting the material facts

When a situation is first examined, more than one problem area can usually be seen. It is necessary to try to differentiate between those areas that merit more detailed investigation and those which are irrelevant to the main issues. This preliminary survey familiarizes the O. and M. staff with the main work areas to be investigated, and enables their terms of reference for the assignment to be finalized.

16.2.1.2 Recording the facts

The terms of reference being agreed, the relevant facts are recorded. This often involves direct observation of people in a work situation. Staff may be interviewed as to their duties and responsibilities, questionnaires may be completed and statistical returns analysed.

16.2.1.3 Examining the information obtained

The information obtained at the previous stage is critically examined, in order to obtain answers to the questions: What is done? Where is it done? When is it done? Why is it done? How is it done? Who does it?

16.2.1.4 Developing ideas for improvement

Ideas for improving the situation are discussed with management and the employees concerned. This discussion helps to reveal any potential snags or problems and to identify the costs involved in the changes, e.g. for re-training. In other words it helps to ensure that the new systems are practical and capable of implementation.

16.2.1.5 Implementing recommendations

The ideas for improvement, modified as required in the light of the discussions, are incorporated in a report. If the report is accepted by the management responsible, the O. and M. staff then have to assist with the introduction of their new ideas. This is often a salutary experience which involves overcoming people's built-in resistance to change. This implies that O. and M. staff must have analytical skills and must also be able to 'sell' their ideas and develop good personal relationships with all types of people.

16.2.1.6 Maintaining new systems

As circumstances and individuals change, the newly introduced systems may have to modified. To ensure that this happens, O. and M. staff undertake a monitoring role. The need for constant monitoring is the main reason why larger organizations employ their own full-time O. and M. staff rather than calling in outside consultants.

16.2.2 Work study

Work study was pioneered by Frederick Taylor (see Chapter 2) in his attempts to improve efficiency in a factory unit, and has been developed ever since. The basic technique is work measurement, designed (a) to provide management with information to aid the planning and control of work and (b) to offer an individual a financial incentive for an above average work performance.

Work is measured using either a stop watch or more sophisticated systems incorporating micro-chip technology. The procedures usually adopted are:

1 The job or operation is broken down into easily identifiable sections or elements.
2 The time taken to complete each element of the work is measured.

Because some people work faster than others, and because some employees may try to mislead the work study officer as to the normal pace of work required (e.g. by working more slowly than usual to make the job appear to require longer time and hence a greater allowance), the work study officer applies a 'rating estimate' to his study. The aim of this 'rating' is to assist with a true estimate of the time necessary to complete the task in a normal work situation with an average employee working at an average pace.

Because of the personal judgement involved in this rating exercise, the factor is often the cause of subsequent disputes. Studies are taken of a variety of employees doing that same job in a variety of work situations to ensure that all types of work situations and conditions are covered.

3 The results are analysed and a time or target is issued for the completion of a particular job or operation. This time will include allowances for rest and relaxation, harsh working conditions etc. The work study officer also advises on the best way to do the job, drawing on his observations of perhaps several working methods. On the basis of this

information management can plan its work schedules, allocate manpower and equipment, train employees to do an operation in the most effective way, and offer them a financial incentive to increase their productivity.

The trade unions, particularly in the public sector in the 1960s and 1970s, welcomed work study as a measure of increasing their members' take-home pay. It also suited many public sector organizations to encourage work study as a means of retaining skilled craftsmen and other manual workers who were, at that time, on lower wage levels than comparable employees in the private sector. It was not until the early 1970s that the efficiency aspects, and the advantages of work study as a management aid, came to be fully appreciated.

It is beneficial for the staff who work in these areas to undertake the training required for membership of the Institute of Management Services. But to be really successful in these areas of work, personal qualities of a particular type are also required. Since people are the focus of both O. and M. and work study, the main qualities required are impartiality, an enquiring mind, patience and the ability to persevere in periods of adversity, a realistic approach to problem solving, and an understanding of and liking for people.

16.2.3 Operational research

This is a problem-solving technique which uses analytical and statistical techniques to try to measure the factors of change in a given situation, and to compare alternative courses of action. O.R. is now applied to a wide range of issues, e.g. the best route for school buses, optimum stock levels, refuse collection systems and the location of warehouses. The Local Government Operational Research Unit operates a central service to local government and has developed considerable expertise in the use of O.R. techniques in the public sector. For example it will advise local authorities on the feasibility of introducing a waste paper collection system.

16.2.4 Network analysis

This technique, which is used for planning and co-ordinating large projects such as the construction of a new office building, begins by charting each of the activities concerned. Some can be completed concurrently, others are dependent on another activity being completed first. Each activity has to have a start, a duration and an end. The aim of network analysis is to show all these activities visually and to identify the series of key activities which determine the total duration of the project. This series is known as the 'critical path'.

Because of the time involved in drawing up the network and keeping it up to date, management services staff are often involved in its operation. They have the necessary knowledge of the organization, know the key personnel involved, and have the skills and the time required for this project co-ordination role.

16.3 The organization of the management services function

16.3.1 Computerization

In the private sector the computer system is normally controlled by the manager in charge of the management services function, as shown in Figure 16.1. This means that there is no problem in co-ordinating the work of management services staff who may be involved in a computer application to a work procedure and require the assistance of systems analysts (who design the system) and programmers (who write the operating procedures for the computers). In this type of combined management services unit the management services staff may well do the systems work and even the programming work themselves. Even if they do not, the control of a multi-disciplinary project team is easier where the management services manager also controls the computer and allied staff.

In the public sector e.g. local government, the computer section is often within the finance directorate, whereas the management services section is either in the director of administration's department or is directly responsible to the chief executive (Figure 16.2). This split of responsibility can create problems when it has to be decided who should do the 'systems analysis' work for a particular application, or when putting a management services application on to the computer would conflict with the finance department's priorities. The situation is often resolved by joint working arrangements between the two departments.

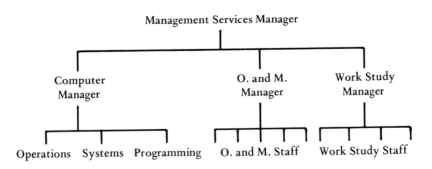

Figure 16.1   A private sector management services unit.

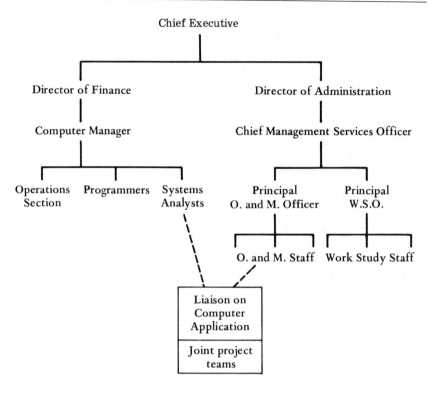

Figure 16.2   A local government management services unit.

16.3.2 The local authorities' management services and computer committee

In addition to individual management services units in local government, there exists a large central unit, LAMSAC. This operates as a central consultancy unit carrying out research, and developing computerised systems in areas of interest common to all local authorities. It also undertakes specific assignments for individual authorities.

LAMSAC operates on private sector lines in combining management services and computer skills and it may be a forerunner of smaller combined units in individual local authorities. But one of the authors, who spent some years in charge of management services units in local government, feels that progress along these lines will be very slow, if only because finance departments will be reluctant to surrender the powers inherent in the control of the computer and its information systems.

16.4 Internal versus external consultants

Provided that there is sufficient work to occupy staff on a full-time basis, there are several advantages in having an internal management services unit:

1 As staff of the organization they are more likely to have managers' best interests at heart when carrying out their work.
2 They have to 'live with their mistakes', and will therefore be more careful in framing their reports and implementing their recommendations.
3 Internal staff get to know their own organization's workings and develop good relationships with other employees and managers. This helps to overcome mistrust and many of the worries brought about by change.
4 Maintenance of incentive schemes and of re-organization processes is easier when management services staff are on site all the time. They are well placed to pick up problems at an early stage.

Outside consultants have a number of advantages:

1 The organization pays for them only when they are needed; the continuing costs of an internal unit are avoided.
2 Managers can hire consultants with expertise in a particular area rather than having to rely on what is available from within their own unit.
3 Outside consultants are independent, and divorced from 'office politics'. They also have experience of other organizations that they can bring to bear on a particular problem.

On the other hand outside consultants' fees for a given job are usually well above the corresponding cost of an internal unit. Moreover they have to spend some time — at the client's expense — getting to know the organization and its management. Furthermore, however effectively they undertake the initial assignment, 'maintenance problems' are likely to arise. The organization is then faced with either recalling the consultants (at a fee of course) or trying to correct problems with which internal staff may not be fully familiar.

16.5 The operation of incentive schemes and productivity agreements

Incentive schemes and productivity agreements are often a major outcome of the work of management services personnel. Before introducing any scheme of this nature management must (a) be clear about what it hopes the scheme will achieve, (b) weigh up the costs of the scheme and (c) try to identify any disruptions that may result.

Incentive schemes and productivity agreements frequently have the following objectives:

Increased output and earnings
Better management control and planning
Increased labour mobility between jobs
Better work methods
Better quality
Reduced absenteeism and staff turnover
Reduced overtime working.

Experience has shown that, whatever the type of scheme or the expected benefits, the scheme will only operate successfully if, when designing it, management and the management services staff pay close attention to the following issues:

1 The scheme must be simple to understand and have a minimum of documentation.
2 Employees must accept the work targets as being realistic.
3 There must be a clear relationship between increased performance and increased pay.
4 The calculation period and the pay period should be as short as possible and coincide with the normal wage or salary period.
5 Attention should be given to the impact of the scheme on (a) supervisory staff and (b) staff not directly concerned with the scheme but having some input into the work of those who are. The loss of 'differentials' by first time supervisors is an issue that arises time and time again.
6 A system must be set up to deal with queries and disputes.
7 A decision must be made concerning:
   (a) waiting time — when employees are willing to work but are prevented from doing so by factors beyond their control, e.g. machine breakdown or bad weather.
   (b) unmeasured work — where no work study target exists.
   (c) sickness and holidays.
8 Should the scheme have an individual or a group basis? If a group scheme is chosen, will problems arise in groups containing older, slower workers and younger faster workers?
9 The introduction period of the scheme must be realistic.
10 Other departments (e.g. finance or accounts) will be affected by the scheme and may need increased staff, e.g. to pay the bonus and prepare documentation for the computer.

16.6 The results

Given the time and effort required to deal with such issues — and the above list is by no means exhaustive — the question arises as to whether incentive schemes, productivity agreements, and the other outputs of management services units are worth the cost involved.

The answer will obviously depend on the results obtained in a given organization. But experience suggests that the benefits often outweigh the costs. The main benefits fall into three groups.

First, a work study or O. and M. exercise gives management a great deal of information about their organization, its workings and, most important, the people involved. This is valuable even if no attempt is made to use the information for incentive payment purposes.

Second, it obliges management, trade unions, employees' representatives and employees to discuss together the issues raised. The benefits of this inter-personal communication spill over into other areas and can be vital in overcoming the 'them and us' attitudes still prevalent today.

Third, such assignments can lead to greater efficiency and competitiveness, and can assist in the introduction of new work methods and equipment. By enabling higher wages and salaries to be paid to employees, in return for greater productivity, management is able to seize the advantage in this area from the trade unions and groups of militant workers.

16.7 Summary and conclusions

In this chapter we have looked at various aspects of the management services function. We have shown what the function involves and how it operates in the public and private sectors. We have also examined some of the issues connected with incentive schemes and productivity agreements. We concluded that although these, and other areas of management services, involve the expenditure of considerable time and effort, many organizations consider these costs to be outweighed by the benefits.

Revision questions and exercises

1   Answer *briefly:*
A   What is meant by the term management services?
B   What is work study?
C   What is O. and M.?
D   Give the first two stages in carrying out an O. and M. assignment.
E   What is operational research?
F   How can network analysis help managers?

G   What do management consultants do?
H   What is a productivity agreement?
I   How can one measure productivity?
J   What is waiting time?

2   You are the Assistant Chief Finance Officer in the technical section of the Finance Department of a large county council. The Director of Administration presents a report to the personnel committee supporting the setting up of a management services unit in his department, saying that this unit will help to improve the overall efficiency of the council. The Director of Finance informs you that while he is not against the idea in principle, he wonders if an internal unit, as opposed to the use of outside consultants, is the answer to the problem. He asks you to prepare a report that he can show the Chief Executive, detailing the advantages and disadvantages of using external consultants as opposed to setting up an internal unit. Write the report.

3   'Incentive schemes lead to higher wages and lower productivity in the long run'. Discuss.

4   List the main functions of an O. and M. section and explain which you think are the most important.

5   Outline the main stages in carrying out an O. and M. assignment. At which stage would you expect the greatest difficulty to occur?

6   Discuss the main aims of incentive schemes and say whether you think they are achievable in practice.

7   Outline the main criteria for the successful operation of incentive schemes.

Further Reading

ANDERSON, R. G. *Organization and Methods* (Macdonald Evans: London, 1979).

BENTLEY, T. *Making Information Systems Work* (Macmillan: London, 1981).

CURRIE, R. and FARADAY, J. *Work Study* (Pitman: London, 1980).

LACEY, T. *Management Information Systems* (D. P. Publications: London, 1981).

MACE, R. *Management Information and the Computer* (Accountancy Age Books: London, 1978).

NIGHTINGALE, N. *Method Study* (Institute of Management Services: London, 1980).

ROWAN, T. G. *Managing with Computers* (Heinemann: London, 1982).

SHEARMAN, T. P. *O and M in Local Government* (Pergamon: Oxford, 1969).

WHITMORE, D. *Work Measurement* (Heinemann: London, 1981).

17

Management in the Office

17.1 Introduction

Many readers of this book will eventually pursue careers involving work within an office type of environment. Be they purchasing or personnel officers, architects or engineers, designers or computer managers, insurance brokers or investment analysts, the office will be their second home.

In this chapter we try to give the reader an understanding of what it means to work in an office environment, and discuss some of the management functions involved in this important central department.

17.2 The office and its work

The office refers to the place that staff work in, and also to the grouping of a particular set of administrative functions that are central to the efficient operation of most organizations.

The administrative office is concerned with two main areas of work:

1 *Information* This function involves the collection and analysis of information and the presentation of information in a suitable format to management.
2 *Services* The administrative office provides a variety of services to line and professional managers. The most common of these are:
  Office location, layout and maintenance.
  Filing and information systems,
  Reception and telephone arrangements,
  Mail and messenger services,
  Secretarial services,

254

Reprographics,
Publicity and Transport.

17.3 The organization

17.3.1 The company secretary

In the private sector, the manager normally in charge of office-type functions and administrative procedures is the company secretary. Whilst this position may be regarded as a 'staff function', in that it provides services to senior and line management, the appointment of a company secretary is required by law and therefore has an importance and responsibility somewhat different from other appointments.

The company secretary is normally responsible for:

1 The company's compliance with all aspects of the law: company, industrial, employment, contract, tax, commercial, environmental.
2 Proper recording of the meetings of the board of directors.
3 Administration of patents, licences and constraints.
4 Insurance and pensions.
5 Registers of members (shareholders), loans and mortgages.
6 Legal aspects of any company clubs (e.g. sports and social).
7 Any administrative matters not falling to other specialized departments.

The Company Secretary has been described as an 'all rounder' and in many respects this is particularly true. The main professional body concerned, The Institute of Chartered Secretaries and Administrators, has members not only in private sector organizations, but is rapidly increasing its membership in the public sector, especially in local government, the health and water services.

This recognises the administrative role of the professionally qualified secretary in both the public and the private sector. The secretary is, in many cases, an organization's chief administrative officer, a mixture of lawyer, administrator, personnel officer and financial manager. Because of their varied skills, company secretaries often act as the bridge between top directors and other levels of the organization, particularly the more specialist ones. Company secretaries are the lynch pins to the day-to-day administration of organizations; convening and attending board meetings, recording and communicating decisions, keeping the statutory books and register of shareholders, arranging for the payment of dividends and loan interest as well as making arrangements for new issues of capital. They are often the managing director's right-hand man, or woman, in providing wide-ranging advice as well as day-to-day control of the running of all the administrative arrangements, without which any organization would soon grind to a halt.

In an era when specialists abound, more and more organizations are realizing the value of the company secretary as a communicator between all the sections and departments of the organization, as someone who has the broad base of skills and knowledge to advise the most senior of managers on the most appropriate option to be followed, and as a key manager who knows the organization's intricate day-to-day workings better than anyone else.

17.3.2 The director of administration

In the public sector, administration and management have always been closely linked and the Director of Administration plays a key role in the management of local authorities and other public sector bodies. We can take as an example the responsibilities of the Director of Administration in a typical London Borough:

1 To act as legal advisor to the council and to head the legal department.
2 To be responsible for public control including the administration of civil defence, Rent Act administration and local elections.
3 To act as functional head of all administrative officers of the council; maintain a staff relationship to administrative personnel in other departments and take responsibility for their procedures.
4 To encourage and introduce standard administrative procedures between departments and to provide centralised services where appropriate.
5 To balance the seasonal and temporary peak needs of the various departments for clerical and administrative staff, and to seek economies by temporary transfers between departments and by the use of temporary staff.
6 To be responsible for such office services as the administration of office buildings, telephonists, managers, reception staff, office cleaning, security, printing and stationery.
7 To head the council's publicity department and develop a system of internal staff communication and publicity.
8 To supervise the work of the road safety officer.
9 To act, in the absence of the Chief Executive, as the council's principal officer.
10 To control the operation of the council's committee system, provide agendas, prepare and circulate minutes, and liaise with councillors on any issues that may affect the efficient operation of the administrative machinery of the authority.

17.4 Centralization versus De-centralization

Provided the various departments of an organization are situated in one location, there is much to be said for centralizing many of the administrative functions listed above. The reasons are:

1 Better use can be made of staff and equipment in terms of efficiency, flexibility, job satisfaction and career progression. Specialist staff can be employed and trained; this is not possible in smaller offices where one person may have to carry out several staff functions. Specialist equipment can be justified because of the increased workload in one location and under one manager's control, e,g. franking machines instead of manual postage methods.
2 Management control is made easier; this is particularly important in the 'service' function provided by the administrative office to other departments.
3 Consultation, communication and standardization of administrative procedures is easier where all the staff are based in one office and personal contact is possible.

17.5 The office functions

Each of the main functions or areas of responsibility of the office manager, or person similarly responsible, will now be discussed in more detail.

17.5.1 Office location

Certain general issues on location of organizations have already been dealt with in Section 13.5.1 and so we will restrict our comments in this section to issues particular to the office situation. The main factors to take into account are:

1 The convenience of the location to other departments within the organization. Where all departments are in one building there is much to be said for locating the administrative office on the ground floor where its major functions of reception, telephones, security and mail need to be positioned.
  Where the other departments are in more than one location, e.g. where production and sales units are located in several regions, the main decision is whether the administrative office should be organized on a centralized or de-centralized basis. The general advantages of centralization were outlined above; if it is decided that there should be an administrative head office, a London location has several advantages. It facilitates contact with the financial and commercial

institutions of the City, with government departments and with the head offices of other companies. (On the other hand the cost of office accommodation and staff costs are higher in London than elsewhere in the U.K.).

2 Space for expansion should be available; the building should have good communication systems, be close to the necessary services, have adequate car parking and good access to public transport facilities.

3 The office should be in an area where suitable staff can be attracted and retained. Since there is a high proportion of management, secretarial and clerical staff, the availability of leisure facilities, shops, schools, etc., is often important.

4 Rent or buy decisions will be made on financial grounds; the availability of purpose-built or specially designed buildings should also be taken into account.

17.5.2 Office layout

The reader has already been introduced to some aspects of organizational layout in Section 13.5.2. The comments that follows relate, in the main, to an office as opposed to an industrial situation. Whether a ready-made office is taken over or a purpose-built one contemplated, the basic choices remain the same.

Should the layout be open plan or have cellular offices? Open plan offices have a number of advantages:

1 They allow design changes to take place with the minimum of disruption as departments change in size and requirements.

2 They economize on heating, light and floor space.

3 They allow easier communication and consultation, and better supervision to be exercised without the 'them and us' attitude often associated with private offices.

However, there are also disadvantages to open plan offices. Noise, people walking through the office and other distractions can reduce working efficiency. Moreover, a lack of privacy may mean that individual offices still have to be provided for certain purposes, e.g. disciplinary interviews. Such offices are likely to be under-utilized for most of the time.

To overcome these disadvantages, open plan offices have been designed using special furniture and facilities. This system, pioneered on the Continent and known as Bureaulandschaft (office landscaping), utilizes screens, plants, filing cabinets etc., to create smaller work areas and minimize the problems mentioned above. Office landscaping is expensive, and must be carefully designed if corresponding benefits are to be obtained. Arising from the personal involvement of one of the authors in the design of an office landscaping system for a large local authority, it is suggested that the following guidelines be followed:

1 The furniture and landscaping equipment should be used in such a way that employees can still relate to their group or section. Rest areas should also be provided. Lighting and air conditioning must be appropriate to the requirements of each work (or rest) area.

2 The system should apply to all staff, including senior and junior managers, if the advantages of the open plan office — such as good communications and the development of a common interest — are to be fully realized.

3 Time must be spent training employees in the different working habits that their new environment will require, and familiarizing them with the planned layout. A guided tour can do more to gain employees' acceptance of the new system than hours of discussion and pages of information.

17.5.3 Office maintenance

Whether an organization owns a purpose-built building or rents space in an office block, certain maintenance issues have to be dealt with. Where the accommodation is rented, the landlords or letting agents will often provide some maintenance services as part of the lease. But the administrative office will still have to deal with queries and arrange for the work to be carried out.

There are several broad types of office maintenance activity, connected with:

1 The provision of services: gas, electricity, water, oil etc. for heating, lighting and power facilities.

2 Structural maintenance: the repair of broken windows, leaking roofs etc., the painting and maintenance of the interior and exterior of the building's fabric.

3 Cleaning; an organization may choose to employ an outside contract cleaning service or recruit its own cleaning staff. The choice will depend on costs and the standard and range of services required, e.g. towels in the washrooms, soap etc.

4 Security; we live in troubled times and few organizations can afford to have unrestricted entry to their premises. Careful design of the building, control over entry and exits and, where appropriate, a night patrol system will reduce the chances of unauthorized entry with its consequential dangers.

5 Car parking; some local authorities insist on a minimum provision. Even if this is not so, organizations will usually provide car parking for

senior executives, salesmen etc. to avoid their time being wasted. It is also important to provide access roads for deliveries and facilities for visitors.

6 Entertainments/Social; it is usually the responsibility of the administrative office to organize the Christmas party, control the finances of the social club (if one exists) and to decide the policy on luncheon vouchers.

7 Catering; the scale of the facilities provided will depend upon the size of the organization and the provision in the surrounding area. But even in the smallest organizations staff are likely to want drink and snack facilities. These may be provided by the organization's own staff or by specialist contract caterers. The choice will be influenced by the range of services required and by the cost.

17.5.4 Filing

A major function of the office is the collection, maintenance and provision of information, Although computerized information systems are becoming increasingly common, all organizations remain dependent on filing systems, and efficient filing is one of the most vital operations in an organization's success. Because of this and because filing is a link between the office and all other departments of the organization we discuss it at some length.

17.5.4.1 The essentials of a good filing/records system

The system should be easy to understand and to operate. Its location should be convenient for main users. Especially important is the ability to find quickly the required information; this implies adequate indexing and cross-referencing, and a classification system that is neither too detailed nor too broad.

The system should be compact, in terms of equipment and layout, since space costs money. However it should be flexible enough to allow for future growth. Another aspect of flexibility is that it should be possible to remove 'dead' files and, where appropriate, to store them elsewhere.

The staff operating the system should, of course, be of a good calibre, well trained and supervized.

17.5.4.2 Centralization versus De-centralization

The *advantages* of a system based in a central administrative office are as follows:

(a) Control, updating and maintenance are made easier.
(b) It allows for standard classification systems and procedures.
(c) Duplication of files is minimized.

(d) Space can be used to its full advantage.

(e) Full time, specialist staff can become familiar with the system and save managers' time by providing them with information.

The *disadvantages* of a centralized system are:

(a) Time may be wasted, e.g. because of delays in obtaining files, working to the central point.

(b) Since files may be required by more than one person at the same time, duplicate systems may be established (thus negating advantage (d) above).

(c) If paperwork requisition systems operate, the overall paperwork burden of the organization could increase.

(d) If the filing staff are not acquainted with the detail of the work, they may lose interest in it.

A possible compromise is to have a mix of centralized and de-centralized files, all on a common index:

(a) All non-current files to be central, but current files in departments.

(b) All files to be kept locally but the classification and indexing to be centralized.

17.5.4.3 The office and central administration

There is often a case for grouping other common services with the central filing system and this often comes under the heading of a 'filing' or 'deeds' registry, e.g. mail, reception and dispatch, internal and external messenger services, reprographic service. The objective should be to minimize on staffing costs and to link common services that closely relate to the information held on the filing system.

17.5.4.4 Filing classification

Filed material is usually of three broad types: (1) current correspondence, records or registers; (2) subject and policy files; (3) cases, e.g. personal case files.

The material is usually classified in one or more of the following ways:

1 *Alphabetical.* General correspondence, names of firms, staff files etc., are usually classified alphabetically.

2 *Chronological.* This can also be used in conjunction with some other classification, e.g., chronological/alphabetical systems.

3 *Numerical.* This would be used for motor car numbers, insurance policy numbers etc. It has the advantage that new files can be added at the end instead of being inserted into the middle of the series.

4 *Geographical.* This system is useful in large national and multinational organizations. It is normally used in conjunction with another system, e.g., geographic according to country, alphabetical according to organization, name, e.g., Australia/Perth/North Churchlands College

(AUS/PER/CH).

5 *Subject.* With this system it is usual to use some alpha/numerical coding to provide the index, e.g., the Library Dewy/Decimal system.

17.5.4.5 Types of filing

Correspondence Files
Memos, letters etc., are normally housed in one of the following types of unit:

1 A four drawer filing cabinet with the files suspended vertically in specially designed pockets.
2 A lateral filing cabinet with the files suspended horizontally.
3 An automatic system with rotating racks of files which occupy the minimum amount of floor space but which reach from floor to ceiling. The mechanism rotates the files until the relevant rack or shelf is available, at desk height, to the operator.

Card index files
This type of filing is often used for personnel records, health records etc., and the cards are stored in either drawers, carousel units or automatic filing systems.

Plan filing
Those organizations with architectural, engineering, drawing and other similar staff require filing systems for plans, drawings and maps. There are three main methods available.

1 *Plan chests.* A plan chest is a series of drawers in a chest allowing plans to be stored free from dust and without folding. (Plans that are to be photocopied or microfilmed cannot be folded).
2 *Tubular storage.* The plans are rolled, placed in tubes and stored in a 'honeycomb' type filing cabinet.
3 *Vertical filing.* Plans are held vertically via direct suspension; this makes indexing and retrieval easy and makes maximum use of floor space.

Microfilm
The original information is photographed and held on miniature lengths of film (rolls, strips, sheets, cassettes etc.) and a viewer or reader is used to view the information. Photocopies can also be taken.

The main *advantages* of microfiling are:

1 Saving in space: 3,200 letters held on a normal 100 foot reel of microfilm takes 21 cubic inches of space compared with 1,300 cubic inches in a conventional filing system.
2 Safety. Fireproof storage units or a duplicate set of films can be kept at

another location. This is vital when an organization depends on its
information for its existence.

3 Time. Retrieval of information is rapid via modern indexing systems,
e.g. the catalogue system in use in libraries.

4 Long life. Microfilm has an almost indefinite life.

Disadvantages include:

1 The equipment is expensive, and perhaps prohibitive for small
organizations. However rental, leasing and the use of outside agencies
can help to overcome this problem. The equipment comprises a
camera to film documents and index them, a processor, the most costly
item, and a viewer/reader, (the projection type, which is durable and
easy to read, being the most common).

2 Legal difficulties may arise, since microfilm is not always admissible as
evidence.

3 Specialized staff are required to do the initial filming and indexing.
(But any staff can use the retrieval system).

Nowadays microfilm is used extensively in recording the massive
paper output of computers and storing this for ease of reference. This is
very expensive and can only be justified for those very large installations
where security is a vital factor.

17.5.4.6 Filing in operation

Whatever system is eventually chosen, management must decide:

1 Which person(s) has responsibility for opening and closing files and
for selecting titles.

2 Who does the indexing and positioning.

3 Who puts the papers into the file and removes them.

4 What, if any, materials are to be excluded from the files.

5 What is the system for borrowing, using and returning files.

6 What size of paper for correspondence is to be used; (international
paper sizes now help, and the most common size used in
correspondence is A4 which has replaced the old foolscap size).

7 Who decides on the method and equipment.

8 Who keeps copies of the classification and index and is responsible for
updating it.

9 Who decides on a 'weeding out' of files and liaises with an archivist or
similar person before deciding whether to destroy documents.

An absence of clear management decisions on these matters may cause
users to lose confidence in the system, and to a proliferation of filing
systems.

17.5.4.7 Summary

Information is vital to the efficiency of any organization. An effective filing system is usually the responsibility of the administrative office or the office manager. There are a variety of filing systems available and there is no doubt that computers, with remote terminals at the users' workplace and home, will revolutionize filing arrangements in the next few years. Here the decision what to file is determined not so much by storage constraints, but by considerations of confidentiality. Restrictions may be imposed with respect to personnel records, health records, police and security information etc.

17.5.5 Reception and telephones

These two functions are closely related; indeed in smaller organizations the staff who work on the reception desk also operate the switchboard. There is a lot to be said for combining or interchanging reception and telephone duties. The staff have similar knowledge about the organization, e.g. names of people, departments, functions etc. But the telephonist's job is somewhat impersonal when compared with the receptionist who actually sees the people he or she deals with, and an interchange of duties provides a welcome variety.

The staff involved in these functions are often the first contact between the organization and its customers, the general public etc. Staff should be specially chosen for their personality, ability to maintain an overall knowledge of the organization and its people, and for their manner, appearance and attitude. It may be difficult to overcome a bad initial impression caused, for example, by delays in answering the telephone or an unhelpful attitude towards a query at reception. Organizations often employ disabled people in these duties, since attitude and knowledge is more important than physical effort.

Receptionists and telephonists can only do their job properly if they are notified of changes in rooms, titles, or staff, new projects, new customers etc. It is particularly useful for new employees to be introduced personally to these staff so that they are physically known and not just a voice on the telephone.

17.5.6 Mail and messenger services

A centralized mail room has the advantage that it can:

1 Employ specialized staff who can operate full time and (particularly in the case of messengers) get to know locations and individuals.
2 Use specialized equipment that saves time and money, e.g. franking machines, letter opening systems, scanning devices, letter insertion and

folding machines etc.

3 Enable the most appropriate postal and parcel methods to be utilised following the advice of the Post Office.

4 Enable close links to be maintained with e.g. reprographics and filing, whose needs are closely linked with document transmission and retrieval.

Certain departments may argue that their needs are specialized, e.g. the finance department may object to money being handled by another department. Such arguments should be resisted so that the services operate at maximum overall efficiency as central units.

In large organizations an internal messenger service, using 'pick up' and 'disposal' points strategically placed throughout the office, can provide a speedy service for mail and other documents, e.g. it can be used for photocopying, plan printing, file return and retrieval. Once again the use of specialist full-time staff should avoid mistakes and also provide a useful training ground for newcomers to the organization. They can get to know individuals, sections and the work involved, as well as providing a vital central service.

17.5.7 Secretarial services

There is a great deal of waste in the way many organizations use their secretarial and typing staff. Senior managers may require full-time secretaries to undertake personal assistant duties, e.g. making travel arrangements as well as typing. But a secretary is a status symbol in many organizations and there is often room for increased efficiency by having a secretary work for a number of executives.

With reference to typing, the recent trend has been towards centralized typing units (or pools), audio as opposed to shorthand dictation, and the use of word processing equipment rather than simple typewriters. We briefly discuss each of these in turn.

17.5.7.1 Units

Centralized units maximize the usage of specialized equipment. They enable staff to be kept fully occupied and allow for adequate supervision and control of work. However, most women dislike working in a large unit in a 'battery hen' environment. There is much to be said for large organizations having a number of units, no larger than four or six typists, spread across departments but under centralized control to allow work to be re-scheduled should the need arise.

Special attention should be paid to the lighting, acoustics, decoration, furniture and equipment used, as the staff concerned spend the majority of their time at one desk.

17.5.7.2 Audio versus shorthand

It has long been recognized that shorthand-taking wastes the time of a typist and the use of audio dictating equipment is now commonplace. However, the higher up the organizational hierarchy one goes, the more likely the executive is to use shorthand dictation. It is therefore not surprising that those typists who hope to become secretaries to executives, try to retain their shorthand knowledge. Full benefit is obtained from audio dictation systems only if all executives use them all the time, and in this respect senior managers often fail to set a good example.

There is a variety of equipment on the market and it is important to ensure that the manufacturer has standardized equipment that covers portable, individual desk machines and remote centralized systems. An organization may start off with one type and add another at a later stage. Compatibility of the two types is obviously desirable. The purchaser should also check that the system has been proved in pre-operational trials and that the supplier will provide adequate training and servicing.

17.5.7.3 Word processing

The day is not far off when one will be able to speak directly into a typewriter and see the words transmitted onto a sheet of paper. Indeed, the technology already exists but such a facility has not been developed commercially. The word processors currently on the market can store, edit and correct and thus offer considerable advantages over the standard and electric typewriter. They are, of course, much more expensive and should not be used as ordinary typewriters.

The technology is fast changing and there is much to be said for renting or leasing equipment, since this gives maximum flexibility to update. Ground rules for installation include:

1 A thorough survey of needs and uses, costs and benefits.
2 Proper training and remuneration of staff.
3 Care in the design of the working environment to minimize health hazards, e.g. eyestrain, fatigue.
4 Purchase from a reputable manufacturer with good repair and maintenance as well as training services.
5 Proper supervision and control of work going on to the system.

Finally, consultation and negotiation with unions is becoming more important. In the public sector in particular, unions are waking up to the implications for employment of word processors and are demanding job safeguards, good working conditions and adequate remuneration as conditions to be met before word processors are introduced.

17.5.8 Reprographics

Reprographics involves the use of expensive equipment operated by trained staff. In most organizations this calls for centralization to ensure that the right equipment is used for a particular purpose — to obtain maximum cost advantages.

17.5.8.1 Photocopies

The market leader, Xerox, achieved its dominance through rental contracts. But equipment can now be rented, leased or bought. The cost per copy depends upon the number of copies taken, whether copies are single or double-sided, whether the machine has a sorter etc. Consequently, careful monitoring of the use of the machine can yield substantial savings.

17.5.8.2 Duplicating

This is now out of favour in larger organizations. But in smaller firms and offices the stencil or spirit duplicator still provides a cheap and effective means of multiple document production.

17.5.8.3 Printing

This is a highly specialized area and any organization that has needs beyond photocopying and duplicating should, until it is very large, use outside facilities as and when required. The print unions are very powerful, wages are high, and there is considerable resistance to the introduction of new technology. These factors make any management extremely wary of establishing an 'in house' print unit.

17.5.8.4 Plan printing

Like printing, plan printing requires specialized equipment and trained staff and can only be justified in larger organizations.

17.8.5.5 Microfiling

This has been dealt with above.

17.5.9 Publicity/information

The public relations function is often located within the central administration department, since this department has the relevant information and controls the means of dissemination, i.e. mail, reprographics etc. Moreover the department acts as the unofficial P.R.O.

via its reception and telephone staff.

Public relations is now a professional function with its own professional body and training scheme. Only the largest organizations are able to justify the use of a full-time public relations officer. But all organizations should have some individual, adequately briefed, who is available to answer queries on subjects that are not the clear responsibility of any member of the organization, and who can take a positive role in projecting the corporate image of the organization to the outside world.

The basic requirements of public relations is good communications. This area was dealt with at length in Chapter 4 and 5, and only a few additional points need to be made here with reference to public relations.

The organization should develop friendly, mutually beneficial relationships with the media. All employees are unofficial PROs and must be kept informed about the organization's activities. However, managers have a special responsibility to take positive action to create a favourable image in the mind of customers, suppliers and the general public.

As part of this image the organization should develop a house theme, or logo, that can be used on all written communications, packaging, uniforms, advertisements, signs etc. This is made easier when public relations is the responsibility of the central administrative office which controls these work areas. The modern trend is for people to want to be involved, to be consulted, to be notified and to have their own views listened to. This means having a good public relations policy, and governments as well as companies are realizing the importance of spending time and money in this important area of communications.

17.5.10 Transport

An organization's policy relating to personal transport embraces mileage allowances for private car users, the use of company cars and taxis, the use of public transport, and the choice between car purchase and rental.

The policy will also cover arrangements for land, sea and air travel as appropriate. In overseas travel, there are considerable advantages in developing good working relationships with a local travel agent who has the local contacts and can become familiar with the organization's needs. The same can be said for car hire and taxi services; a regular customer often gets preference and a better deal.

In all these functions of the central administrative office, organizations should make use of their own management services staff (see above). These staff have the appropriate training and expertise in these areas and know the personal requirements of their colleagues. They are independent of any particular supplier and can offer unbiased advice. Finally, they have to live with their recommendations and so have an incentive to meet the organization's needs as effectively as possible.

Should an organization not be large enough to have its own management services unit, use can be made of outside consultants, and of the free advice and information offered by most equipment manufacturers.

17.6 Summary and conclusions

In this chapter we have examined the importance and operation of the central administrative office. We considered the arguments for centralization and de-centralization and discussed the main responsibilities of the office, relating to position, layout, maintenance, filing, microfiling, reception and telephones, mail and messenger services, secretarial/typing facilities, reprographics, publicity, and transport.

Revision questions and exercises

1   Answer *briefly:*
A   Give two work areas which are often the concern of the administrative office.
B   Give two work areas under the control of the Company Secretary.
C   Why is administration more efficient when it is centralized?
D   On what grounds does one make a rent-or-buy decision for office accommodation?
E   What is an open plan office?
F   What are the essentials of a good filing system?
G   Give one method of classifying files?
H   What is meant by secretarial services?
I   What is meant by word processing?
J   What is the basic requirement of good public relations?
2   Compare the functions of a company secretary in the private sector with those of a director of administration in a public sector organization.
3   Discuss the advantages of centralized administration.
4   'Head offices should always be situated in London'. Discuss.
5   'Open plan offices have the advantage of flexibility at the expense of privacy'. Discuss.
6   You are asked to advise an organization on the various factors it should take account of in maintaining its buildings. Write your report.
7   Your local authority is moving all its departments to a new county hall and the question of centralization of filing is raised at the management team meeting. As O. and M. officer you are asked to prepare a report on the issue, summarizing both the advantages and disadvantages of centralization. Write the report.
8   'Administrators are not managers. They merely carry out instructions and operate procedures'. Discuss the validity of this statement with reference to a public sector organization.

Further Reading

BREALEY, R. *An Activity Course in Office Management* (Longman: Harlow, 1980).

CARTER, R. *Business Administration* (Heinemann: London, 1981).

DENYER, J. C. *Office Management* (Macdonald Evans: London, 1979).

HARRISON, J. *Secretarial Duties* (Pitman: London, 1981).

HOWARD, W. *The Practice of Public Relations* (Heinemann: London, 1982).

JONES, R. and HOBDAY, I. *Commerce* (Pan: London, 1980).

SALMON, G. *The Working Office* (B.I.M: London, 1980).

SHAW, J. *Office Organization for Managers* (Macdonald Evans: London, 1978).

TOWNSEND, K. *Choosing a Word Processor* (Gower: London, 1981).

VINNICOMBE, S. *Secretaries, Management and Organizations* (Heinemann: London, 1980).

18

The Future

18.1 Introduction

In this chapter we look to the future. We consider some of the changes likely to occur in the final decades of the twentieth century, concentrating on certain key areas: information technology, the industrial and commercial environment, and attitudes to work and leisure. We discuss the implications of these changes for the structure of organizations, the role of managers and, briefly, for government policy.

18.2 Information technology

The greatest technological changes will continue to occur in the gathering, storage, retrieval and transmission of information. We are coming to accept the home television set with its access to the mass of data stored on central computers in such systems as 'Ceefax' and 'Oracle'. Change in this area will continue to be rapid with the formulation and implementation of plans for 'the wired society'. This term refers to a telecommunications network bringing to the home, via the telephone service, multi-channel television, electronic mail and opportunities for trading (push button shopping, banking etc.)

A report submitted to the government by the Cabinet's Information Technology Advisory Panel in 1982 proposed a cable television system to cover the whole country. It would comprise a series of local networks, with every street being served by optical fibre cables, which can carry large volumes of information. It was envisaged that a monthly subscription of between £5 and £10 would give the householder access to 20 entertainment channels and a further 10 for consumer services. The operation would cost an estimated £10 billion, and would provide a huge impetus to Britain's cable and electronic industries.

Considering the impact of such a system in more detail, we can envisage a consumer examining a selection of goods on her television monitor (where they can be portrayed in a much more realistic fashion than in, say, a mail order catalogue), making her decision what to buy, ordering the goods from the retailer of her choice (who would deliver them or pack them ready for collection), and charging these to her bank account by tapping out her account code number.

The daily newspaper may become a thing of the past as far as news transmission is concerned. The television provides more up-to-date coverage of events, using cameras and equipment that can now relay world events as they are happening, via satellites and cable transmission systems. (To compensate for this, newspapers will have to give more space to comment and to feature articles).

The daily letter delivery and the traditional mail systems are bound to suffer as the costs of transmitting documents electronically continues to fall, and as more homes acquire the facility to receive and send messages electronically throughout the world.

Entertainment patterns are already being affected by the new equipment. Cinema audiences continue to fall as more people choose to watch a video film in the comfort of their own home in preference to going to a cinema with its higher costs, in terms of money and/or effort.

Banking is seeing a gradual change from a system based on coins and paper to one based on credit cards and computers. These changes will continue and as information systems develop further, the 'cashless society' will become the norm rather than the exception. Nearly all the population will have bank accounts and will make use of new financial services and accounting systems based on computers. To utilize the new system is fully as possible, each bank will try to attract more customers by a variety of means including, perhaps, a reduction in bank charges.

Education is also being transformed by the new information systems. Work on distance learning systems, pioneered by the Open University, will be extended and will reach new sectors of the population. It is already possible to learn golf, chess, bridge and a variety of other leisure activities via specialized video tapes, and this market will expand into many other areas. Students are now familiar with borrowing video tapes, and the new video discs and other learning systems are transforming the traditional public library system from one based on books, to one that uses various information media.

The teacher or lecturer will still continue to be needed to provide help and advice, (at least the two authors hope so!), but the traditional lecturing role may be at least partly replaced by video learning packages using the latest presentation techniques and skilled actors or expert lecturers. The advantage of these packages is that they can be referred to repeatedly, as required.

Educational courses will become packaged and hence available to a much wider cross section of the population. People will be able to study in their own time, contact their academic counsellor via confravision for help and advice, and use their television set to obtain up to the minute information on practically any issue or item whatsoever.

This will in turn cause the traditional method of learning, i.e. remembering and notetaking, to be questioned. If it is possible to have information instantly and visually available, why bother to learn facts and figures in the traditional way? A few years ago the idea that young schoolchildren would be at ease using pocket calculators rather than logarithm tables would have been incomprehensible; now it is an accepted everyday fact. These changes in education and learning are probably one of the most exciting consequences of the new information technology, and readers of this book will be very much a part of this change process.

Although improved access to information will give rise to many opportunities, there are also signs of mistrust of the power that access to information can give. Fears about the possible mis-use of information relating to people have been mentioned in previous chapters. To this must be added the effects of improved access on people's reactions to decisions taken by governments, organizations and managers. People might accept unpopular decisions taken by others with more information, but are less likely to do so when they have access to exactly the same information as the decision taker.

In future power may reside with those who decide 'who gets what information'. This process has, in fact, already begun as interested parties seek to preserve their power, position and influence by restricting the information available to their critics.

18.3 The industrial and commercial environment

The last twenty years have seen a dramatic change in the industrial and commercial environment. Employment has declined in traditional industries such as shipbuilding, steel, coal mining and textiles and also in some newer industries such as vehicle manufacture. The decline in the relative importance of manufacturing and the increase in the relative importance of the service sector is not confined to Britain, as can be seen from Table 18.1.

Although the growth of the service sector is likely to slow down in the 1990s, it will continue to be the major employer. Whilst certain public sector services might be regarded as unproductive, other service industries (e.g. banking, insurance, tourism, scientific services) supply products that

Table 18.1 Employment in the E.E.C. by major areas of activity %

	1960	1970	1979
Forestry, fishing, agriculture	13.5	10.5	7.7
Mining, quarrying	2.6	1.2	1.0
Manufacturing	35.9	33.4	28.8
Electricity, gas, water	1.1	1.0	0.9
Construction	8.5	8.6	8.2
Services	38.4	45.3	53.4

N.B. 1960 and 1970 figures exclude Denmark and Luxembourg.

Source: *ILO Yearbook of Nation Statistics.*

are sold in domestic and overseas markets in the same way as manufactured items. These 'tradeable' services now account for nearly 25 per cent of the total employment in E.E.C. countries, and will continue to grow in importance with the development of new information services and the increase in leisure.

It is impossible to foresee all the effects of this change in the industrial environment. But it is obviously going to have important consequences for the mix of occupations, training requirements, the geographical distribution of jobs and (following from all of the above) requirements for government assistance.

These changes in the industrial and commercial environment are partly due to changes in technology, as already indicated. Technological change, especially in biotechnology, has other important implications in terms of the dangers that can arise when the frontiers of science are breached on an almost daily basis. The ethics of research and development used in such areas have been subject to constant debate in recent years.

The changes considered in this and the previous section suggest that constant attention will have to be paid to the need to reconcile the objectives of commercial and industrial organizations with public accountability. As people become better educated and have improved access to information they will be in a better position to study and assess the implications of the changes initiated by organizations. Managers will have to look beyond their own industrial and commercial horizons and become more socially responsible. In certain cases the pace of change may have to be reduced to fit in with social attitudes. (This has already happened in some medical areas such as cloning and the use of certain types of transplants).

18.4 Attitudes to work and leisure

Perhaps the biggest challenges facing organizations in the coming years will arise from changes in attitudes towards work and employment. For much of the post-war period it was generally accepted as desirable that organizations should introduce new equipment and working methods in order to increase efficiency. The economy was expanding at a rapid rate (by previous standards), and workers released by one organization soon found alternative employment. But as the rate of economic growth slackened in the 1980s, workers who were made redundant remained unemployed for longer periods. Moreover young people seeking employment for the first time found it more difficult to obtain work.

Although social security payments ensure that unemployed workers and their families escape the worst of the privations suffered by the unemployed in the 1930s, there is a substantial and growing gap between the living standards of those with and those without jobs. Furthermore, people's expectations have risen as a result of almost a quarter of a century of economic growth, combined with an emphasis on material possessions from a variety of sources, ranging from Prime Minister Macmillan's 'You have never had it so good' to the advertisements broadcast by the independent television companies. (The inability of the unemployed to fulfil these increased expectations, together with the boredom associated with unemployment, might have contributed to the increase in crime in recent years.)

One benefit to employers of the higher unemployment has been a curbing of the power and influence of the more militant trade unions. There have been several instances, in the car industry, road transport etc., of workers rejecting the advice of shop stewards or national union officials to strike for higher wages.

The effect of higher unemployment on workers' attitudes towards new technology is more problematic. On the one hand, the scarcity of alternative jobs might make workers reluctant to accept changes that would lead to job losses. On the other hand, obstruction of the changes, especially by strikes, could harm the organization's competitive ability and thus, in the longer term, give rise to even more job losses.

This illustrates the fact that there is no easy answer to the questions posed by changes in technology. As an international trading nation we must remain competitive and so cannot afford *not* to take advantage of improvements in technology, even though the immediate effect may be to reduce employment opportunities. Nor is there an easy answer to the problems arising from unfulfilled expectations. We mentioned that television advertising has played a part in raising expectations. We must also recognize that insofar as advertising is successful in persuading people to buy more products, it thereby contributes to an increase in employment.

Another aspect of higher unemployment levels is that it becomes less obviously beneficial to work hard. Limited promotion opportunities reduce personal incentives, while working more hours per day reduces job opportunities for the unemployed. Changing attitudes may mean that managers find it more difficult to obtain positive co-operation from workers, e.g. in 'pulling out the stops' in order to meet deadlines.

The problems facing school leavers have already been referred to. Some young people are responding to the lack of opportunities in traditional occupations — in the office or on the factory floor — by taking part-time employment in pubs, cafes, with pop-groups etc. There will have to be a greater degree of social acceptance of such patterns including, perhaps, a change in government policy making it possible for part-time workers to supplement their income with social security benefits in certain instances.

The government may also be forced to reduce the age at which retirement pensions become payable, to provide an incentive for workers to retire earlier, thus creating more opportunities for young workers.

A lowering of the official retirement age would have important implications for organizations. They would be especially important in relation to managerial posts, where early retirement could mean the loss of staff whose experience makes them especially valuable to the organization.

Finally there is a range of tasks — gardening and shopping for the elderly and handicapped, the creation of children's playgrounds from derelict areas, providing advice and information to holiday-makers etc. — which are mainly undertaken on a voluntary basis at present, but which in future may form the basis of regular, paid employment. New types of organizations will be required to administer and operate such schemes.

18.5 Summary and conclusions

In this chapter we have considered the implications for managers and organizations of changes in information technology, in other aspects of the industrial and commercial environment and in attitudes towards work and leisure. These changes will require changes in the structure of organizations and the role of managers. But whatever changes occur in managers' roles, they will continue to spend much of their time dealing with people; indeed the 'people aspects' of managers' work will assume even greater importance as a result of some of the changes considered above. As we said at the beginning of the book, as people's attitudes, lifestyles and aspirations change, managers and organizations must change in response. Choosing the most appropriate response has always been, and will always be, the major challenge facing managers and organizations.

Revision questions and exercises

1   What effects do you think the growth of information systems, available via the television set, will have on the way managers and organizations operate

in the future?
2   What benefits will a 'wired society' bring to organizations?
3   Will there ever be a cashless society? If so how would this affect the financial function of organizations?
4   What changes do you think the new information technology and learning systems will have on education?
5   What will be the growth industries of the future?
6   'Leisure is a growth industry'. Discuss.
7   Will micro-technology help to solve unemployment, or make it worse?
8   What effects are the current social and economic conditions likely to have on the demand for the services offered by the public sector?

Further Reading

CHRISTOPHER, W. *Management for the 80s* (Prentice Hall: New York, 1980).
COOPER, P. *Developing Managers for the 1980s* (M.B.S.: London, 1980).
DRUCKER, P. *Towards the Next Economics* (Heinemann: London, 1980).
FOY, N. *The Yin and the Yang of Organizations* (Grant McIntyre: London, 1980).
GERSHUNY, J. *After Industrial Society: The Emerging Self-Service Economy* (Macmillan: London, 1978).
SAMPSON, A. *The Changing Anatomy of Britain* (Hodder & Stoughton: London, 1982).
TOFFLER, A. *The Third Wave* (Collins: London, 1980).

Index